LITERARY
TOPICS

ISSN 1526-1549

LITERARY TOPICS

Volume **2**

Ernest Hemingway and the Expatriate Modernist Movement

Kirk Curnutt

A MANLY, INC. BOOK

GALE GROUP

Detroit
San Francisco
London
Boston
Woodbridge, CT

ERNEST HEMINGWAY AND THE EXPATRIATE MODERNIST MOVEMENT

Matthew J. Bruccoli and Richard Layman, *Editorial Directors*

The Gale Group

27500 Drake Road

Farmington Hills, MI 48331

ISBN 0-7876-3963-X

ISSN 1526-1549

Printed in the United States of America

10 9 8 7 6 5 4 3 2 1

TABLE OF CONTENTS

MODERNISM

A NOTE TO THE READER

Gale Study Guides are designed to be helpful by being informative, by removing tedious and unnecessary obstacles, and by pointing you toward further thought. They are also designed to be responsive to the changed conditions of reading literature which have arisen in the past fifteen or twenty years in schools, colleges, and universities. What are these conditions?

by Denis Donoghue, Henry James Professor of English and American Letters, New York Unviersity

They are mainly imposed by Theory. There was a time when students read literature—and were instructed to read it—without a theory of reading or a theory of literature. Even a critic as far-reaching as William Empson seemed to play it by ear and to trust to his hunches. It was assumed that everybody knew what a work of literature was and what reading such a work entailed. Teachers tried to offer a persuasive interpretation of the work, and that was that. One interpretation might be more interesting than another, but both interpretations were in the same field of assumption and reference. These assumptions don't hold any longer. If we say that such-and-such a book is a work of literature, we have to explain what we hold a work of literature to be, why it is such, and how it has become such. No attribute of the book can be taken for granted. Theory asks not, primarily, what the book is or what it means or how it works but what are the conditions under which it has come into being. Those conditions are deemed to be social, political, economic, linguistic, formal—and perhaps most insistently, cultural. A novel, a play, or a poem is said to be a work of cultural production. What does that mean? It means that many diverse forces have come together to produce the book. Not just the intention of an author.

One result of this emphasis is that the context of a work of literature is not deemed to be a static "background" or scene. In a celebrated essay called "The Historical Interpretation of Literature" (1941), Edmund Wilson assumed that "history" could be called upon to steady the work of literature, to curb its mobility, and to ground it in some value more ascertainable than the author's intention or the formal properties of the work. History is no longer thought to provide such a ground. If there is a contemporary sense of history, it features rather the conviction—or the fear—that history itself is partly fictive. There are histories, but there is no single or stable History. A history of the French Revolution is not a sequence of characters and actions, transcribed. What or who is the real Julius Caesar? In the second chapter of James Joyce's *Ulysses* Stephen Dedalus asks himself: "Had Pyrrhus not fallen by a beldam's hand in Argos or Julius Caesar not been knifed to death?" and in answer to himself he murmurs: "They are not to be thought away. Time has branded them and fettered they are lodged in the room of the infinite possibilities they have ousted." Yes: in some sense, yes. But it is hard to establish "Julius Caesar" as an entity independent of my sense of him, or your sense of him. Granted that he was knifed to death. But that is not enough to establish him or to remove from the image of him the taint of fictiveness. The philosopher E. M. Cioran asserted, in *Précis de décomposition* (1949), that "history is merely a procession of false Absolutes, a series of temples raised to pretexts, a degradation of the mind before the Improbable." We are not obliged to agree with Cioran, but we can't shrug off his skepticism or assume that we are free to invoke History, as Wilson did, without misgiving. The concept of History is, as we have been schooled to say, problematic. History may be everything that is the case, but the force of fictiveness in constituting it can't be ignored.

So a question arises: is literary history possible? If it is: is it necessary or desirable? Why do we talk about literary movements and schools, if the very concept of History is questionable? Was there ever such a thing, for instance, as Romanticism or Modernism?

There was, but not in any fixed or steady sense. Writers who live at a particular time often feel a certain commonality of purpose. They respond in similar ways to the conditions they face. They share, in some degree, a conviction of the expressive possibilities. The revolutionary writers are those few who intuit or divine, among those possibilities, the ones that clamor to be fulfilled. T. S. Eliot saw the possibility of putting fragments of verse together in a seemingly arbitrary or at least unofficial way which would make a rather esoteric kind of sense: the result was *The Waste Land*, a kind of poetry no other writer thought of writing. It soon began to emerge that *The Waste Land*, Ezra Pound's *Cantos*, W. B. Yeats's *The Tower*, Hart Crane's *The Bridge* and a few other poems had something in common—a distinctive sense of their time—despite their formal and rhetorical differences. The concept of Modernism seemed to be called for, to note similarities of purpose among such writers: Eliot, Pound, Valéry, Yeats, Rilke, Joyce, Proust. This does not mean that these writers thought of themselves as associates. Pound and Eliot did, but not Eliot and Yeats. The concept of Modernism is a worthy one, provided we deal with it flexibly: it is not a place of residence for the writers it designates. Differences, then, persist and have to be acknowledged; but they are folded within a grand sense of "the modern spirit" or Modernism. So we can still use this word. It is more useful to think of a certain consanguinity of purpose among various writers than to assume that one writer is utterly separate from other writers.

So too with the concept of the author, another once-steady notion that has come into question. Of course Shakespeare or Emily Dickinson or F. Scott Fitzgerald or James Dickey wrote the book, but not in utter freedom or sky-blue autonomy. They had to deal with the exigencies of cultural performance: specifically, with questions of language, communication, ideology, audience, readership, money patronage, publishers, genre, literary form, the social forces issuing in taste. Not that any one of these was absolutely coercive. Pierre Bourdieu has maintained, in *A Theory of Literary Production* (1966), that "a writer never reflects mechanically or rigorously the ideology which he represents, even if his sole intention is to represent it; perhaps because no ideology is sufficiently consistent to survive the test of figuration." Otherwise put: the force of an ideology is not irresistible, it must yield in some degree—bend if not break—to the force of the language, the figures of speech and thought, which are entailed by writing in English, French, Greek, Latin, or another language. Total freedom is not available in the production of literature. Writers may proceed as if such freedom were available. They would be wise not to capitulate to the social, economic, or cultural forces at large. A certain measure of resistance is possible. Kenneth Burke maintained, in *Counter-Statement* (1931), that the motto of the imagination is: "When in Rome, do as the Greeks." But it's not quite as straightforward as that.

It is hoped that these *Gale Study Guides* will help you to negotiate these and other issues. They won't tell you what to think about, say, *The Great Gatsby,* or dictate the limits of your experience in reading that book; but they will open up new possibilities.

ACKNOWLEDGMENTS

This book was produced by Bruccoli Clark Layman, Inc. R. Bland Lawson is the series editor and Penelope M. Hope is the in-house editor.

Production manager is Philip B. Dematteis.

Copyediting supervisor is Phyllis A. Avant. Senior copyeditor is Thom Harman. The copyediting staff includes Brenda Carol Blanton, James Denton, Worthy B. Evans, Melissa D. Hinton, William Tobias Mathes, and Jennifer Reid.

Indexing specialist is Alex Snead.

Layout and graphics supervisor is Janet E. Hill. Graphics staff includes Karla Corley Brown and Zoe R. Cook.

Photography editors are Charles Mims, Scott Nemzek, Alison Smith, and Paul Talbot. Digital photographic copy work was performed by Joseph M. Bruccoli.

Systems manager is Marie L. Parker.

Typesetting supervisor is Kathleen M. Flanagan. The typesetting staff includes Mark J. McEwan, Kimberly Kelly, and Patricia Flanagan Salisbury.

COPYRIGHTED PHOTOGRAPHY

Ford Madox Ford, James Joyce, Ezra Pound, and John Quinn, Paris, early 1920s, photograph.

Ernest Hemingway at Shakespeare and Company, photograph. Princeton University Library. Reproduced by permission.

Ernest Hemingway, Hadley, John Dos Passos, and the Murphys, photograph. John F. Kennedy Library.

Ernest Hemingway in a suit and tie, photograph. John F. Kennedy Library.

Ernest Hemingway on a motorcycle, Paris, photograph. Department of Rare Books and Special Collections, Princeton University Library. Reproduced by permission.

Ernest Hemingway sitting in front of bookshelves, photograph. Department of Rare Books and Special Collections, Princeton University Library. Reproduced by permission.

Ernest Hemingway with son on skis, photograph. Department of Rare Books and Special Collections, Princeton University Library. Reproduced by permission.

Hadley Hemingway and Ernest Hemingway, photograph. Department of Rare Books and Special Collections, Princeton University Library. Reproduced by permission.

Pauline Hemingway and Ernest Hemingway, photograph. Department of Rare Books and Special Collections, Princeton University Library. Reproduced by permission.

Henry McAlmon in arena at Ronda, Spain, photograph. Department of Rare Books and Special Collections, Princeton University Library. Reproduced by permission.

"Le Violin d'Ingres" by Man Ray. © Coll.Treillard-ADAGP 1987. © 1999 Man Ray Trust / Artists Rights Society, N.Y. / ADAGP, Paris. Reproduced by permission.

Gertrude Stein and Alice B. Toklas, photograph. Reproduced by permission of the Gertrude Stein Estate.

Gertrude Stein and Virgil Thomson, photograph. Reproduced by permission of the Gertrude Stein Estate.

Gertrude Stein, portrait by Pablo Picasso. Reproduced by permission of the Gertrude Stein Estate.

CHRONOLOGY: MODERNISM

1900 Sigmund Freud publishes *The Interpretation of Dreams*; Joseph Conrad's *Lord Jim*, Stephen Crane's *Whilomville Stories*, and Theodore Dreiser's *Sister Carrie* are published.

1901 Pablo Picasso's first exhibition opens at Galeries Vollard in Paris; American experimental composer Charles Ives completes his Symphony No. 2.

1902 Photographer Edward Steichen has a one-man show in Paris; Claude Debussy's *Pelleas et Melisande* premieres in Paris; Conrad's *Heart of Darkness* is published.

1903 Gertrude Stein moves to Paris; Henri Matisse exhibits paintings at the Salon des Indépendants in Paris.

1904 Conrad's *Nostromo* is published.

1905 Albert Einstein proposes his theory of relativity; Matisse exhibits *La Femme au Chapeau* at the Autumn Salon; Isadora Duncan opens her modern-dance academy in Berlin; Alfred Stieglitz opens the first show at his Photo-Secession gallery in New York; Claude Debussy composes *La Mer*; Freud publishes *Three Contributions to the Sexual Theory*.

1906 Ruth St. Denis introduces modern dance to Americans on her U.S. tour.

1907 New York galleries feature the works of American impressionist Mary Cassatt.

1908 Italian artist Emilio Marinetti publishes the *Futurist Manifesto*; Matisse publishes *Notes d'un peintre*, setting forth his artistic principles.

1909 Picasso begins his portrait of Stein, which ushers in his Cubist period. Sergei Diaghile's Ballets Russe performs for the first time in Paris; Stein's *Three Lives* is published.

1910 Artists Wassily Kandinsky and Franz Marc publish *The Blue Rider* in Munich, inaugurating the Postimpressionist movement; Picasso has a one-man show at Stieglitz's 291 Gallery in New York.

1911 Pound's *Canzoni* and Thomas Mann's *Death in Venice* are published; Georges Braque paints *Man with a Guitar.*

1912 Ezra Pound establishes Imagism with H.D. (Hilda Doolittle) and Richard Aldington; Marcel Duchamp completes *Nude Descending a Staircase;* *L'Après Midi d'un Faune,* featuring dancer Vaslav Nijinsky of the Ballets Russes, has its premiere in Paris; Carl Jung's *Theory of Psychoanalysis* is published.

1913 The Armory Show opens in New York. Igor Stravinsky premieres *Le Sacre du Printemps,* a ballet commissioned for Sergei Pavlovich Diaghilev's Ballets Russes; *Swann's Way,* the first volume of Marcel Proust's seven-volume *Remembrance of Things Past,* is published; D. H. Lawrence's *Sons and Lovers* is published.

1914 World War I begins; Duncan's modern-dance company performs in New York City; James Joyce's *Dubliners* and *A Portrait of the Artist as a Young Man* are published.

1915 Franz Kafka's *Metamorphosis* is published; the Provincetown Players stage their first performance in Provincetown, Massachusetts.

1916 Hugo Ball and Ricard Hülsenbeck launch the Dada movement in Zurich.

1917 Pound, living in London, becomes foreign editor of *The Little Review;* Pound and Wyndham Lewis found vorticism; America enters World War I.

1918 Germany surrenders, ending World War I.

1919 Sylvia Beach opens her bookstore, Shakespeare and Company, at 8, rue Dupuytren (later moves to rue de l'Odeon; Paris Peace Conference results in the Treaty of Versailles; Sherwood Anderson's *Winesburg, Ohio* is published.

1920 Pound's *Hugh Selwyn Mauberley* is published.

1921 Avant-garde artist-photographer Man Ray arrives in Paris; Picasso paints *Three Musicians.*

1922 Beach's Shakespeare and Company publishes Joyce's *Ulysses* in Paris; T. S. Eliot publishes the first issue of his journal, *The Criterion,* which includes his poem *The Waste Land; The Little Review* moves its operation to Paris; E. E. Cummings's *The Enormous Room* is published.

1923 Robert McAlmon establishes the Contact Publishing Company; The "Exiles Number" of *The Little Review* appears, including works by Ernest Hemingway, Cummings, and Stein; Hemingway's *Three Stories and Ten Poems* is published by McAlmon; *Within the Quota,* a ballet by Cole Porter and Gerald Murphy premieres in Paris; William Carlos Williams's *Spring and All,* which includes "The Red Wheel Barrow," is published.

1924 Hemingway helps edit Ford Madox Ford's *transatlantic review;* Hemingway's *in our time* is published; André Breton publishes the *Surrealist Manifesto.*

1925 Stein's *The Making of Americans* is published; George Antheil's *Le Ballet mecanique* has a preview in Paris (the official premiere is in 1926); F. Scott Fitzgerald's *The Great Gatsby,* John Dos Passos's *Manhattan Transfer,* Pound's *A Draft of XVI. Cantos,* and Virginia Woolf's *Mrs. Dalloway* are published.

1926 Hemingway's *The Torrents of Spring* and *The Sun Also Rises* are published; William Faulkner's *Soldiers' Pay* is published.

1927 Charles Lindbergh completes the first solo transatlantic flight.

1928 Harry Crosby publishes his *Shadows of the Sun* at his Black Sun Press; Pound's *Selected Poems* with an introduction by Eliot is published; D. H. Lawrence's *Lady Chatterley's Lover* is published.

1929 Stein and Virgil Thomson's opera *Four Saints in Three Acts* is published in *transition;* Faulkner's *The Sound and the Fury* is published; Black Sun Press publishes Kay Boyle's first book, *Short Stories;* the stock market crashes; the Great Depression begins.

1930 Dos Passos's *42nd Parallel,* the first volume of his *U.S.A.* trilogy, is published; Faulkner's *As I Lay Dying* is published; Hart Crane's *The Bridge* is published by Black Sun Press in Paris; Pound's *A Draft of XXX Cantos* is published in Paris by Nancy Cunard's Hours Press; Tristan Tzara's Dadaist prose poem *Approximate Man* is published.

1931 Salvador Dalí paints *The Persistence of Memory;* Henry Miller's *Tropic of Cancer* and Woolf's *The Waves* are published.

1932 Dos Passos's *Nineteen-Nineteen,* the second volume of his *U.S.A.* trilogy, is published.

1933 Stein's *The Autobiography of Alice B. Toklas* is published.

1934 Fitzgerald's *Tender Is the Night* is published.

1935 *Four Saints in Three Acts* debuts in New York.

1936 The Spanish Civil War begins; Djuna Barnes's *Nightwood* is published; Dos Passos's *The Big Money*, the third volume of the *U.S.A.* trilogy, is published.

1937 Breton's Surrealist novel *L'Amour fou* is published; Paul Klee paints *Revolutions of the Viaducts*; René Magritte paints *The Pleasure Principle*; Joan Miró paints *Still Life with Old Shoe*; Wallace Stevens's poetry collection *The Man with the Blue Guitar* is published.

1938 Germany marches into Austria; Jean-Paul Sartre's *La Nausée* is published.

1939 Joyce's *Finnegans Wake* is published; Abstract Expressionist painter Willem de Kooning exhibits his *Seated Man* in New York

1940 Jung's *Psychology and Religion* is published; Stravinsky composes his *Symphony in C Minor.*

HISTORY OF EXPATRIATE MODERNISM

Some years before his death in 1961, Ernest Hemingway began a series of autobiographical sketches describing his rise to literary eminence four decades earlier. As *A Moveable Feast* (1964) illustrates, an inspirational environment was essential to his success. No matter how skilled or disciplined, a writer cannot mature without surroundings that invigorate the imagination. For Hemingway, satisfying this need meant abandoning Chicago, where he worked as a writer for the *Cooperative Commonwealth,* for Paris, France, "the town best organized for a writer to write in that there is."[1] Once free to roam the scenic streets of Paris, he could carry his notebook and pencils in his coat until he happened upon an inviting café whose marble-topped tables and lingering aroma of café au lait were conducive to artistic creation. Yet, the subject of his writing was not necessarily the exciting sights and sounds of the *ville lumière* or "city of light." While the French capital provided the setting for some early prose sketches, the woods and rivers of northern Michigan where Hemingway learned to hunt and fish in his youth also preoccupied him.[2] Why journey all the way to Paris to write about Michigan? "I had already seen the end of fall come through boyhood, youth and young manhood," he explains, "and in one place you could write about it better than in another. That was called transplanting yourself, I thought, and it could be as necessary with people as with other sorts of growing things" (5). As *A Moveable Feast* makes clear, for Hemingway to become a great American writer, he first had to leave America.

Hemingway was one of dozens—hundreds even—of aspiring American artists who transplanted themselves to Europe in the 1920s. The actual amount of time he lived in Paris was relatively brief—roughly six of his sixty years, with additional extended stays in later periods of life (1929, 1937–1938, and 1956). Many of his novels, stories, and essays offer vivid descriptions of other exotic locales he visited during his life-long adventures, from the battlefields of Italy and Spain to the plains of

Hemingway's passport photo, c. 1930.

Africa and the seas surrounding Cuba. Yet, no matter how widely he traveled, Hemingway always retained a special affection for Paris. "There is never any ending to Paris," reads the final paragraph of *A Moveable Feast.* "Paris was always worth it and you received return for whatever you brought to it" (211). Because the city so shaped Hemingway's sensibility, his works cannot be fully understood without appreciating its effect on him. Equally important, Paris was not a vacuum. Hemingway never could have plied his craft there had the city not provided sanctuary for a loose affiliation of writers and poets whose literary aims complemented his. Although he hated to acknowledge the fact—like most writers, Hemingway believed himself wholly unique and individual—he was part of a literary movement.

No classification adequately encapsulates the diverse themes and goals of such disparate writers as Hemingway, Gertrude Stein, Ezra Pound, F. Scott Fitzgerald, John Dos Passos, E. E. Cummings, Sherwood Anderson, and Djuna Barnes, who congregated in Paris throughout the 1920s. Historians dub them the "Lost Generation," borrowing a phrase from Stein that Hemingway made famous in *The Sun Also Rises* (1926). On the other hand, because it reveals nothing about their artistic intentions and because Hemingway regarded it as an albatross around his generation's neck, this label is insufficient for conveying the role of this movement in American literature. A better designation might be *expatriate modernism,* for it identifies both the broader literary movement in which these authors participated and the experience of life abroad that is central to much of their writing.

To *expatriate* means to abandon one's homeland out of some fundamental dissatisfaction with its morals, attitudes, or character. In discussions of Hemingway and his peers, the word is used interchangeably with *exile,* in part because of the influence of Malcolm Cowley's *Exile's Return* (1934), an early study of the movement. But a slight difference in connotation renders these terms imperfect synonyms. "In early use an exile was a banished man, a wanderer or roamer: *exsul,*" Mary McCarthy explains. "The exile is essentially a political figure, though the offense he has committed may have been in the sphere of morals. . . . He is an unhealthy element sent to lonely quarantine in some remote spot."[3] One of the most famous literary exiles is the Italian poet Dante, who was banished from his native city Florence in the early fourteenth century. Dante's bitterness at being condemned to a rootless, vagabond existence is evident in his greatest achievement, the section of *The Divine Comedy* (ca. 1307–1320) called the *Inferno,* in which he imagines a journey through Hell, where the newest residents are the political foes responsi-

EXILES VS. EXPATRIATES

Famous literary exiles:

Ovid (43 B.C.-A.D. 18), Roman poet exiled in A.D. 8 to the Black Sea by Emperor Augustus for ambiguous crimes against the empire.

Dante Alighieri (1265-1321), Florence-born poet and writer banished from his native land in October 1301 when a coup d'etat unseated the reigning party he supported.

Voltaire (1694-1778), French satirist and philosopher exiled to England in the 1720s for his attacks on the French crown and nobility.

Jean-Jacques Rousseau (1712-1778), French philosopher and novelist whose theories on the sanctity of the individual earned him exile to Switzerland. He was allowed to return to France in 1770 only when he agreed to write nothing displeasing to the government or the Church.

Thomas Mann (1875-1955), German author of *The Magic Mountain* (1924) who voluntarily left Germany for Switzerland when Hitler's Nazi party assumed power in 1933. His expatriation officially became exile when the Nazis revoked his citizenship. He became an American citizen in 1944, after lecturing for more than a decade against fascism.

Vladimir Nabokov (1899-1977), Russian-born writer whose politically prominent family went into exile in the wake of the Bolshevik revolution.

Alexander Solzhenitsyn (1918-), Russian-born novelist deported from the Soviet Union in 1974 for his exposés of life in Communist *gulags*, or prison labor camps.

ble for his predicament. The expatriate, by contrast, is a self-imposed exile. "His main aim," according to McCarthy, "is never to go back to his native land or, failing that, to stay away as long as possible. His departure was wholly voluntary. . . . The average expatriate thinks about his own country rarely and with great unwillingness. He feels he has escaped from it."[4] Exiles and expatriates may criticize their native cultures with equal fervor, but the type of displacement each suffers is different. For the exile, life abroad is a judicial sentence that carries the stigma of punishment, whether merited or not. *Emigrés* (those who voluntarily emigrate from their native country to another) are more likely to experience their border crossings as an opportunity, an adventure, or—in the artist's case—as a stimulus to the imagination.

Modernism is much harder to define with specificity because it encompasses an international array of movements in literature, painting, and music, few members of which regarded each other with much affection or esteem. In general, this classification is an umbrella term describing the response of the arts to a bewildering conflux of political, social, and technological changes that engulfed the globe at the turn of the century. A short list of these changes includes the following:

- *The rise of radical theories in the natural sciences, psychology, philosophy, and physics that eroded belief in the power of humanity to determine its destiny.* Among the most influential of these theorists were Friedrich Nietzsche, Charles Darwin, and Sigmund Freud. Nietzsche (1844–1900) rejected Christian virtues such as humility and servitude, insisting that aggression, will, and power were the most important human instincts. Darwin (1809–1882) advanced the theories of evolution and natural selection. His argument discounted any divine influence in the rise of the human species and insisted that nature was a product of chance rather than design. For his part, Freud (1856–1939), by arguing the unconscious mind's dominion over human behavior, imagined the existence of a psychic underworld where uncontrollable impulses rather than reason ruled. Combined, these three thinkers undermined faith in civilization's ability to evolve through discipline and self-control. By insisting that human motives could be reduced to a universal schema (or organized framework) of complexes and disorders, they struck a major blow against the idea that individuals are inherently unique, a notion central to much nineteenth-century political and social thinking. The three are representative of a shift in the sciences toward dehumanization, which rejected the premise that humanity was intuitively moral and capable of imitating a divine ideal. Other discoveries, such as Albert Einstein's theory of relativity and Ernest Rutherford's model of the atom, likewise demystified the universe by reducing it to an impersonal world of mathematical systems, theorems, and formulae.

- *The proliferation of new technologies that altered the experience of time, distance, speed, and other perceptual measures.* Innovations such as the automobile, the airplane, the telephone, the cinema, and electricity collapsed spatial and temporal boundaries between cultures while accelerating their pace. Technology made the world a smaller place by linking remote locations. It also abetted the dehumanization process by mechanizing the rou-

Famous literary expatriates:

George Gordon, Lord Byron (1788-1824), British baron and author of *Childe Harold's Pilgrimage* (1812) who traveled abroad to Spain, Portugal, and Greece, abandoning England forever in 1816 after financial problems and rumors of incest destroyed his reputation.

Joseph Conrad (1857-1924), Ukrainian-born author of Polish descent who became a British subject in 1886; his years as a sailor inspired his classics such as *Lord Jim* (1900) and "Heart of Darkness" (1902).

Federico García Lorca (1898-1936), Spanish poet and dramatist whose *Poet in New York* (1940) was inspired by his expatriation to America in the late 1920s. García Lorca eventually returned to Spain, where he was executed by fascists in August 1936 during the Spanish Civil War.

Richard Wright (1908-1960), African-American novelist and short-story writer best known for his 1940 novel *Native Son.* Wright relocated to Paris shortly after the end of World War II, where his interest in the black experience of the rural American South broadened to colonial African politics.

V. S. Naipaul (1932-), author of *In a Free State* (1971) and *A Bend in the River* (1979), among other works. Born in Trinidad but has lived in England since 1955.

Salman Rushdie (1947-), best known for *The Satanic Verses* (1988), which provoked calls for its author's death from the devout Muslim government of Iran. Born in India, educated in England, he lived in seclusion for more than a decade, until the Iranian government announced in 1998 that it would no longer seek to have the death sentence carried out.

Hadley and Ernest Hemingway, shortly after their September 1921 wedding. Late in life, Hemingway nostalgically recalled their marriage in several works, including *A Moveable Feast* and *Islands in the Stream.*

---

tines of daily life. Although celebrated for making the conditions of human existence more comfortable, the unceasing flow of inventions demanded that people accept instability and rapid change as necessary byproducts of progress. As a result, the idea of tradition appeared an impossibility in a dynamic age characterized by impermanence and perpetual transition.

- *The rise of mass markets that trumpeted the pleasures of consumerism while devaluing thrift and frugality.* An expanding range of goods competing for consumer attention, increased availability of credit, and the professionalization of the advertising and public-relations industry all effected a striking change in economic and financial attitudes. As sociologist Thorstein Veblen argued in *The Theory of the Leisure Class* (1899), middle-class Western culture no longer valued work and was becoming obsessed instead with lifestyle. Veblen coined several famous phrases, including "conspicuous consumption" and "pecuniary emulation," to describe an outbreak of materialism by which individuals defined their social status through external trappings. Because the working class aspired to the leisure and possessions traditionally reserved for the wealthy, communal ties eroded as households competed against each other with ostentatious displays of affluence. Other critics complained of a more odious effect of mass consumption: as consumer products were distributed across a nationwide network of retailers, communities began to lose their regional peculiarity and assume a generic sameness. Consumerism threatened to rob America of a prized resource—its diversity.

Such changes came so rapidly at the dawn of the twentieth century that a wedge appeared to split the past and present into irreconcilable halves. Many commentators dramatized the sheer suddenness of these transformations by ascribing a date to the moment older traditions and beliefs became irrelevant. "On or about December 1910 human nature changed," Virginia Woolf wrote in 1924. "All human relations shifted—those between masters and servants, husbands and wives, parents and children. And when human relations change there is at the same time a change in religion, conduct, politics, and literature."[5] D. H. Lawrence suggested that 1915 was the actual *annus mirabilis,* or miracle year, while still others pointed elsewhere on the calendar. Such estimates were not seriously aiming to identify the actual inauguration of the new epoch but to suggest the flicked-light-switch speed with which it occurred. Everyday life became so different on so many levels that one observer suggested that the world had changed more in the previous thirty years than it had since the days of Jesus Christ.

Because the rupture with tradition was so drastic, artists recognized that existing forms of expression were obsolete. Accordingly, modernists defined themselves, in Herbert Read's words, as the "tradition of the new."[6] Seeking to document the uncertainty around them, they experimented with radical, innovative styles intended to re-create in language the experience of discontinuity. These innovations included such literary techniques as fragmentation (breaking a narrative into disconnected parts), juxtaposition (placing clashing elements against each other), and stream of consciousness (descriptions of the mind's flow of thought). Thematically, modernist texts are often pessimistic about the break with the past. Many are even apocalyptic. William Butler Yeats's poem "The Second Coming" (1921) conveys the ominous feeling that history now measured civilization's decline rather than its progress: "Things fall apart; the centre cannot hold; / Mere anarchy is loosed upon the world, / The blood-dimmed tide is loosed, and everywhere / The ceremony of innocence is drowned."[7]

Despite their gloomy tone, modernists believed that art was the lone resource by which humanity could transcend its confusion. Some modernist factions such as the futurists, Dadaists, and Surrealists exploited the shock of the new for sensational purposes.[8] But most sought to reconnect readers with the past that now seemed so distant and antiquated. Poets such as Pound, T. S. Eliot, and H. D. (Hilda Doolittle) maintained ties to tradition by incorporating many allusions to classical mythology and literature into their work. As Eliot wrote of the Irish novelist James Joyce's method in *Ulysses* (1922), "manipulating a continuous parallel between contemporaneity and antiquity" provided writers a "way of controlling, of ordering, of giving a shape and a significance to the immense panorama of futility and anarchy which is contemporary history."[9] Not all modernists agreed with this approach. Hemingway found it too academic, and, like Fitzgerald, he preferred to describe the dramatic struggle of individuals to uphold values in a world of shifting standards.

Not all writers in 1920s Paris, however, can be classified as modernists. As Jean Méral's *Paris in American Literature* (1989) documents, several popular novels such as Homer Croy's *They Had to See Paris* (1926) and Lyon Mearson's *The French They Are A Funny Race* (1931) exhibited little literary merit; their only aim was to cash in on the reputation of Paris as a bohemian hotbed of decadence. By the same token, not all American modernists were expatriates. Despite the examples of such writers as Hemingway, Stein, and Pound, important writers such as Robert Frost, Wallace Stevens, and Marianne Moore rejected the idea that American literature was better when written abroad. Still others—including William Carlos Williams and William Faulkner—made brief, unproductive forays to the city but found life in their home communities more inspiring. Nor was Paris the only foreign capital to host an American literary colony. Before the 1920s, London was the most influential site of expatriate modernism, while Berlin, Vienna, and Mexico City at various times proved popular destinations for aspiring artists. Despite these qualifications, historians agree that expatriate Paris was a dominant influence on American literature in the 1920s. Accordingly, a more specific set of characteristics typical of Hemingway and his peers can be formulated.

1. *Expatriate modernists depict displacement as a fundamental condition of life in the early twentieth century.* Because Hemingway (born 21 July 1899) and the majority of his expatriate contemporaries came of age during the first two decades of the century, they experienced the tumultuous transformations of the era in a distinctly generational way. "We

were the last group to grow up under the formidable discipline of the nineteenth century," explains Winifred Ellerman, pen name "Bryher," in her autobiography *The Heart to Artemis: A Writer's Memoirs* (1962). "All of us had been taught as soon as we could speak that abnegation and hard work give us security and peace. The battle of the trenches cracked this myth from one end of Europe to the other. The Armistice offered us influenza, inflation and loss. In such a seething epoch of personal tragedy, the only thing left to believe in was art."[10] As Fitzgerald explained in his first novel, *This Side of Paradise* (1920), this generation had "grown up to find all Gods dead, all wars fought, all faiths in man shaken."[11] As a result, they imagined themselves dispossessed, cast out of the security of cultural continuity. Living in such a transitional time left them without guidelines or traditions to follow.

Foreign travel became a pastime in the 1920s in part because it provided a perfect metaphor for expressing this orphanlike sense of not belonging. Anyone voyaging abroad confronts innumerable cultural differences, from languages one cannot speak to social customs that seem unusual and even to food that seems unappealing. These differences engender anxious feelings of alienation and loneliness. Most travelers compensate by imagining their comfort upon returning home. But expatriate modernists did not believe a homecoming was possible. Because their childhood world was now so old-fashioned and irrelevant to the contemporary scene, they saw themselves cut loose from their moorings, doomed to drift from port to port in search of a stability they were not sure they would ever find.

2. *Expatriate modernists denounce America as a land of repressive morality where puritanical attitudes render the nation incapable of acknowledging the uncertainties of the age.* Contributing to the modernists' sense of displacement was their belief that the vast bulk of Americans failed to appreciate the complexities of modern life. Mainstream America, they insisted, was too business-minded, too conservative and pragmatic, and too rooted in its inflexible presumption of moral superiority to comprehend the disruptions brought about by cultural and technological change. For many critics, Warren G. Harding's 1920 election to the presidency symbolized the national mood. Inarticulate, unassuming, and inoffensive, Harding struck many as less a visionary leader than a bumbling uncle. His installation in office corresponded with a series of treatises condemning America for its similarly dull, obtuse demeanor. Titles such as *The Wine of the Puritans* and *The Puritan's Will to Power* suggest that the heritage of the pilgrim founders offered a convenient target for ridiculing the country as sexually

SINCLAIR LEWIS AND "BABBITTRY"

Perhaps the most enduring symbol of writers' disdain in the 1920s for the American middle class is George F. Babbitt, the main protagonist of Sinclair Lewis's best-selling 1922 novel *Babbitt.* As an endlessly enterprising "middleman," Babbitt symbolized the mindless conformity of white-collar workers who embodied the belief—first articulated later in the decade by Calvin Coolidge, who succeeded Warren G. Harding in the White House in 1923—that "the business of America is business." As *Babbitt's* vitriolic satire insisted, the ambitions of the average American were limited to joining the Chamber of Commerce, accumulating newfangled inventions (in one hilarious episode, Babbitt becomes enthusiastic over his new water cooler), and reveling in gas-bag orations on the nobility of the Protestant work ethic. By the middle of the novel, however, Babbitt becomes dissatisfied with the rat race; suddenly aware of the emptiness of his existence, he indulges in an affair, socializes with a debauched coterie known as "the Bunch," and openly tangles with a civic group with the ominous moniker of "the Good Citizens' Brigade." Although Babbitt ultimately returns to his complacent job and marriage, he can never again accept the notion that prosperity and happiness are synonymous. "I've never done a single thing I've wanted to in my whole life!" he tells his son in the closing paragraphs. "I don't know 's I've accomplished anything except just get along." By confessing the ultimate banality of business and civic duty, *Babbitt* established a powerful stereotype that lingered throughout both the decade and the century. Indeed, "Babbittry" has entered the popular vernacular as a term describing the hollow rhetoric of middle-class ambition.

repressed and intellectually ignorant. As William Carlos Williams argued, the Puritan race was "incapable of flowering," and, as a result, the "American grain" remained primitive and unrefined, a land of "gross know-nothingism, of blackened churches where hymns groan like chants from stupefied jungles."[12] Harold Stearns (whom Hemingway parodied as Harvey Stone in *The Sun Also Rises*) expressed the same sentiment but more vehemently: "The institutional life of America," he complained in *America and the Young Intellectual* (1921), "is a combination for the blackjacking of our youth into the acceptance of the *status quo* not of 1920, but of the late eighteenth century in government, of the early nineteenth century in morals and culture, and of the stone age in business."[13] The backward mentality of America was further confirmed by the adoption of the Eighteenth Amendment in 1919, which made prohibition law for the next thirteen years. In a nation in which bobbed hair, jazz, and dancing prompted efforts to legislate morality, the successful outlawing of alcoholic beverages struck intellectuals as repressive. Given the growing conservatism of the country, Stearns ended his book with advice that became the battle cry of the expatriate artist: "Get out!"

3. *Although expatriate modernists condemned American conservatism, they did not renounce their nationality. Rather, they regarded Paris as a foreign realm in which they could create new identities, craft new values, and explore unconventional and taboo behaviors.* Few Americans were drawn to Paris out of an interest in French history, traditions, or customs. The point of living and writing abroad was not to become a citizen of another country but to free oneself from the restrictions of home. (It also helped that the exchange rate made living in

France unusually cheap; in the mid 1920s, one could rent a comfortable apartment for less than fifty dollars per month). Expatriation was a means of opening one's eyes, of learning to question authority and truth, and, perhaps most important, of experimenting with life-styles that across the Atlantic would provoke condemnation or carry legal consequences.

For women writers, expatriation allowed greater social mobility by freeing them from the obligation either to marry or to take up a traditionally female occupation such as schoolteaching. Gays and lesbians also fled to Europe because they could more openly express their sexual preference there. Homo-sexuals in America lived closeted lives, hiding their orientation either by posing as room-mates or by entering marriages of convenience. In Paris, however, one could maintain a same-sex relationship without fear of arrest or harassment. Wealthier expatriates such as Natalie Barney (1876–1972) established liter-ary salons where lesbian writers gathered to read their work to a sympathetic audience. Other couples, including Gertrude Stein and Alice B. Toklas, and Sylvia Beach and Adrienne Monnier, lived less flamboyantly in domiciles that were models of domestic monogamy. Afri-can Americans also found Paris a haven; jazz clubs thrived in a section of Northern Paris called Montmartre, where writers such as Lang-ston Hughes and Claude McKay enjoyed the racial tolerance of the city. Jessie Fauset explained in 1925 why writers of color were drawn to the city: "I am in Paris where nobody cares—not even Americans, it seems—whether an artist is white, black or yellow."[14] For those who felt like exiles while living in their own homeland, the appeal of Paris rested in its reputation for tolerance. The only people not welcome were chaperones and snoops.

But expatriation did not just provide an escape from American puritanism. It was also seen as a means of creating a new American type—more cosmopolitan or internationally minded, more politically aware,

Hemingway with his oldest son Jack, called "Bumby," skiing in Austria, mid 1920s.

THE GREAT WAR: A STATISTICAL OVERVIEW

Number of German fatalities	1.8 million
Number of Russian fatalities	1.7 million
Number of French fatalities	1.4 million
Number of Austrian-Hungarian fatalities	1.2 million
Number of British fatalities	947,000
Number of American fatalities	48,000
Number of Americans dead from postwar outbreaks of influenza	56,000
Total estimated cost of the war	$180 billion (in 1920 dollars)

Important literary works on World War I: *Collected Poems,* Wilfred Owen (1920, British); *1917: One Man's Initiation,* John Dos Passos (1920, American); *The Enormous Room,* E. E. Cummings (1922, American); *A Son at the Front,* Willa Cather (1923, American); *All Quiet on the Western Front,* Erich Maria Remarque (1928, German); *A Farewell to Arms,* Ernest Hemingway (1929, American); *A Testament of Youth,* Vera Brittain (1933, British); *Seven Pillars of Wisdom,* T. E. Lawrence (1935, British).

Source: Hew Strachan, *World War I: A History* (New York: Oxford University Press, 1998).

more appreciative of art. In truth, the theory worked better than the practice. Most expatriates congregated on and around the Boulevard du Montparnasse on the Left Bank in Paris, an enclave known for housing poets and writers of different nationalities. There one could pass an entire day lounging in cafés that catered to Americans while reading English-language newspapers. One need not know much French to get by, for ordering meals and negotiating tips with waiters, taxi drivers, and concierges required only rudimentary familiarity with the language. At one point, a Chicago cab company even imported American taxis to make the city more like home.

Because Americans were detached both from their homeland and from their adopted home, they were able to experiment with their identities, adopting and discarding different aspects of them, all the while exploring in their writing the philosophical question of how personality is determined by one's setting. As J. Gerald Kennedy suggests, living in Paris allowed expatriates to ponder the "ancient human predicament" of "the ungrounded self":

> A lengthy stay in an alien place must produce certain changes in the way one feels, thinks, sees, and writes. In the difference between the immediate scene of exile . . . and those real, remembered scenes of homeland, one confronts the anxiety of the ungrounded self. No mere homesickness, this condition exposes a radical uncertainty about one's relation to "home" and to the self one has been. . . . The experience of exile reveals a different, foreign self while disclosing the stranger whom one no longer resembles.[15]

This conflict between the former self and the foreign self is a major theme in modernist writing. This process of transformation, which typically leads to identity crises and confusion, is not caused, however, by the site of expatriation. Rather, the source of anxiety is the individual's awareness that identity is unstable and prone to shift when placed against different backdrops. Thus, in Hemingway's most famous exploration of expatriation, *The Sun Also Rises*, Paris is depicted, in Kennedy's words, as "a town without pity suffused by sexual ambivalence, inversion, masochism, and despair; a site of frenetic and seemingly random movement." Hemingway is not saying that these troubling characteristics are inherent to the metropolis itself. His characters view the *ville lumière* through their own disturbed perspectives and convert it into what Kennedy describes as a symbol or "index of" their "moral confusion."[16] In essence, a foreign locale comes to represent whatever temptations and indulgences expatriates must suppress while on their native soil.

4. *Expatriate modernists also explore the consequences of World War I, depicting it as a major cause of their disillusionment and disaffection.* Of the many displacements experienced by Hemingway's generation, none affected them as intensely as "the Great War," as World War I was called before the rise of Adolf Hitler guaranteed its gruesome sequel. Often described as the first modern military exchange, this international conflict (1914–1918) left some fifteen million people dead, decimated vast stretches of Europe, and introduced such fearsome tools of destruction as the airplane, machine gun, poison gas, and the landmine to modern weaponry arsenals. Perhaps the greatest casualty was the idea that war was a noble endeavor fought for patriotism, the honor and glory of sacrifice, and the valiant defense of one's principles and convictions. Of course, to suggest that World War I was the first war ever in which soldiers questioned the reasons for fighting would be a gross exaggeration; every military contest suffers crises of purpose when idealized notions of heroism confront grim battlefield realities. Yet, the battle between the Central Powers (Germany, Austria-Hungary, and Turkey) and the Allies (England, France, Italy, Russia [1914–1917] and the United States) resulted in unprecedented cynicism toward the motives for armed conquest. The looming reality that the conflict was a war of attrition fought from immovable trenches was partly responsible. Whole battalions were sacrificed for yards of territory at a time. Four hundred thousand British soldiers died for five miles of land at Ypres in Belgium; more than one million died in the battle of the Somme in Northern France in 1916. Amid such massacres, clearly the ultimate winner would be whichever side could sustain the greatest losses without surrendering. Soldiers also grew bitter over censored press accounts from the front. Believing newspapers romanticized the conditions troops faced, they grew distrustful of any authority figure, military or civic, who believed that obscuring the reality of life on the front lines was necessary for maintaining morale.

Long before America joined the campaign in April 1917, a sense of discontent was rampant among such British soldier-poets as Siegfreid Sassoon and Wilfred Owen. In detailing the grueling world of the infantryman, these writers hoped to expose the naiveté of the visions of glory that inspired them to enlist in the war effort. "If you could hear . . . the blood gargling from froth-corrupted lungs," Owen admonished parents in "Dulce et Decorum Est" as he described the effects of mustard gas, "You would not tell with such high zest / To children ardent for some desperate glory, / The old Lie: Dulce et decorum est / Pro patria moria [Great and glorious is it to die for one's country]."[17] Americans who witnessed equal brutality also began publishing novels and stories informing readers of the miseries of war. Works such as John Dos Passos's *Three Soldiers* (1921), E. E. Cummings's *The Enormous Room* (1922), and Hemingway's *A Farewell to Arms* (1929) protested the carnage of the war and detailed the psychological scars of those who survived the slaughter. "I was always embarrassed by the words sacred, glorious, and sacrifice," the narrator of *A Farewell to Arms,* Frederic Henry, says amid the wreckage of the Italian front. "I had seen nothing sacred, and the things that were glorious had no glory and the sacrifices were like the stockyards at Chicago if nothing was done with the meat except to bury it."[18]

The Great War influenced modernist literature in many ways. It inspired writers to experiment with techniques to convey the accelerated pace and disorienting absurdity of trench life. Exposure to battle also drove authors toward more graphic prose styles that described in detail the bloodshed and gore soldiers witnessed. But the most striking effect of the war on American writing was its tone. Paul Fussell remarks that "the most pervasive contribution of war to modernist culture is irony," meaning that soldiers' shell-shocked detachment became the dominant attitude or "normative mentality" of expatriate modernism.[19] In several works, including Hemingway's, characters cope with the cataclysm of battle by disengaging their emotions and affecting a hard-boiled facade. This aloof, alienated aura is not reserved just for soldiers. Postwar expatriate characters also retreat into indifference to avoid grappling with the enormity of the war. The result is that in modernist writing the *dramatis personae* seem more like spectators than participants in the action. They observe events but are not moved by them; in many cases they are powerless to respond other than to acknowledge the strangeness of what they witness.

This passive, observational attitude also owes something to the fact that many American writers who witnessed the war firsthand did so not as soldiers but as volunteers for various relief agencies. Hemingway, Dos Passos, and Cummings are just a few of those who later became novelists and poets who made their way overseas as drivers for different ambulance services, including the American Red Cross. Others such as Stein, who had already lived in Europe for a decade when the hostilities erupted, worked for the American Fund for the French Wounded, which distributed care packages to hospitals and shelled villages. Cowley's *Exile's Return* explains how observing warfare as relief workers contributed to these writers' detachment:

> One might almost say that the ambulance corps and the French military transport were college-extension courses for a generation of writers. But what did these courses teach? . . . They carried us to a foreign country, the first that most of us had seen; they taught us to make love, stammer love, in a foreign language. They fed and lodged us at the expense of a government in which we had no share. They made us more irresponsible than before: livelihood was not a problem; we had a minimum of choices to make; we could let the future take care of itself, feeling certain that it would bear us into new adventures. They taught us courage, extravagance, fatalism, these being the virtues of men at war; they taught us to regard as vices the civilian virtues of thrift, caution and sobriety; they made us fear boredom more than death. All these lessons might have been learned in any branch of the army, but ambulance service had a lesson of its own: it instilled into us what might be called a *spectatorial* attitude.[20]

As chapter 4 demonstrates, Hemingway criticizes this observational detachment, even when his sympathetic characters succumb to it. For him, the moral struggle of modern life was to resist what Cowley describes as the apathetic pose of "monumental indifference" that became fashionable in the postwar years.[21] Nor was he alone in this criticism. The best expatriate modernists recognized that, although the war made belief in the values their elders bequeathed them impossible, to craft new ideals that would impose order and clarity upon the confusions of modern life remained the responsibility of the younger generation.

5. *Expatriate modernism is a youth-culture movement.* It arose in part from a generation gap in American society that divided Victorian parents from young people raised amid modernity's tumult. The restlessness and confusion that expatriate writers express also reflects this generation's uncertainty over the value of maturation. In a world in which adulthood seemed an initiation into little more than hypocrisy and deceit, growing up for them signaled a fall from innocence into moral corruption.

With the exceptions of Stein and Sherwood Anderson, many expatriates were still in their youth when they experienced the twin onslaughts of modernity and World War I. The vast cultural and technological transformations they witnessed as teens made the mores of their Victorian upbringing obsolete without providing alternatives to direct their *paysage moralisé,* or "moral passage," to maturity. Nor were they

"THEY WANT TO KNOW": YOUTH, IDEALISM, REBELLION

Countless articles in the 1920s debated the rebelliousness of the Lost Generation, pondering in particular whether modern youth represented a threat to American morals or a rejection of out-moded, hypocritical ideals. In December 1926 *The New Republic* began its inquiry into "hard-boiled youth" with a passage from *The Sun Also Rises* in which Jake Barnes wonders about "how to live in it": "Maybe, if you found out how to live in it," Jake says, "you learned from that what it was all about." For the magazine, Jake's ruminations confirmed that young people in the 1920s were not outlaws or hooligans but pragmatists who understood that religion, morality, and idealism no longer governed the postwar world: "Assuming . . . that young people wake up to find themselves in a world without a plan and without authoritative instruction, how do they propose to get their bearings? At present, so far as we can see, they do not bother much about it. They are quite content to eat and drink, swear and sing, work and love and now and then pretend to be sorry for themselves. Yet without any relapse towards subordination to doubtful authority, they can try another route. Scepticism cannot rob them of life itself and their animal faith in life. Perhaps, as Mr. Hemingway says, they can learn by living. They are not sure that they can learn by living, but they feel sure they cannot learn without living. The only way to find out is to try to behave as if they are able to live and learn. Their scepticism, instead of being a handicap to the acquisition of this experimental knowledge, is transformed into a preparation and a stimulus. . . ."

"They Want to Know Why," *The New Republic*, 49 (29 December 1926): 151.

sure they wanted to grow up, for age commanded little respect by the time they entered their early twenties. "The older generation pretty well ruined this world before passing it on to us," John F. Carter Jr. declared in the *Atlantic Monthly* in 1920. "My generation is disillusionized and, I think, brutalized, by the cataclysm which *their* complacent folly engendered. . . . And now they are surprised that a great many of us, because they have taken away our apple-cheeked ideals, are seriously considering whether or not *their* game be worth *our* candle."[22] Old before their time but disdainful of adults, young people found themselves drifting in the no-man's land separating the child and the adult. Expatriation allowed them to act out this sense of displacement, for going abroad, as Cowley notes, encouraged irresponsibility. Freed from parental supervision, expatriates could indulge in debauchery while eluding initiation rituals such as work or marriage that, back home in America, would mark them as adults.

Hemingway and his peers were hardly the first writers to abandon America for Europe. Indeed, as chapter 3 documents, there is a rich tradition of expatriation in American literature; authors from Washington Irving and Nathaniel Hawthorne to Henry James and Edith Wharton analyzed the effect of living abroad long before the Lost Generation crossed the Atlantic. Nor was Hemingway's generation the last to relocate to foreign shores. In the late 1940s, as Europe struggled to rebuild itself after the devastation of World War II, American writers such as James Jones, George Plimpton, and James Baldwin (all with well-worn copies of *The Sun Also Rises* in their travel bags) flooded Paris anew in hopes of establishing a literary revolution akin to that of the 1920s. The romantic myth of expatriation continues to exert a powerful appeal among young Americans. *The Cimarron Review,* a literary journal, dedicated a 1992 issue to the work of writers dubbed "The New Expatriates" because they explore American life abroad "thirty years A. H. (After Hemingway)":

> Why do they come? Where do they come from? And did they come to be in Europe or to get away from the States? They come, of course, from everywhere, every corner of every state. . . . Some leave America because of a company relocation, others—perhaps most—because of love, or a lack of same, still others leave to flee a dead-end job, or a job that is *too* good, that is keeping them from writing what they care about. . . . Still others come because they are attracted by the northern light or the lush landscape, the music, the art, the food, the café life. Some leave seeking sexual freedom or religious or racial freedom, only to find it necessary to move on elsewhere to avoid something worse than what they left.[23]

Such passages suggest that recent expatriates have expressed the same sense of drift and detachment as Hemingway's generation. Whether written in the 1920s or today, stories of life abroad testify to the instability of their times. In them, readers find characters trapped between a desire for peace and permanence and the reality of relentless change that was the twentieth century.

NOTES

1. Ernest Hemingway, *A Moveable Feast* (New York: Scribners, 1964), p. 182. Subsequent references to this work will be cited parenthetically in the text.

2. Hemingway does not specifically name the text he remembers writing here; however, because he claims that the "wild, cold, blowing" weather inspired him to make it "that sort of day in the story," several critics assume he refers to "The Three Day Blow," a tale published in *In Our Time,* in which two young men sit out a Michigan thunderstorm.

3. Mary McCarthy, "A Guide to Exiles, Expatriates, and Internal Emigrés," in *Altogether Elsewhere: Writers on Exile,* edited by Marc Robinson (Boston: Faber & Faber, 1994), p. 49.

4. Ibid., p. 51.

5. Virginia Woolf, "Mr. Bennett and Mrs. Brown," in her *The Captain's Death Bed and Other Essays* (New York: Harcourt, Brace, 1950), p. 96.

6. Herbert Read, *Art Now* (New York: Pitman, 1936; revised and enlarged as *Art Now: An Introduction to the Theory of Modern Painting and Sculpture,* 1968), p. 51.

7. William Butler Yeats, "The Second Coming," in his *The Poems of William Butler Yeats,* edited by Richard J. Finneran (New York: Macmillan, 1983), p. 187.

8. Definitions of the different modernist schools can be found in the glossary of this study.

9. T. S. Eliot, "*Ulysses,* Order, and Myth," in his *Selected Prose of T. S. Eliot,* edited by Frank Kermode (New York: Harcourt Brace Jovanovich, 1975), p. 177.

10. Winifred "Bryher" Ellerman, *The Heart to Artemis: A Writer's Memoirs* (New York: Harcourt, Brace & World, 1962), p. 203.

11. F. Scott Fitzgerald, *This Side of Paradise* (New York: Scribners, 1920), p. 282.

12. William Carlos Williams, "The Voyage of the Pilgrims," in his *The William Carlos Williams Reader,* edited by M. L. Rosenthal (New York: New Directions, 1966), pp. 343, 345.

13. Harold Stearns, *America and the Young Intellectual* (New York: Doran, 1921), p. 166.

14. Quoted in *The Left Bank Revisited: Selections from the Paris Tribune, 1917–1934,* edited by Hugh Ford (University Park: Pennsylvania State University Press, 1972), pp. 47–48.

15. J. Gerald Kennedy, *Imagining Paris: Place, Writing, and American Identity* (New Haven, Conn.: Yale University Press, 1993), pp. 27–28.

16. Ibid., pp. 97–98.

17. Wilfred Owen, "Dulce et Decorum Est," in *The Norton Book of Modern War,* edited by Paul Fussell (New York: Norton, 1991), p.166.

18. Ernest Hemingway, *A Farewell to Arms* (New York: Scribners, 1929), p. 196.

19. Paul Fussell, "World War I," in *The Norton Book of Modern War,* edited by Fussell (New York: Norton, 1991), p. 24.

20. Malcolm Cowley, *Exile's Return: A Narrative of Ideas* (New York, 1934); revised and enlarged as *Exile's Return: A Literary Odyssey of the 1920s* (New York: Viking, 1951), p. 38.

21. Ibid., p. 43.

22. John F. Carter Jr., "Those Wild Young People," *Atlantic Monthly,* 126 (1920): 302–303.

23. Thomas E. Kennedy, "The New Expatriates: American Writers in Europe Today," *The Cimarron Review,* 100 (1992): 10–11.

REPRESENTATIVE WRITERS

When Ernest Hemingway arrived in Paris in late December 1921, he could hardly call himself a writer. For more than two years, since his return to Oak Park, Illinois, from Milan, Italy, where he had recuperated from his wounding at the Italian front, he had tried to break into the commercial short-story market. Without exception, magazines such as *The Saturday Evening Post* and *Red Book* rejected his early efforts; even for editors who prized generic romance plots and stock characters, Hemingway's apprentice fiction was derivative and unsubstantial. "No matter how hard he worked at his stories," according to biographer Michael S. Reynolds, "Hemingway had not yet learned to invent out of his own experience. He used settings that he knew—Kansas City, Chicago, Italy—but the characters remained weak imitations from other men's work."[1]

Had Hemingway not relocated to Paris, he might have abandoned fiction writing and contented himself with newspaper work, as many would-be authors his age did. Expatriation supplied the isolation and time necessary for him to focus on his craft and develop his own vision and voice. Paris also introduced him to a community of expatriate modernists who encouraged and taught him. Within three years, members of this community published two small-press collections of Hemingway's work, *Three Stories and Ten Poems* (1923) and *in our time* (1924). Several other Paris friends helped Hemingway secure a commercial publisher for an expanded version of *In Our Time* in 1925 and *The Sun Also Rises* in 1926. After the publication of *The Sun Also Rises*, Hemingway's popularity overshadowed most of his peers' achievements. Because he became the standard against which they were measured, the general reader may possess little knowledge of other important expatriate modernists of the 1920s. An overview of Hemingway's Paris years thus serves as an introduction to the lives and work of these sometimes overlooked authors.

From left to right: Ford Madox Ford, James Joyce, and Ezra Pound with modernist patron John Quinn in Paris, early 1920s.

Probably Hemingway would not have chosen Paris as the site of his expatriation had he not befriended Sherwood Anderson in Chicago in early 1921. Although Hemingway had visited the French capital in 1918 on his way to war, his emotional ties were to Italy, where he had been wounded and where, during his recuperation, he had fallen in love with an American Red Cross nurse named Agnes von Kurowsky who encouraged and then rejected his matrimonial advances (an experience that inspired *A Farewell to Arms*). Anderson was a former paint-factory manager who at thirty-six had walked out of his job and abandoned his wife and family to pursue a literary career. When he met Hemingway, Anderson was at the peak of his influence. His short-story collection *Winesburg,*

Ohio (1919) was cited as a modernist remedy for the Victorian sentimentalism plaguing American literature. As a series of stark portraits of the repression and despair festering beneath the placid facade of small-town life, it was revered for its depiction of "grotesques," characters suffering debilitating emotional deformities. Because of the critical regard for the book and its follow-up, *The Triumph of the Egg* (1921), Anderson in 1921 received a prestigious $2,000 award from *The Dial,* a leading literary publication; the award placed him in the vanguard of American authors.

Anderson was also known for his unfailing patronage of fellow writers. He was an important advocate of Gertrude Stein in America, and when he met Hemingway, Anderson was also advising Hart Crane, whose epic poem *The Bridge* (1930) is an ambitious celebration of America. Anderson's initial advice to Hemingway was to expand his reading tastes; like most young American men, Hemingway grew up reading Rudyard Kipling and Horatio Alger, writers whose Victorian sensibilities rendered them out of date by the 1920s. For more appropriate role models, Anderson recommended European realists such as Fyodor Dostoevsky, Ivan Turgenev, and Anton Chekov—all of whom Hemingway compared himself to in later life. Anderson's greatest contribution to his friend's career, however, was to extol the creative atmosphere of Paris. After a six-month stay there, Anderson returned to Chicago in November 1921 with alluring stories of cafés, bookstores, and a coterie of modernist luminaries who welcomed promising arrivals. Anderson's 1921 journal, posthumously published as *France and Sherwood Anderson* (1976), offers ample evidence of his affection for Paris and its American literary scene.[2] His enthusiasm is as infectious as it must have been for Hemingway, who quickly convinced his wife, Hadley (whom he had married in September 1921), that their future lay in the City of Light.

Anderson supplied the Hemingways with letters of introduction to Stein, Ezra Pound, and Sylvia Beach, whose Shakespeare and Company bookstore was an important hub of modernist activity. During their initial months in Paris, Hemingway kept his sponsor informed of his gradual entry into the circle of expatriate artists in the city, sharing gossip and reporting on their impending projects. While Anderson assumed his influence over the young author had been exhausted, Hemingway was drawn to his mentor's fiction as he struggled to develop his own style. In the summer of 1922, he completed "My Old Man," a short story reminiscent of Anderson's short story "I Want to Know Why," from *Triumph of the Egg.* To Hemingway's chagrin, critics for years compared the similarities of the works. Both are set in the world of horse racing; both are narrated from the perspective of an adolescent boy; and both end with the sudden revelation that the jockeys are morally corrupt and unworthy of esteem. The revelation in "My Old Man" is more poignant because the narrator's fallen hero is his father, but Hemingway nevertheless found in "I Want to Know Why" a potent example of the "initiation story," also called the "coming-of-age tale," in which a young protagonist loses his or her innocence through a sudden, dramatic exposure to adult hypocrisy. Anderson had only recently begun to experiment with this form. His more characteristic stories in *Winesburg Ohio* and his later collection *Death in the Woods* (1933) de-emphasize plot, exploring instead the disturbed psychology of eccentric characters. For Hemingway, by contrast, the plot of "My Old Man" became a recurring story line. As Michael S. Reynolds notes, "It is his first story in which the father fails the son. In his Chicago juvenilia, he wrote several stories in which the son could not please the demanding father or some other figure whose admiration he sought. After 'My Old Man,' Hemingway's fictional fathers seldom meet the expectations of their needy sons."[3]

In Hemingway's stories, the drama of failed expectations is heightened by the major difference between "I Want to Know Why" and "My Old Man"—the latter's Paris setting. At the end of "My Old Man," the narrator, Joe, is orphaned in a city that he finds "all balled up" and alienating.[4] Unlike Milan, where he and his jockey father can make a living at "easy courses," Paris is a world of temptation and moral ambiguity. Although Joe is attracted to the girls strolling its boulevards, the city is also where his father's race-fixing is revealed. In "I Want to Know Why" locale is not symbolic. Clearly, Hemingway was tapping into expatriate feelings of isolation to underscore the theme of alienation. This underlying theme is perhaps why, despite the many affinities of the two stories, he insisted that they were nothing alike. "Sherwood has written about boys and horses," he wrote Edmund Wilson in 1923. "But very differently. . . . I know I wasn't inspired by him."[5]

Early reviewers, nevertheless, failed to see beyond the superficial similarities. As *Three Stories and Ten Poems* and *in our time* attracted attention, the association between the two writers was often discussed— a comparison that irked Hemingway. Subtly, he began to distinguish himself by criticizing the older writer's latest productions. Reviewing Anderson's autobiography, *A Story Teller's Story* (1924), Hemingway acknowledged that Anderson was "a great writer" but added that "his talent and his development of it has all been toward the short story or tale and not toward that highly artificial form, the novel."[6] He reiterated the judgment throughout his life. Anderson, for his part, was nonplused both by the criticism and by Hemingway's dislike for Anderson's novel *Many*

Marriages (1923). In fact, Anderson continued to aid his young friend's career by recommending him to publisher Horace Liveright. After Hemingway contracted with Liveright's firm in spring 1925 to publish *In Our Time,* he sheepishly thanked Anderson for his support while admitting that "probably" he "was wrong about the *Many Marriages.*"[7] Nevertheless, Hemingway's disdain for Anderson's writing erupted with even greater ferocity later that year. Not only was Anderson's novel *Dark Laughter* (1925) outselling *In Our Time,* but reviewers also again mistook Hemingway for a disciple of the older author. Even Hemingway's own mother—whom he had not seen in nearly four years—insisted on pointing out his debt to Anderson. As Hemingway complained, "My mother sends me everything that shows up Sherwood or when he gets a divorce or anything because she has read that I am much the same thing only not so good and she naturally wants me to know how the Master is getting along."[8] In Hemingway's mind, the time had come to unseat the master.

Over Thanksgiving week 1925 Hemingway composed an unfunny, vicious parody of Anderson's work called *The Torrents of Spring* (1926). The purpose of the satire was twofold. It would halt any further comparisons between the two authors, and it would have the more practical effect of freeing him from Liveright, whom Hemingway blamed for the meager sales of *In Our Time.* (Anderson was one of Liveright's most profitable writers; Hemingway rightly reasoned that the publisher would never risk offending such an important asset for his sake.) Although Hadley and many of Hemingway's Paris friends discouraged the publication of the parody, others (including Pauline Pfeiffer, who became Hemingway's second wife in 1927) agreed that Anderson was past his creative peak and was guilty of inferior art. In May 1926 Hemingway wrote to Anderson explaining that *The Torrents of Spring* was not a personal attack but a professional courtesy. Hemingway claimed that to point out the failures of *Dark Laughter* was his job as a fellow writer:

> You see I feel that if among ourselves we have to pull our punches, if when a man like yourself who can write very great things writes something that seems to me, (who have never written anything great but am anyway a fellow craftsman) rotten, I ought to tell you so. Because if we have to pull our punches and if when somebody starts to slop they just go on slopping from then on with nothing but encouragement from their contemporaries—why we'll never produce anything but Great American Writers i.e. apprentice allowance claimed.[9]

Anderson's response to this astonishing mixture of condemnation and condescension was reserved. "You always speak to me like a master to a pupil," he answered. "It must be Paris—the literary life. You didn't seem like that when I knew you."[10] By suggesting that the aspiring Oak Park artist had succumbed to the insular superiority of the expatriate crowd,

GERTRUDE STEIN AND GRACE HEMINGWAY

"Grace was born in 1872; Gertrude, who was old enough to be his mother, in 1874. Both had the same imposing, statuesque appearance. Both, according to Hemingway, had emotional problems that were connected to their change of life [menopause] and that provoked quarrels with him. . . . Both were extremely egocentric. Both were highly talented artists who felt irritated by their thwarted careers and lack of recognition."

Jeffrey Meyers, *Hemingway: A Life* (New York: Harper & Row, 1985), p. 76.

"Grace Hemingway, a large woman driven to perform as musician, singer and painter, was the genetic source of her son's creativity and a disturbing presence in his early Oak Park years. She championed women's rights, marched for the vote and was constantly in the public eye or ear. No one who knew her ever forgot her sometimes eccentric but always commanding presence, for she filled whatever stage was available. Grace Hemingway may have been the 'all-American bitch,' as Ernest later called her, but he was undoubtedly her son.

"Thus on that March afternoon when he first met Gertrude Stein, Hemingway found the Paris mother he needed. Like Grace Hemingway, Gertrude was imperious, headstrong, talented and over-weight. Both women dominated conversations and lived as they pleased."

Michael S. Reynolds, *Hemingway: The Paris Years* (New York: Blackwell, 1989), p. 35.

Anderson indulged in an understated counter-attack, for he knew how hard Hemingway had worked to distinguish himself from bohemian poseurs who delighted in condemning mainstream writers. For the most part, Anderson publicly treated *The Torrents of Spring* as a minor annoyance. Nearly twenty years later, in his posthumously published *Memoirs* (1942), he dismisses the parody by suggesting that it might "have been humorous had it been condensed into twelve pages."[11] In private, though, Anderson was deeply wounded, for the satire echoed his own fear that his career was over. Unfortunately for Anderson, Hemingway's judgment was accurate, for Anderson's talents were better suited to the short story than to the novel. While critics continue to study *Winesburg Ohio* and a select group of stories (including "I Want to Know Why"), today Anderson's novels attract little attention. Those who analyze *Many Marriages* and *Dark Laughter* are usually scholars seeking evidence of the artistic offenses that inspired Hemingway's parody.

Despite the visibility of their feud, Hemingway's most troubling literary acquaintanceship was not with Anderson. His relationship with Gertrude Stein haunted him more, for her influence extended beyond a single story to the core of his style. As he wrote in his posthumously published memoir, *A Moveable Feast*, Stein taught him "many truths about rhythms and the uses of words in repetition."[12] Some modernists—Wyndham Lewis most notably—dismissed Hemingway as unoriginal for adopting her expressive habits as his own. Stein did little to discourage this perception. In *The Autobiography of Alice B. Toklas* (1933)—a peculiar memoir in which she writes her life story from the third-person perspective of her long-term companion—Stein takes credit for "inventing" Hemingway. In retaliation, Hemingway claimed that he taught her to write dialogue and that she abandoned him out of jealousy over his commercial success. As always, the truth is more complex than either author could acknowledge. Although their relationship dissolved into mutual acrimony, in the early and mid 1920s they regarded each other with affection.

When they met in early 1922 at Anderson's encouragement, Stein had lived in Paris for nearly twenty years. She resided at one of the best-known expatriate addresses in the city—27, rue de Fleurus—which since 1913 had been recognized in Europe and America as an important meeting place for modernist painters such as Pablo Picasso, Henri Matisse, and Juan Gris. As the daughter of German-Jewish immigrants to America, Stein had come to Paris in 1903 after studying psychology under William James at Radcliffe College and attending Johns Hopkins Medical School, where she was one of a handful of female students. Her medical career floundered, however, when she failed a crucial obstetrics course; that experience, coupled with a crushing lesbian love affair, left her nearing thirty, adrift and purposeless. Originally, the intent of her expatriation was to follow in the footsteps of her older brother, Leo, a dandyish dilettante who vented frustration with his undisciplined attempts at an artistic career by denouncing his sister as an imbecile. But life abroad energized Stein's creativity and made her want to be a writer. Within a few years, she was producing volumes of experimental prose that challenged the interpretive habits by which readers typically make sense of words and sentences.

Shari Benstock offers a productive summary of Stein's aims:

> Rather than trying to master the movements of language, to discover the perfect match of word and meaning through image, metaphor, and symbol, Stein began by careful observation of linguistic nuance and submitted herself to the rhythms and sounds of language, listening carefully to the speech around her, allowing herself to be educated by language. She did what no other writer has quite had the courage to do: to relinquish the right to make language submit to the writer's will.[13]

In other words, Stein did not use words to describe people, objects, or actions. She used them for their sound and syllabic rhythms, fashioning sonic tapestries in which the music of language took precedence over its meaning. Detractors thought her writing was mere gibberish, but artists interested in the craft of literature considered Stein a formidable stylist who demonstrated the effects one could achieve in a verbal medium.

By the time Hemingway arrived in Paris, Stein was in a curious position: she was well-known but rarely read. Her first two books, *Three Lives* (1909) and *Tender Buttons* (1914), inspired equal parts reverence and ridicule among reviewers. Yet, except for whatever excerpts newspapers might print, her work was virtually unavailable to the average reader. Because commercial publishing houses saw little potential for profit in her work, she was forced to resort to the vanity press, meaning she had to pay for the privilege of seeing her name on a title page. Self-published books were poorly distributed and enjoyed little, if any, advertising support. Moreover, there was (and remains) a stigma attached to such outlets, for paying to print one's own work implies that nobody else will. The result was that Stein's writing was deemed valuable more for its influence than for its own merits.

Whenever Hemingway and his wife visited Stein's studio, they were subjected to an unusual ritual. Stein would lead him to view the paintings by Picasso and Paul Cézanne decorating her walls, while Alice B. Toklas occupied Hadley in a far corner of the studio. During their meetings, Hemingway showed Stein his tentative efforts, most of which she disliked. She considered the short story "Up in Michigan," which culminates in a graphic rape, *inaccrochable* (inappropriate for public viewing) and encouraged him to abandon a premature effort at a novel. Despite the harsh advice, he continued to frequent the rue de Fleurus, often encountering Stein during her afternoon forays through the Luxembourg Gardens. Biographer James Mellow describes the connection they shared:

> Gertrude Stein was old enough to be Hemingway's mother, just a year and four months younger than Grace Hemingway. The relationship that developed between the two in those early years of friendship might have passed for that of a son and a proud and approving mother. . . . But where Grace Hemingway was suspicious and disapproving of her son . . . Stein was flattered by Hemingway's attentiveness and encouraged their relationship. . . . Their relationship was based on a mutual interest in the writer's craft, the French sense of *métier*, a dedication to the practice of one's trade. It was a concept that Stein had adopted and one that Hemingway took up as well.[14]

From 1922 through 1924 Hemingway curried Stein's favor, writing a flattering review of her poetry collection *Geography and Plays* (1923) and updating her on his literary progress. "I've been working hard and have two things done," he reported in February 1923. "I've thought a lot about the things you said about working and am starting that way at the beginning."[15] While critics debate the extent of her influence, clearly Stein heightened Hemingway's appreciation for modernist painting; introduced him to bullfights in Pamplona, Spain, that would provide important settings for *In Our Time* and *The Sun Also Rises;* and taught him the importance of literary technique. (He also claimed in *A Moveable Feast* that she lectured him on sex). As a sign of their closeness, Hemingway asked Stein and Toklas to serve as godmothers for the Hemingways'

F. Scott Fitzgerald with wife, Zelda, and daughter, Scottie, in Rome, 1924.

child, John Hadley Nicanor, born in October 1923. But the real evidence of their relationship is found in his work. Several passages in early Hemingway stories echo Stein's style; her "Miss Furr and Miss Skeene" (1922) and his "Mr. and Mrs. Elliot" (1924) illustrate such similarities:

> Helen Furr had quite a pleasant home. Mrs. Furr was quite a pleasant woman. Mr. Furr was quite a pleasant man. Helen Furr had quite a pleasant voice a voice quite worth cultivating. She did not mind working. She worked to cultivate her voice. She did not find it gay living in the same place where she had always been living. She went to a place where some were cultivating something, voices and other things needing cultivating.[16]

> Mr. and Mrs. Elliot tried very hard to have a baby. They tried as often as Mrs. Elliot could stand it. They tried in Boston after they were married and they tried coming over on the boat. They did not try very often on the boat because Mrs. Elliot was quite sick. She was sick and when she was sick she was sick as Southern women are sick. (109)

In both cases, the strategic repetition of key words and short sentence structures creates a rhythmic effect. Stein and Hemingway used these devices, however, to achieve different ends. For her, they were tools of abstraction that allowed her to generalize her meaning, while he employed them to narrow his meaning and make it more concrete.[17] Despite this difference, echoes of Stein's rhythms were so prevalent in Hemingway's work that reviewers quickly pronounced the young writer the newest foster child of the "Mother Goose of Montparnasse."

As he had with Anderson, Hemingway grew frustrated at constant comparisons to Stein and felt the need to challenge her authority. In February 1924, while helping British expatriate Ford Madox Ford edit a literary journal called the *transatlantic review,* Hemingway arranged for the serialization of Stein's novel *The Making of Americans.* This self-described "eternal hymn to repetition," which ran some nine thousand pages in manuscript, was a Parisian legend. Written nearly a decade and a half earlier, it had circulated among baffled publishers, who recognized isolated passages of genius but found the sheer bulk of the manuscript unreadable. With only the pamphlet-sized *Three Stories and Ten Poems* in his professional portfolio, Hemingway assumed the role of seasoned editor and agent for his literary matron. His correspondence, once deferential, assumes a new authoritative tone as he notifies her of the modest fee the *transatlantic* would pay for her work. Ford "is under the impression that you get big prices when you consent to publish. I did not give him this impression but did not discourage it."[18] Stein was upset to discover that the magazine would only publish selected excerpts, not the entire magnum opus. Hemingway had either failed to inform her that the *transatlantic* could not commit to such a vast undertaking, or he had misinformed Ford as to its size. Most likely, he stretched the truth to both parties. While Stein was grateful for getting any portion of *The Making of Americans* in print, she began to doubt Hemingway's influence in the publishing world, especially when his attempts to persuade Horace Liveright of the merits of her manuscript resulted in another rejection. A decade later, Stein voiced suspicion over Hemingway's motives in her autobiography: "She [Gertrude Stein] says, yes sure I have a weakness for Hemingway. After all he was the first of the young men to knock at my door and he did make Ford print the first piece of *The Making of Americans.* I myself [Alice B. Toklas, the narrator of the book] have not so much confidence that Hemingway did do this. I have never known what the story is but I have always been certain that there was some other story behind it all."[19]

Other evidence suggests Hemingway's growing disenchantment with Stein in 1924–1925 grew out of their disagreement over the violence depicted in his writing. An allusion to her poem "Accents in Alsace" (published in *Geography and Plays*) appears in "Soldier's Home," a story about a son's alienation from his mother, who fails to appreciate how his exposure to the brutality of World War I has embittered him. The story may also be a response to her poem, "Hemingway: A Portrait" (1923), which mocks his preoccupation with war and brutality: "Is there any memorial of the failure of civilization to cope with extreme savagedom?" [20] Stein's piece concludes. As she later remarked, she believed Hemingway doomed to go "the way so many other Americans have gone before. He became obsessed with sex and death." [21] Her Hemingway poem seems an effort to steer the young writer away from "savagedom" toward less-pessimistic subjects. By contrast, he thought Stein's dislike of such topics revealed an unwillingness to acknowledge the harshness of modern life. As he declared in *A Moveable Feast*, Stein "wanted to know the gay part of how the world was going; never the real, never the bad" (25).

Despite disagreements over what was appropriate subject matter, Hemingway continued to value Stein's advice. In late October 1924 he showed her a long story about a one-man fishing trip in upper Michigan called "Big Two-Hearted River" (1925). While Stein appreciated the slow, steady picture of the woods and river, the story ended with a jarring series of comments on writing, marriage, and the Paris literary community. Telling him that "remarks are not literature," Stein encouraged him to cut these unnecessary passages and maintain the most powerful feature of the story, its reticent tone. [22] Had the original ending remained, "Big Two-Hearted River" probably would not have become one of the greatest short stories of the twentieth century.

Stein made one more memorable contribution to Hemingway's work before their relationship eroded. Over the fall of 1925, he was considering possible titles for what became his second published novel (*The Torrents of Spring* was his first). While listing his options, he recalled a story Stein had told him about a French garage owner who insisted that the war had spoiled young people under thirty. "C'est un génération perdu," the old man had complained. Although Hemingway eventually chose to call his book *The Sun Also Rises* (a phrase from Ecclesiastes), he used the quote as one of the epigraphs of the novel and credited it to Stein. The pithy pronouncement captured reviewers' attention when *The Sun Also Rises* was published in America in October 1926; it encouraged them to interpret the story as a declaration of generational discontent and gave youth in the 1920s their enduring nickname, the "Lost Generation."

Almost immediately, Hemingway began to qualify the significance of the phrase, deriding it as an example of Stein's "splendid bombast" and tendency to assume "prophetic roles." As he wrote his editor, Maxwell Perkins, in November 1926, "Nobody knows about the generation that follows them and certainly has no right to judge."[23] Hemingway never wanted to be identified as part of a literary movement, and he began to suspect that Stein was positioning herself in the media as the mother superior of expatriate writers. In "The True Story of My Break with Gertrude Stein," a parody published in *The New Yorker* in early 1927, he pokes fun at Stein's eagerness to accumulate disciples, even when they are poseurs and not true artists. At one point, as Hemingway articulates his literary goals, Stein interrupts to declare "all you young men are alike." The judgment offends his sense of individuality, but other fawning admirers visiting the rue de Fleurus are overjoyed with the declaration because "what times we would all have then."[24] The implication is clear: by questioning Stein's authority, he distinguishes himself from young writers flocking to Paris to join the expatriate fad. Hemingway was telling readers he was not just another enlistee in Stein's literary corps.

Accounting for Hemingway's need to distinguish his writing from Stein's after 1926 is problematic since there is no single disagreement or argument that initiates their break. Most likely, as Reynolds suggests, after the four years Hemingway had spent in Paris "Gertrude was no longer the writer he so admired."[25] Nevertheless, residual feelings of dependency lingered; as if to assure himself that he was not a mere pupil, he repeatedly reflected on their relationship to catalogue the many differences separating them. For the rest of his life, he insisted that Stein lacked discipline and that she wrote too quickly, ignoring the responsibility of revising to sharpen her point. "I have never been able to write longer than two hours," he remarks in one 1928 letter. "If I could only take the slight plunge to going in for not making sense I could work ten and twelve hours a day every day and always be perfectly" satisfied "like Gertrude Stein who since she has taken up not making sense some eighteen years ago has never known a moment's unhappiness with her work."[26] At his least generous, he dismissed Stein's art by alluding to her lesbianism, or he attributed her peculiar style to her being the daughter of immigrants and thus lacking familiarity with the English language. As for Stein, she seems to have enjoyed inflaming the bitter feelings. In *The Autobiography of Alice B. Toklas,* she describes Hemingway as "ninety percent Rotarian," as smelling like a museum, and as "yellow" as "the flat-boat men on the Mississippi River as described by Mark Twain." More provocatively, she targets his biggest vulnerability by claiming he was a product of her and Sherwood Anderson: "Hemingway had been formed by the two of them, and they were both a little proud and a little ashamed of the work of their minds."[27]

Throughout the 1930s Hemingway addressed the question of Stein's influence in several minor published and unpublished pieces, the most remarkable aspect of which is the divergency of their tones. At times he brutally denigrates her talent, while in other places (especially in an unpublished parody of her memoir called "The Autobiography of Alice B. Hemingway") he seems genuinely saddened by their broken friendship.[28] Even a decade after her 1946 death, Stein's specter haunted him as he worked on *A Moveable Feast*. In a notorious chapter, Hemingway implies that his admiration for her ended when he overheard a lesbian squabble between her and Alice. The revelation of the couple's physical intimacy is suspect, since Stein and Toklas's relationship was an open secret among expatriates. More subtly, he suggests that he was repulsed by Stein's emotional dependence on her lover. Listening to Alice berate Gertrude as "I had never heard one person speak to another; never, anywhere, ever" (118), he claims that Stein was not as confident and secure as her public persona portrayed her. Behind closed doors, he informs us, she was not a literary "master" at all, but weak and needy, traits that in Hemingway's world were character flaws.

Unlike Anderson and Stein, Ezra Pound was one mentor whose influence Hemingway never repudiated. Born in Hailey, Idaho, Pound abandoned America for Europe in 1908 after being fired from the small Indiana college where he taught.[29] (A woman had been discovered in his living quarters.) Con-

WYNDHAM LEWIS ON THE "STEINING OF HEMINGWAY"

First published in April 1934, Wyndham Lewis's essay "The Dumb Ox: A Study of Ernest Hemingway" is perhaps the most vicious critical assault the author suffered in his lifetime. Despite its condemnatory tone, it is also one of the most intriguing analyses of Gertrude Stein's influence on Hemingway. According to Lewis, Hemingway unconsciously suffered Stein's "overmastering influence" to the point where her "gibbering and baboonish" techniques dominate his writing, even when the tone they create clashes with the seriousness of his dramatic scenarios:

"With Stein's bag of tricks he takes over a Weltanschauung, which may not at all be his, and does in fact seem to contradict his major personal quality. This infantile, dull-witted dreamy stutter compels whoever uses it to conform to the infantile, dull-witted type. He passes over in the category of those to whom things are done, from that of those who execute—if the latter is indeed where he originally belonged. One might even go so far as to say that this brilliant, Jewish lady has made a clown of him by teaching Ernest Hemingway her baby-talk! So it is a pity. And it is very difficult to know where Hemingway proper begins and Stein leaves off as an artist." Literary legend has it that Hemingway was so angered upon reading the essay at Sylvia Beach's Paris bookshop that he broke a lamp.

Reprinted in *Hemingway: The Critical Heritage*, edited by Jeffrey Meyers (London: Routledge & Kegan Paul, 1982), p. 193.

vinced of the puritanism of his native country, he toured Italy before settling in London, where he resided until the early 1920s. In England he associated with both established poets such as William Butler Yeats and younger rebellious artists eager for literary revolution. By the mid 1910s, he was a tireless champion of modernism—reviewing, advising, and helping publish the works of poet friends such as H.D. (Hilda Doolittle), William Carlos Williams, and T. S. Eliot. Pound even offered unlikely assistance to Robert Frost, whose homespun American-oriented verse could not be more different from Pound's formal, classically steeped poetry. Pound also had a penchant for initiating literary movements. In 1912 he announced the birth of Imagism, a school of poetry devoted to verbal simplicity and visual immediacy. But as soon as followers began subscribing to the Imagist principle of conveying complex emotions through concrete language, he and Wyndham Lewis founded vorticism. More aggressive and revolution-minded than the Imagists, vorticists despised cultural conservatism, rejected the idea that poetry should be regulated by meter, and in the visual arts celebrated geometric abstraction over realism. (Its most lasting contribution has been in the area of page design and layout. The text of the vorticists' short-lived literary journal, *Blast,* was printed in different typeface sizes, a technique previously unheard of in the publishing industry.)

Throughout his years in England, Pound grew increasingly disenchanted with the intellectual conservatism of the country, which he believed discouraged experimentation and innovation. Before relocating to France and later Italy, he completed his best-known poem, "Hugh Selwyn Mauberley (Life and Contacts)," a fictional autobiography protesting the indifference of England to poetry, the vulgarity of its popular culture, and its inability to acknowledge the devastation of World War I. Developing the techniques of fragmentation, juxtaposition, and allusion with which he later helped Eliot shape *The Waste Land,* Pound suggested that his alter ego wasted his time trying to "resuscitate the dead art / Of poetry" in Great Britain. The culture preferred cheap "plaster" to Greek "alabaster" and the trendy "pianola" to "barbitos" (Greek poetry sung to the accompaniment of a lyre). In later sections, Pound calls Anglo-Saxon civilization "an old bitch gone in the teeth" and ridicules leading British writers of the 1910s as fools, drunks, and sellouts.[30] So pungent is the bitter attitude of the poem that it remains one of the most powerful declarations of discontent in modernism.

Pound had lived in Paris only a year when he and Hemingway met. Hemingway's initial impression was not favorable. Disdainful of bohemians, he was ill prepared to see beyond Pound's pointy goatee and affected gestures. Had a mutual friend not discouraged him from publishing a hastily composed caricature of the poet, Hemingway might have burned an important bridge to his future. Fortunately, he recognized that, however outlandish Pound's persona, this modernist was definitely not a poseur. Indeed, Pound's advice proved vital. By discouraging the use of adjectives and adverbs, Pound introduced the younger writer to the regime of paring and compressing that became his trademark style. In a 1933 letter Hemingway acknowledged Pound's influence, claiming to have "learned more about how to write and how not to write from you than from any son of a bitch alive."[31] (As another measure of Hemingway's affection, Pound is one of three contemporaries remembered affectionately in *A Moveable Feast;* the others were Sylvia Beach and expatriate poet Evan Shipman.) Additionally, Pound was generous in introducing unpublished authors to literary journals where they could build a reputation. One of Pound's first acts of friendship was to send several Hemingway poems to *The Dial* with a strong endorsement. Although *The Dial* rejected the submissions, Pound served as a talent scout for other small, experimental magazines, including the *Little Review,* an early outlet for Hemingway's writing. In 1923 Pound invited Hemingway to contribute to a series of limited-edition books called "*The Inquest* into the state of contemporary English prose" that he was organizing for another expatriate, William Bird, who ran a small printing press when not working as an overseas correspondent for an American news service. The resulting collection, *in our time,* along with his previously published *Three Stories and Ten Poems,* advanced Hemingway's literary stature by placing his name alongside established modernists such as William Carlos Williams and Pound himself, who also contributed to the project.

As important a professional connection as Pound proved to be, however, Hemingway was not influenced by Pound's writing. (The exception is the minor poem "The Age Demanded," published in a German little magazine called *Der Querschnitt* [The Cross Section], inspired by a line in "Hugh Selwyn Mauberly."[32]) Pound's characteristic work is built out of obscure allusions; untranslated fragments of Latin, Greek, and Chinese; and an erudite vocabulary requiring constant reference to the dictionary. Rarely establishing a consistent plotline, his poems may employ characters, but there is usually little effort to humanize them through psychological or emotional description. A typical passage reads

> *Casus est talis:*
> Filippo, commendatary of the abbazia
> Of Sant Apollinaire, Classe, Cardinal of Bologna
> That he did one night (*quadam nocte*) sell . . . marble, porphyry, serpentine.[33]

Pound was frequently criticized for such obscurity; yet, as a dedicated classicist, he believed modern works must be based on ancient forms of expression if they were to attain the status of literature. This passage comes from his lifelong work-in-progress, the *Cantos,* which he began in 1917. Julian Symons explains the intent behind this formidable effort: The *Cantos* "represent . . . his passionate concern with history and romance. . . . What he hoped to do by mixing past and contemporary, classical and modern, chatty autobiography and lyrical desire, was to produce a work that combined history and autobiography so that it was finally a comment on the nature of civilization."[34] As a young writer prone to feelings of intellectual inferiority, Hemingway was ill-suited to appreciate such a lofty goal. While he agreed that the *Cantos* included "some Christwonderful poetry," he felt the poems were also bloated with "quite a lot of crap" and that Pound could not "leave any erudition true or false out of a poem." Hemingway believed that knowledge of ancient history and classical tradition should inform the writing, not obscure it. "Erudition," he insisted, "shouldn't show."[35]

Hemingway and Pound maintained contact throughout the 1920s, even after Pound abandoned Paris for Rapallo, Italy. In the 1930s Pound drifted into a self-imposed isolation, cutting himself off from American friends and immersing himself in Italian culture. By the onset of World War II he was a devotee of Benito Mussolini's fascist regime and the anti-Semitism he shared with many American writers (including Hemingway) deepened into paranoia over Jewish influence in banking and economics. (Pound titled one newspaper article he wrote in this period "The Jew, Disease Incarnate.") Hemingway, like many of Pound's friends, was bewildered by anti-American tirades the poet broadcast from Rome in the early 1940s, an offense that in July 1943 earned him an indictment for treason. "He has a long history of generosity and unselfish aid to other artists and he is one of the greatest living writers," Hemingway wrote, clearly conflicted. "It is impossible to believe that anyone in his right mind could utter the vile, absolutely idiotic drivel he broadcast. His friends who knew him and who watched the warping and twisting and decay of his mind and his judgment should defend him and explain him on that basis."[36]

After his postwar arrest, Pound was held for six months in a military prison camp, spending a portion of the time in a zoolike outdoor cage. There he completed what are widely considered the best of the *Cantos* (known as the *Pisan Cantos*) before being deemed unfit for trial and committed to a Washington mental-health facility. When Pound was released thirteen years later, Hemingway sent a $1,000 check to finance

Pound's return to Italy. Rather than cash it, Pound hung the gesture of goodwill on his wall. Hemingway declared his continued loyalty in a 1958 letter: "During the P. Harbor to A. Bomb war . . . I wrote . . . that if there should arrive any question of you being hanged I would get up onto the gallows and make it clear that I should be hanged with you."[37]

Pound's dense, difficult style of poetry exemplifies a type of modernism (called "High Modernism" for its obscurity) that also includes works by James Joyce and T. S. Eliot. During Hemingway's initial months in Paris, the city was abuzz with talk of Joyce's *Ulysses* (1922), voted in one recent survey as the most important novel of the twentieth century. As a retelling of the Odysseus myth recast in modern-day Dublin, Ireland, the book provided modernists an exhilarating encyclopedia of possible themes and styles. Its much-publicized plot parallels to Greek legend elevated modernist feelings of displacement to mythic status, sending poets scurrying to the ancient classics in search of archetypes and analogues. Additionally, Joyce's dynamic wordplay, which includes countless puns and neologisms (invented words), dramatized the dexterity of language and suggested how authors might convey characters' internal moods, feelings, and thoughts in disarmingly original ways. Even the book's sexual bawdiness and bathroom humor (including a descriptive outhouse interlude) inspired modernists. By sticking a finger in the eye of Victorian decorum, Joyce opened the genre of the novel to investigating previously taboo arenas of human existence. Even before publication, the revolutionary status of the book was cemented when a New York judge deemed excerpts printed in the *Little Review* obscene. Because of that judgment, *Ulysses* was banned in America until 1933.

Hemingway spoke highly of *Ulysses* throughout his Paris years. During a four-month return to North America as a *Toronto Star* correspondent in late 1923, he even smuggled contraband copies of it through Canadian customs for distribution in the United States. Whether he read the entire novel is unclear. In his copy roughly half the pages remain unopened, suggesting he was familiar only with the beginning and end.[38] Nevertheless, critics have identified various Hemingway passages indebted to *Ulysses*. Like Joyce's novel, "The Snows of Kilimanjaro" (1936) and *To Have and Have Not* (1937) include passages of "stream of consciousness," a technique that dramatizes the unedited flux and flow of a character's thought patterns. Hemingway incorporates some Odyssean allusions into *The Sun Also Rises* that critics such as Carlos Baker suggest owe a debt to Joyce, including an overt reference to Brett Ashley as Circe, the enchantress who tempts sailors into intoxication so she may turn them into swine.[39] *Green Hills of Africa* (1935), a nonfiction meditation on the twin arts of game hunting and writing, includes more overt references to *Ulysses*, including one passage in which Hemingway proclaims Joyce the greatest of living writers.

Despite his praise for *Ulysses*, Hemingway was more influenced by Joyce's earlier book, *Dubliners* (1914). Like *Winesburg, Ohio*, Sherwood Anderson's short-story collection, *Dubliners* is a series of narratives linked together by recurring themes, characters, and geographical setting. Whereas most story collections are composed of unrelated tales, the story cycle weaves its contents together to create a novelistic sense of unity. During the early 1920s, when Hemingway concentrated on short stories before attempting a longer narrative, *Dubliners* offered a model for connecting shorter pieces. Both the Paris-edition version of *in our time* and the trade book *In Our Time* (1925) suggest that Hemingway studied the way that Joyce linked his stories together. *Dubliners* also demonstrated the need for a concluding tale that summed up the themes of the overall collection. With "The Dead" Joyce not only created a story brilliant on its own merits but one that, when read in the context of the entire sequence, seemed a key to decoding the contents. Hemingway designed "Big Two-Hearted River" to serve just such a function; he "saw how Joyce had used his massive story, 'The Dead,' to weld the themes of *Dubliners* together, placing it last to anchor the collection. Ernest needed such a story to end his book, a story bringing together everything he had learned."[40]

Hemingway was far less impressed with the London-based Eliot, whose influence among Paris expatriates was more professional than personal. In early 1922, passing through the city after recovering in Switzerland from an emotional breakdown, Eliot entrusted Pound with a poetry manuscript titled "He Do the Police in Different Voices." Using techniques like fragmentation and juxtaposition that he had employed in "Hugh Selwyn Mauberly (Life and Contacts)," Pound cut the more accessible passages of the poem to emphasize its kaleidoscopic discontinuity. The result was *The Waste Land*, perhaps the single most famous modernist work. First published in late 1922 in *The Dial*, Eliot's vision of modern life as barren and meaningless inspired controversy over its fragmented form and allusions to classical and Renaissance literature. For some aspiring modernists, the poem was a perfect expression of the despair and detachment of the century. Others, including Hemingway, were suspicious of Eliot's erudite approach, which, like Pound's, borrowed from a half-dozen different languages and possessed no discernable plot.

Contemptuous of Eliot's intellectual and conservative persona, Hemingway perpetually misspelled his name as "Elliott" and often referred to him as "Major Eliot" in Pound's presence. (Pound was an admirer of an economist named Major Douglas.) Around November 1922, on the eve of the publication of *The Waste Land*, Pound began soliciting funds from various expatriates to relieve Eliot of his full-time job at a London bank. In *A Moveable Feast*, Hemingway sarcastically portrays himself as an enthusiastic conscript in this volunteer effort: "In my dreams I had pictured" Eliot coming to Paris " . . . to live in the small Greek temple and that maybe I could go with Ezra when we would drop in to crown him with laurel." Hemingway's commitment to the project seems suspect, however, for he goes on to lose his donation at the racetrack: "I would have been happier if the amount of the wager had gone to Bel Esprit"—the name of the endeavor. "But I comforted myself that with those wagers which had prospered I could have contributed much more to Bel Esprit than was my original intention" (112–113).

The first public acknowledgment of Hemingway's dislike of Eliot came in 1924 during Hemingway's tenure at the *transatlantic review*. In an issue dedicated to the recently deceased writer Joseph Conrad, Hemingway took aim at Eliot's reputation: "If I knew that by grinding Mr. Eliot into a fine dry powder and sprinkling that powder over Mr. Conrad's grave Mr. Conrad would shortly appear . . . I would leave for London tomorrow morning with a sausage grinder."[41] Hemingway could not resist insulting Eliot whenever possible. Another slur came in early 1925 when Hemingway changed the names of the main characters in a short story called "Mr. and Mrs. Smith." As a mean-spirited vignette based on gossip about an expatriate couple's marital woes, the story could

T. S. ELIOT ON HEMINGWAY

Hemingway's derisive comments on Eliot raise an obvious question: how did the author of *The Waste Land* feel about Hemingway? Strikingly, Eliot never retaliated for Hemingway's notorious 1924 "sausage grinder" remark; nor does he seem to have taken offense at the short story "Mr. and Mrs. Elliot," which satirizes the poet as effete and asexual. Eliot's public comments on Hemingway are, in fact, uniformly positive. As the following passage from one 1933 essay suggests, Eliot admired Hemingway's style, finding in its terse rigidity an authentic expression of disillusionment that he preferred to the more stylized despair of French writers such as Anatole France and André Gide:

"In America, this pseudo—or not quite good mannered sophistication takes the form of what they call hard boiling. To each climate its own illusion; but the illusion which pervades the whole various-climated American continent is the illusion of the hard boiled. Even Mr. Ernest Hemingway—the writer of tender sentiment, and true sentiment, as in *The Killers* and *A Farewell to Arms* . . . has been taken as the representative of hard boiling. . . . Mr. Hemingway is a writer for whom I have considerable respect; he seems to me to tell the truth about his own feelings at the moment when they exist. He does not belong in the class in which I have placed France, and Gide, and (tentatively) Mr. Aldous Huxley. He has, at the moment, a popularity which I think (it is a high compliment) is largely undeserved."

T. S. Eliot, "A Commentary," *Criterion*, 12 (April 1933): 471.

not be printed in *In Our Time* for fear that the real-life Smiths would sue for libel. Recalling his London nemesis, Hemingway retitled the tale "Mr. and Mrs. Elliot." For those familiar with Eliot's tortured marriage to Vivien Haigh-Wood, who suffered from an inherited nervous disorder, the story now seemed a malicious exposé of Eliot's personal problems.

Hemingway's animus toward Eliot arose from his inveterate sense of competition. Although eleven years Eliot's junior, Hemingway regarded him more than Stein, Joyce, or Pound as a contemporary whose reputation as a leading modernist threatened to overshadow his own. A similar feeling marks his attitude toward his most important Parisian peer, F. Scott Fitzgerald. When the two met at a Paris bar called the Dingo in April 1925, Fitzgerald's career was at its critical peak. Just two weeks earlier, *The Great Gatsby* had been published, and although its perpetually cash-strapped author was disappointed by its sales, the book was embraced by most reviewers as an artistic breakthrough. Hemingway was familiar with Fitzgerald's literary debut, *This Side of Paradise,* having read it in Chicago in 1920. Later, Hemingway judged this thinly fictionalized account of Fitzgerald's undergraduate days at Princeton unreadable, but early in his career, he, like many young Americans, found its energy exhilarating.[42] Critics recognized that *This Side of Paradise* was a wholly modern tale of growing up. It included frank depictions of such teenage rituals as drinking and petting, and it audaciously communicated young people's anti-authoritarian disdain for adults. The book seemed single-handedly to render obsolete the sweet, obedient image of adolescents found in such Victorian novels as Louisa May Alcott's *Little Women* and Booth Tarkington's *Seventeen.* As a result, between 1920 and 1924 Fitzgerald was celebrated as a spokesman for postwar youth, a generation that—according to a plethora of outraged editorials and articles—was brash, prodigal, and proudly antitraditional.

Fitzgerald also found the success of *This Side of Paradise* limiting, for it stereotyped him as a "flapper novelist" catering to a collegiate audience. After a second novel, *The Beautiful and Damned* (1922), and two story collections predominantly featuring protagonists in their teens and early twenties, *Flappers and Philosophers* (1920) and *Tales of the Jazz Age* (1922), he recognized the need to mature artistically. *The Great Gatsby* more than satisfied this prerogative; in the eyes of many critics, it even came close to achieving Fitzgerald's other goal, which was to produce "a novel better than any novel ever written in America."[43] In telling the story of Jay Gatsby's doomed efforts to win the love of socialite Daisy Buchanan by transforming himself from "Mr. Nobody from Nowhere" into a mysterious millionaire, Fitzgerald tapped into themes at once reflective of the

1920s in particular and the broader American mythology of success in general. On the one hand, the ambiguous origins of Gatsby's fortune dramatize the Jazz Age intrigue with easy money and charismatic personalities; at the same time, the certainty and confidence Gatsby exudes in his single-minded pursuit of Daisy symbolizes the naïveté of the American dream of determining one's own destiny. In the closing passages of the novel, Fitzgerald's narrator, Nick Carraway, compares Gatsby's ambition to America's optimism and belief in progress:

> Gatsby believed in the green light, the orgastic future that year by year recedes before us. It eluded us then, but that's no matter—tomorrow we will run faster, stretch out our arms farther. . . . And one fine morning——
>
> So we beat on, boats against the current, borne back ceaselessly into the past.[44]

Few passages in American literature so succinctly convey the stubborn idealism of the national character. As Fitzgerald implies, Gatsby's ultimate tragedy is that he never doubts the tangibility of his dream.

Fitzgerald had barely completed a draft of *The Great Gatsby* when he informed Maxwell Perkins, his editor at Scribners, about "a young man named Ernest Hemmingway [sic], who . . . has a brilliant future. . . . He's the real thing."[45] Exactly when Fitzgerald saw a copy of either *Three Stories and Ten Poems* or the small-press version of *in our time* is uncertain, but his enthusiasm intensified the following spring after the two writers met. By that time, Hemingway had already signed a contract with Liveright to publish the expanded edition of *In Our Time*. Almost immediately, he and Fitzgerald began plotting ways to break the agreement so their work could appear under the same Scribners imprint. By early summer 1925 Hemingway was corresponding with Perkins and expressing his admiration for his new friend's talent: "I've read his *Great Gatsby* and think it is an absolutely first rate book."[46] The degree to which his reading of *Gatsby* influenced *The Sun Also Rises* remains a matter of conjecture. The detached, ironic tone of Hemingway's narrator Jake Barnes may owe a debt to Fitzgerald's Nick Carraway. Several minor allusions to a prominent review of *The Great Gatsby* by *The Dial* (which Hemingway despised for rejecting his submissions) also appear in the novel. But the reception of *The Great Gatsby* also aroused Hemingway's competitive spirit, pushing him to distinguish himself from Fitzgerald. As he drafted his expatriate tale, Hemingway composed a foreword that staked his claim to the subject matter: "This generation that is lost has nothing to do with any Younger generation about whose outcome much literary speculation occurred in times past. This is not a question of what kind of mothers will flappers make or where is bobbed hair leading us.

This is about something that is already finished."[47] Readers of the day came to associate terms such as *younger generation, flappers,* and *bobbed hair* with Fitzgerald, making Hemingway's implicit point clear: nobody should confuse *The Sun Also Rises* with *The Great Gatsby.*

In late 1925 Fitzgerald was among the Paris crowd encouraging Hemingway to publish *The Torrents of Spring,* his Anderson parody. (Fitzgerald also makes a drunken cameo appearance in the story.) In the ongoing effort to steer Hemingway to Scribners, Fitzgerald encouraged him to submit a recent story, "Fifty Grand," to *Scribner's Magazine.* As a seasoned veteran of the fiction market, Fitzgerald advised cutting the opening two and a half pages to make the narrative more sellable. In a 1959 essay called "The Art of the Short Story," Hemingway sarcastically recalls this recommendation as evidence of why writers should trust their own instincts and ignore others' judgments. Attributing Fitzgerald's response to the opening of the story to "the way his mind was functioning that year," Hemingway implies that the cuts were wrongheaded and that he agreed out of humility, realizing only too late "how dangerous that attractive virtue, humility, can be."[48] This remembrance, coming thirty years after the fact, is unreliable. In 1926 Hemingway was willing to take advice. *Scribner's Magazine,* moreover, demanded further excisions that the author would not allow, so "Fifty Grand" remained unpublished for another eighteen months.

Fitzgerald's advice on "Fifty Grand" demonstrates just what a judicious critic of his friend's writing he was. In his various responses to Hemingway's work, Fitzgerald is sensitive to what became his fellow author's greatest stylistic flaw—the tendency to digress from the plot to indulge in editorials and insults. In June 1926, after reading the revised draft of *The Sun Also Rises,* Fitzgerald urged Hemingway to delete several "sneers, superiorities, and nose-thumbings-at-nothing that mar the whole narrative." Fitzgerald tried to soften his critique by admitting he suffered the same stylistic foibles ("I find in you the same tendency to envelope or . . . to embalm . . . that I find in myself"). He also warned Hemingway to accept the criticism in the collegial spirit it was offered: "You know the very fact that people have committed themselves to you will make them watch you like a cat." The problem was the first two dozen pages, which described the main characters' backgrounds in a gossipy tone. Knowing the importance of debut novels for authors' reputations, Fitzgerald encouraged Hemingway to dramatize more: "When so many people can write well + the competition is so heavy I can't imagine how you could have done these first 20 pps. so casually. You can't play with peoples attention—a good man who has the power of arresting attention at will must be especially careful."[49] Hemingway acknowledged the soundness of the advice by removing the first sixteen pages of the draft.

In 1929 Fitzgerald identified similar deficiencies in *A Farewell to Arms*. He singled out passages where the pace of the drama slackened, and he encouraged a revision of Catherine Barkley's character, which he found more stereotypical than previous female protagonists. "Our poor old friendship probably won't survive this," Fitzgerald added, "but . . . better me than some nobody in the *Literary Review* that doesn't care about you + your future."[50] Ten years later, Hemingway sent Fitzgerald a signed copy of *For Whom the Bell Tolls* (1940). While reviewers hailed the novel as a comeback after the lackluster nonfiction of *Death in the Afternoon* (1932) and *Green Hills of Africa* (1935), Fitzgerald perceived what later critics acknowledged were the faults of the novel: "It is not as good as the *Farewell to Arms*. It doesn't seem to have the intensity or freshness nor has it the inspired poetic moments." Yet, in another sense, Fitzgerald recognized that for Hemingway's audience, such concerns were irrelevant. "I imagine it would please the average type of reader," he decided. "It is full of a lot of rounded adventures on the Huckleberry Finn order and of course it is highly intelligent and literate like everything he does."[51] The estimation was accurate; *For Whom the Bell Tolls* became Hemingway's most-popular work to date, selling nearly half-a-million copies in its first year. Fitzgerald, however, did not live to see his prediction come true. Within two months of receiving the book, he died of a heart attack, leaving his last novel "The Love of the Last Tycoon" (published in 1941 as *The Last Tycoon*) unfinished.

While Fitzgerald was a canny critic of Hemingway's deficiencies, he never lost respect for the man as an artist. In the 1930s he allusively described Hemingway in one nonfiction essay as his "artistic conscience": "I had not imitated his infectious style," he added, "because my own style, such as it is, was formed before he published anything, but there was an awful pull toward him when I was on a spot."[52] Flattering descriptions of Hemingway's art occur frequently in Fitzgerald's journals, but his most admiring tribute appears in a peculiar form. In 1934 and 1935 Fitzgerald wrote a quartet of stories about a medieval French hero named Philippe, Count of Villefranche, whose moral determination and strength embody the Hemingway qualities that Fitzgerald envied. Although he hoped to compile enough Philippe stories to construct a full-length historical novel, periodical publishers proved ambivalent to their ninth-century setting, and Fitzgerald returned to more familiar contemporary material.

HEMINGWAY AND ZELDA FITZGERALD

Critics agree that Hemingway's estimation of Fitzgerald was inexorably bound up in his dislike of Fitzgerald's strong-willed wife, Zelda. Zelda's comments on Hemingway reveal how intensely she disdained him as well. In the following excerpts, Fitzgerald biographers discuss why Zelda was so antipathetic toward her husband's literary peer:

"Scott had always had some friend whom he considered his mentor, but Hemingway was the first whom Zelda regarded as a threat to her relationship with Scott. She was unrelenting in her opinion that Hemingway was a poseur. But her jealousy also grew out of her own weakening tie to Scott. . . ."

Nancy Milford, *Zelda: A Biography* (New York: Harper & Row, 1970), p. 122.

"Hemingway had brought his novel, *The Sun Also Rises*, with him, which both Scott and Zelda had read in manuscript.

When I asked what his novel was about, Zelda said, 'Bullfighting, bullslinging, and bullsh—'

Sara Mayfield, *Exiles from Paradise: Zelda and Scott Fitzgerald* (New York: Delacorte, 1971), p. 112.

"Hemingway's self-conscious display of virility both irritated and menaced her. Attracted to more genteel, polished and deferential men, she provoked Hemingway's hostility by questioning his sexual power. She told him 'no one is as masculine as you pretend to be.' She tauntingly called him 'a phony,' 'a sort of materialistic mystic,' 'a professional he-man,' 'a pansy with hair on his chest. . . .'"

Jeffrey Meyers, *Scott Fitzgerald: A Biography* (New York: HarperCollins, 1994), p. 148.

For his part, Hemingway turned an increasingly deaf ear to Fitzgerald's editorial assessments after *The Sun Also Rises*. He declined to allow Fitzgerald to read *A Farewell to Arms* until it already had been serialized in *Scribner's Magazine* in 1929, a gesture that implied Hemingway did not care what his friend thought. When he received Fitzgerald's critique, he was more than unimpressed—in the margin of the letter he scribbled a succinct response: "Kiss my ass." Although Fitzgerald never saw this dismissive reply, he apparently got the message, for he confined future criticism to his private notebooks and letters to discreet friends who would not pass on his comments. But while Fitzgerald no longer served as an unofficial editor, Hemingway needed him in a different way. In his post-*Gatsby* years, Fitzgerald was debilitated by mounting debts, marital crises, and alcoholism. While he assured friends he was making headway on a novel variously called "The Melarky Case," "The Boy Who Killed His Mother," and "The World's Fair," nine years passed before *Tender Is the Night* was completed in 1934. He did write several underrated short stories during this period—including at least one classic, "Babylon Revisited" (1931); yet, these later works are filled with a sense of defeat and despair. For Hemingway, who equated self-pity and melancholy with cowardice, Fitzgerald provided a convenient scapegoat upon which he could excise the self-doubt and depression he found difficult to admit to himself. In his journal Fitzgerald cannily noted the temperamental differences separating the two writers: "I talk with the authority of failure," he wrote, "Ernest with the authority of success."[53] In those moments when Hemingway was plagued by feelings of failure, he ascribed whatever weaknesses he felt he suffered to Fitzgerald.

The most famous example of this tendency in Hemingway's writing occurred when "The Snows of Kilimanjaro," arguably his greatest short story, appeared in *Esquire* magazine in August 1936. One passage included a reference to "poor Scott Fitzgerald and his romantic awe" of the wealthy: "He thought they were a very glamorous race and when he found they weren't it wrecked him just as much as any other thing that wrecked him." The comment was a not-so-subtle allusion to a recent triptych of *Esquire* essays Fitzgerald had written, collectively known as *The Crack-Up* (after the first essay in the series). Unable by his late thirties to continue to write the youth-oriented *Saturday Evening Post* stories that had been his bread and butter for fifteen years, Fitzgerald publicly confessed to emotional crises that left him feeling confused and directionless, both in his life and in his career. When questioned about insulting a friend in such an overt fashion, Hemingway argued that Fitzgerald had already admitted to being "wrecked" and that in his story he merely concurred. (Nevertheless, a painfully hurt Fitzgerald demanded a name change in future printings of the story; as a result "poor Scott Fitzgerald" was replaced by "poor Julian.") Later, biographers suggested a different motive for the reference. In 1935 Hemingway was socializing with Maxwell Perkins and a Key West acquaintance named Mary Colum when he professed his admiration for the rich. Colum purportedly responded, "The only difference between the rich and other people is that they have more money." As Matthew J. Bruccoli suggests, "the mechanism of Hemingway's embarrassment seems clear: a standard way to purge an embarrassment is to assign it to someone else. In this case 'poor Scott Fitzgerald' provided a target of opportunity."[54] For his part, Fitzgerald seemed resigned to serving this role for Hemingway. He explained why he declined to respond publicly to the slur in "The Snows of Kilimanjaro": "To have answered," he wrote Perkins, "would have been like fooling with a lit firecracker. . . . He has completely lost his head and the duller he gets about it, the more he is like a punch-drunk pug fighting himself in the movies."[55]

Hemingway's habit of "fighting himself" by pretending to fight Fitzgerald only partially explains why, with the exception of *The Great Gatsby*, he was incapable of appreciating his friend's fiction. Equally important, the tone and mood of their work differ in significant ways. Fitzgerald was a lyrical writer, and his best work is elegiac as it laments the passing of some irrevocable ideal. His most powerful works evoke what he described in 1924 as "the loss of those illusions that give such color to the world."[56] The sense of defeated expectation essential to

Fitzgerald's greatest prose was, however, antithetical to Hemingway's sensibility. Hemingway could only interpret loss and disappointment as signs of weakness, for he valued strength and perseverance, even when it made him seem belligerent or insensitive. These values help explain his negative reaction to *Tender Is the Night*. Although not as focused and stylistically precise as *The Great Gatsby, Tender Is the Night* is nevertheless an acute commentary on the moral decay and identity crises occasioned by the modern era. As the hero of the book, Dr. Dick Diver, squanders his innate vitality by succumbing to dissipation, Fitzgerald depicts the expatriate lifestyle of the 1920s as symbolic of the broader displacement and loss of certainty associated with the early twentieth century. The novel is distinguished by its theoretical sophistication, with Fitzgerald drawing upon Freudian concepts to explain the dependency of the unstable Nicole Diver upon her husband (a theme inspired by the mental illness suffered by Zelda Fitzgerald in the early 1930s). Moreover, *Tender Is the Night* is its author's most experimental effort. The narrative unfolds in nonchronological order, its use of flashback heightening the pervading mood of confusion. Fitzgerald also employs multiple points of view to dramatize a central modernist theme, the subjectivity of perception.

Hemingway, however, proved obtuse to the innovations of *Tender Is the Night*. For him, the story was too self-pitying. While the Divers were initially based on a glamorous expatriate couple, Gerald and Sara Murphy, whom Hemingway and Fitzgerald had met in the mid 1920s, the couple metamorphosed midway through the book into Scott and Zelda, and the plot became a painful exploration of their marital problems. For Hemingway, public admissions of private woe were distasteful: "Forget your personal tragedy," he lectured Fitzgerald after admitting his ambivalence to the novel. "We are all bitched from the start and you especially have to hurt like hell before you can write seriously."[57] Hemingway was even more critical while airing his opinion to others. "Scott's book, I'm sorry, is not good," he told Gerald Murphy. As if to dismiss Fitzgerald's entire career, he added, "But then I've never read these great books by Scott that he has written."[58] To Perkins, he diagnosed Fitzgerald's problem: "The trouble is that he wouldn't learn his trade and he won't be honest. He is always the brilliant young gentleman writer, fallen gentleman writer, gent in the gutter, gent ruined, but never a man."[59] Two additional facts support the suspicion that Hemingway's personal animus toward Fitzgerald shaped his immediate response to *Tender Is the Night*. In the late 1930s, long after he and Fitzgerald were corresponding only irregularly, a rereading of the novel revised his opinion. "It's amazing how *excellent* much of it is," Hemingway wrote Perkins in March 1939. "If he had integrated it better it would have been a fine novel (as it is) much of it is better than anything else he ever wrote."[60] Fitzgerald's novel also seems to have been on Hemingway's mind in the late 1940s and 1950s as he worked on various versions of *The Garden of Eden* (1986). Catherine Bourne's madness, which undermines her relationship with her husband David, in many ways parallels Nicole Diver's emotional frailty, and both novels explore how the rootlessness of expatriate life erodes marital stability. Yet, one fundamental difference distinguishing the books suggests that Hemingway remained wary of Fitzgerald's fascination with dissipation: whereas life abroad saps Dick Diver of his resources, David Bourne possesses the fortitude needed to resist its temptations, and, in the end, he, unlike Diver, is triumphant.

In the late 1950s, nearly twenty years after Fitzgerald's death, Hemingway wrote anew of his friend's failures in *A Moveable Feast*. Biographers suggest that the virulently dismissive depiction of Fitzgerald in the book marks Hemingway's reaction to the Fitzgerald revival that began in the post–World War II years. When Fitzgerald died, his work was to a large extent forgotten; unsold copies from the second printing of *The Great Gatsby* in 1925 even gathered dust in the Scribners warehouse. But as critics rediscovered his fiction, his reputation was resuscitated until he was properly recognized as a leading American modernist. Hemingway may have grown annoyed by scholars' inquiries into their relationship and may even have resented the sudden attention accorded Fitzgerald's neglected writings.[61] By focusing on the man's personal and professional defects, Hemingway in *A Moveable Feast* again transformed his friend into the embodiment of every literary fault and foible he detested. He describes Fitzgerald as a drunk, a writer who sacrificed his art for money, and a man destroyed by his wife's jealousy. In the most humiliating chapter, Hemingway recalls Fitzgerald asking for reassurance that, contrary to Zelda's complaints, his penis is not abnormally small. "There's nothing wrong with you," Hemingway comforts him. "Just have confidence." But even comparing his anatomy to the nude statues at the Louvre is not enough to alleviate Fitzgerald's sense of inadequacy: "Still he was doubtful about himself," Hemingway reports with disbelief (190–191). For years critics have regarded this scene as proof of Hemingway's need to soothe his own insecurities by demeaning those whom he considered his competitors. By equating sexual and literary prowess, he lambastes Fitzgerald as ill-equipped to succeed, whether on paper or in the bedroom.

Hemingway's treatment of Fitzgerald parallels his equally tempestuous rivalry with John Dos Passos. Despite his productivity (some thirty volumes of fiction and nonfiction), Dos Passos may be the American modernist least-known to general readers. In most memoirs of the 1920s (including his own), he is a self-effacing observer of the literary scene rather than a flamboyant participant in it. His detachment, however, does not mean his writing is second-rate or unworthy of study. Far from it: Dos Passos's novels typically possess a scope and texture that are epic in ambition. Because they aim to illustrate the political, economic, and social forces woven together in the American cultural fabric, they are frequently more complex and experimental than Hemingway's.

The two writers met in Paris in 1924, at which point Dos Passos was already the author of several works, including the much-praised *Three Soldiers* (1921). Dos Passos journeyed with the Hemingways and their friends to the 1924 Pamplona bullfights. Upon returning to New York, Dos Passos helped convince Horace Liveright to publish *In Our Time* in 1925. That same year, he wrote *Manhattan Transfer* (published in 1928), a panoramic vision of metropolitan life, as well as several plays, before returning to Europe just in time to counsel Hemingway against publishing *The Torrents of Spring*. While Dos Passos disagreed with the harsh assessment of Sherwood Anderson in the book, he is described affectionately in its Paris scenes as "a very forceful writer, and an exceedingly pleasant fellow besides."[62]

Despite their similar war experiences, Hemingway and Dos Passos were quite different in their approaches to fiction. Dos Passos's novels are explicitly political, subordinating the unusual nature of his characters to their overarching stance on a broad social problem or concern. Hemingway regarded politics as more intrusive than the erudition he criticized in Pound's and Eliot's poetry. For him, literary drama was compelling when it focused on the test of an individual's moral mettle. Dos Passos is also more flamboyant than Hemingway in his use of literary devices. Dos Passos's most famous extended work, *U.S.A.*, is a trilogy or sequence of three novels—*The 42nd Parallel* (1930), *Nineteen-Nineteen* (1932), and *The Big Money* (1936)—that documents the effects of consumerism, corporate greed, and government corruption on the American working class. More than their plot, the novels are celebrated for the techniques that Dos Passos developed. These include the "newsreel" (headlines and journalistic descriptions of world events that juxtapose history against the action), the "camera eye" (an omniscient or "all-knowing" narrative perspective that, like a movie-camera lens, zooms in and out in scope), and the "compressed biography" (short life stories of major historical figures such as Henry Ford or John D. Rockefeller). Additionally, Dos Passos juxtaposes passages of formal, bureau-

From left to right: John Dos Passos, Ernest and Hadley Hemingway, Sara and Gerald Murphy in Schruns, Austria, 1926. In *A Moveable Feast,* Hemingway blamed Dos Passos and the Murphys for ruining his first marriage.

cratic language to everyday speech in order to dramatize the ways that official discourse distorts and corrupts the truth of experience. The most anthologized chapter of *Nineteen-Nineteen*, "The Body of an American," contrasts dishonest notions of heroism and valor propagated by the government to more realistic depictions of the horrors of battle:

> Whereasthe Congressoftheunitedstates byaconcurrent resolutionadoptedon the4thdayofmarch lastauthorizedthe Secretary ofwar to cause to be brought to the unitedstatesthe body of an American whowasamemberoftheamericanexpeditionaryforcesin europewholosthislife duringtheworldwarandwhoseidentityhasnot beenestablished for burial inthememoiralamphitheatre ofthenational cemeteryatarlingtonvirginia
>
> In the tarpaper morgue at Châlons-sur-Marne in the reek of chloride of lime and dead, they picked out the pine box that held all that was left of
>
> eenie menie minie moe plenty other pine boxes stacked up there containing what they'd scraped up of Richard Roe.[63]

With the possible exception of *In Our Time* (which includes interpolated vignettes or mini-chapters from the Paris edition of *in our time* juxtaposed against longer stories), Hemingway's writing is more straightforward and accessible. Because of their divergent styles, Dos Passos and Hemingway admired each other personally more than professionally. In 1926 Dos Passos wrote an unfavorable review of *The Sun Also Rises,* which he described as a "cock and bull story about a lot of summer tourists getting drunk and making fools of themselves at a picturesque Iberian folk-festival."[64] In his correspondence, Hemingway encouraged Dos Passos to humanize his characters and "keep them people" instead of "symbols" of a particular "economic system."[65] Despite such reservations, Hemingway introduced Dos Passos to a childhood friend whom Dos Passos subsequently married, and the two writers socialized throughout the early 1930s at Hemingway retreats in Key West, Florida, and Havana, Cuba. In this period, Dos Passos proved a valuable critic of Hemingway's drafts. Upon reading *Death in the Afternoon* in early 1932, he encouraged Hemingway to cut the intrusive commentaries in which "Old Hem" turned away from bullfighting to strap "on the longwhite whiskers" and give "the boys the lowdown": "When you . . . give them the low down about writing and why you like to live in Key West," he asked, "don't you think that's all secrets of the profession—like plaster of paris in a glove that oughtn't to be spilt to the vulgar?"[66] Although Hemingway resented the criticism, he nevertheless ceded to the judgment and cut several passages to which Dos Passos objected. "May god damn your soul to hell if it's not right," Hemingway wrote back (though he never mailed the letter). "Seemed the best part of the book to me."[67]

Dos Passos's criticism of *Death in the Afternoon* marks his increasing suspicion that Hemingway was succumbing to literary self-consciousness by pontificating on his artistic ideals. Hemingway tolerated the advice only as long as Dos Passos remained a second-tier competitor. In 1936, however, the less-famous writer published the final installment of his *U. S. A.* trilogy. While *The Big Money* was not a bona fide best-seller, it did sell a more-than-respectable seventeen thousand copies, far more than Dos Passos's previous works. Hemingway's most recent book, *Green Hills of Africa,* meanwhile, had stalled at ten thousand copies and was considered a commercial disappointment. Hemingway's jealousy was further aroused when Dos Passos became the subject of a *Time* magazine cover story. (He had to wait another year, until the publication of his novel *To Have and Have Not,* for that honor.) As if to balance Dos Passos's rising fortunes against his own feelings of decline, Hemingway began to concoct a story he maintained throughout the rest of his life. Dos Passos, he believed, was corrupted by success; after years of nagging Hemingway about the necessity of addressing politics in art, his friend had allowed money to compromise his conscience. The criticism was grossly exaggerated; *The Big Money* had not, as Hemingway insisted, reaped big money for its author. Yet, as with his diagnoses of Fitzgerald's flaws, this complaint against Dos Passos served to deflect Hemingway's own self-doubt. Whenever he feared he might sacrifice his own art for money, Hemingway tended to evoke Dos Passos's image as a prime example of a sell-out writer.

Throughout the fall of 1936 Hemingway vented his negative feelings toward Dos Passos by caricaturing him as the novelist Richard Gordon in *To Have and Have Not*. Gordon, known for a trio of proletarian novels, including *The Ruling Classes, Brief Mastery,* and *The Cult of Violence,* belongs to the "haves" crowd of Key West—a spoiled, promiscuous band whose decadence contrasts sharply to the working-class dignity of Hemingway's hero, Harry Morgan. Gordon's major downfall is his hypocrisy; while critiquing the wealthy, he has no problem socializing with them, even borrowing their money to maintain his ultimately meaningless lifestyle. In a symbolic moment Gordon suddenly succumbs to impotence while making love to Helène Bradley, the *femme fatale* of upper-crust Key West.[68]

Before *To Have and Have Not* was published in October 1937, Hemingway and Dos Passos traveled to Spain to cover that country's civil war, which many at the time considered a dress rehearsal for a second world war. Given Hemingway's seeming indifference toward politics, it is ironic that he criticized Dos Passos for his ambivalence toward the anti-fascist communists struggling to save Spain from a Hitler-supported coup. While Hemingway again complained that profits from *The Big Money* had softened his friend's radical beliefs, Dos Passos cooled toward the leftists for more personal reasons. When the communists executed a close Spanish friend as a traitor, Dos Passos began to believe that Hemingway and other writers supporting the communists willfully overlooked their atrocities, which could be as horrific as the fascists'. The disagreement effectively ended the two writers' friendship; both spent the next several years channeling their mutual anger into barely concealed condemnations of each other. In 1951 Dos Passos published *Chosen Country,* a novel based in part on his recently deceased wife's Michigan childhood. One character, George Elbert Warner, is an obvious caricature of Hemingway. Warner is a blowhard writer who mercilessly condemns those who fail to live up to his high moral standards, though he has no ethical problems with appropriating his friends' lives for his fiction. As if to dismiss the attack, Hemingway once more accused Dos Passos of allowing his bank account to influence his writing: "Have you ever seen the possession of money corrupt a man as it has Dos?" he asked Edmund

Wilson in 1952. "When Eisenhower received his tax free money from the Democrats for his book he became a Republican. His political development, and that of Dos, have very strange parallels."[69] At the time, Hemingway was enjoying the largest commercial success in his lifetime, *The Old Man and the Sea* (1952), which remained on *The New York Times* best-seller list for some forty-six weeks while appearing in its entirety in five million copies of *Life* magazine. He had more money in the bank than Dos Passos ever enjoyed. Hemingway, moreover, convinced himself that this money was a reward for remaining true to his ideals.

Hemingway offered his most vitriolic judgment of Dos Passos in *A Moveable Feast*. In his memoirs, he blames Dos Passos (though not by name) for ruining his first marriage. He and Hadley were an idyllic couple, he insists, until a "pilot fish" introduced him to a wealthy expatriate crowd that distracted him from his truest loves, his wife and his writing: "In those days I trusted the pilot fish. . . . Under the charm of these rich I was as trusting and as stupid as a bird dog . . . or a trained pig in a circus who has finally found someone who loves and appreciates him for himself alone." He reiterates charges leveled at Dos Passos since the late 1930s. Hemingway sees Dos Passos as inconsistent in his beliefs: "He enters and leaves politics or the theater in the same way he enters and leaves countries and people's lives in his early days." Nor was Hemingway above personal slurs; he describes his one-time friend as possessing "the irreplaceable early training of the bastard" (Dos Passos's parents were unmarried when he was born) and of trying to hide his "latent long denied love of money." And no Hemingway reference to Dos Passos would be complete without reiterating the charge of being corrupted by money: "He ends up rich himself," Hemingway writes in an inaccurate statement, "moved one dollar's width to the right with every dollar that he made" (207–209). Many critics suggest that *A Moveable Feast* marks Hemingway's effort to account for the disparity between the dedicated young artist he was in the 1920s and the old man who, three decades later, found his creative faculties in decline. If so, his portrait of Dos Passos (as well as his portrait of Fitzgerald) seems crafted to assure readers that other expatriate writers were also corrupted over the years. Indeed, denigrating his fellow authors to such extremes suggests Hemingway's desire to demonstrate that, to whatever depth he had fallen, his Paris friends had fallen farther.

Obviously, these writers did not constitute the entire population of expatriate modernists. Any number of other artists whom Hemingway either did not know well or whom he did not like also passed through the American colony in Paris. He was never close to poet E. E. Cummings, but he praised Cummings's novel *The Enormous Room* (1922), an account of a three-month internment at a French military prison during World War I. Hemingway also admired the short stories of Djuna Barnes, though he seems not to have read her most famous novel, *Nightwood* (1936). And while he socialized with other writers such as Malcolm Cowley and Dorothy Parker, he did not hold them in high regard. However popular and influential, Hemingway's work represents only one version of the expatriate experience. Chapter 7 offers synopses of important works by other modernists. Nevertheless, in the context of Hemingway's career, Anderson, Stein, Pound, Joyce, Eliot, Fitzgerald, and Dos Passos all stand out undeniably as important teachers, supporters, friends, and foes. Hemingway assimilated their influence and advice and produced a body of work that remains his own.

NOTES

1. Michael S. Reynolds, *The Young Hemingway* (New York: Blackwell, 1986), p. 89. For an analysis of these early stories, see Paul Smith's "Hemingway's Apprentice Fiction: 1919–1921," in *New Critical Approaches to the Short Stories of Ernest Hemingway,* edited by Jackson J. Benson (Durham, N.C.: Duke University Press, 1991), pp. 137–148.

2. "You go into the little park back of Notre Dame," Anderson wrote, "you stand on many bridges, you go to see how that, when the moonlight falls on it, the Louvre looks like a white frozen thing. Everywhere lovers. Lips are being pressed to lips. Women bodies are being pressed closely against the bodies of men. The lovers are all in the little dark places, on the bridges, on the stairway leading to the dark river. . . . " See *France and Sherwood Anderson: Paris Notebook 1921,* edited by Michael Fanning (Baton Rouge: Louisiana State University Press, 1976), p. 44.

3. Michael S. Reynolds, *Hemingway: The Paris Years* (New York: Blackwell, 1989), pp. 58–59.

4. Ernest Hemingway, "My Old Man," in his *The Complete Short Stories of Ernest Hemingway* (New York: Scribners, 1987), p. 154. Unless otherwise noted, subsequent references to Hemingway stories refer to this edition and are cited parenthetically in the text.

5. Ernest Hemingway to Edmund Wilson, 1923, in his *Ernest Hemingway: Selected Letters, 1917–1961,* edited by Carlos Baker (New York: Scribners, 1981), p. 105.

6. Quoted in Reynolds, *The Paris Years,* p. 253.

7. Ernest Hemingway to Sherwood Anderson, 23 May 1925, *Selected Letters,* p. 161.

8. Ernest Hemingway to Archibald MacLeish, 20 December 1925, Ibid., p. 178.

9. Ernest Hemingway to Sherwood Anderson, 21 May 1926, Ibid., p. 206.

10. Quoted in James R. Mellow, *Hemingway: A Life Without Consequences* (New York: Houghton Mifflin, 1992), p. 343.

11. Sherwood Anderson, *Memoirs* (New York: Harcourt, Brace, 1942), p. 475. Although Hemingway and Anderson met briefly in Paris in late 1926 for the first time since their Chicago encounters, their acquaintanceship was effectively over. Anderson's

biographer suggests why Anderson was able to reconcile with William Faulkner, who had also parodied him in the mid 1920s, but not with Hemingway: "In 1937 they [Anderson and Faulkner] were at a party together in New York. Anderson tried to avoid a meeting, but Faulkner persevered, pulling Anderson aside, saying, 'Sherwood, what the hell is the matter with you? Do you think that I am also a Hemmy? . . . As Faulkner said on several occasions, Anderson was the literary father of his generation, and he wanted that known. He had no intention of killing him." See Kim Townsend, *Sherwood Anderson* (Boston: Houghton Mifflin, 1987), p. 231.

12. Ernest Hemingway, *A Moveable Feast* (New York: Scribners, 1964), p. 17. Subsequent references are cited parenthetically in the text.

13. Shari Benstock, *Women of the Left Bank: Paris 1900–1940* (Austin: University of Texas Press, 1986), p. 159.

14. James R. Mellow, *Hemingway: A Life Without Consequences*, pp. 159–160.

15. Ernest Hemingway to Gertrude Stein, 18 February 1923, *Selected Letters*, p. 79.

16. Gertrude Stein, "Miss Furr and Miss Skeene," in her *Geography and Plays* (Boston: Four Seas, 1923), p. 20.

17. For an informative analysis of the stylistic differences between Stein and Hemingway, see Marjorie Perloff, "Ninety-Percent Rotarian: Gertrude Stein's Hemingway," *American Literature*, 62 (December 1990): 682–683.

18. Ernest Hemingway to Gertrude Stein, 17 February 1924, *Selected Letters*, p. 111.

19. Gertrude Stein, *The Autobiography of Alice B. Toklas* (New York: Harcourt, Brace, 1933), pp. 215–216.

20. Gertrude Stein, "He and They, Hemingway," in her *Portraits and Prayers* (New York: Random House, 1934), p. 193. The original title of the person was revised when included in this poetry collection.

21. Quoted in John Hyde Preston, "Gertrude Stein: A Conversation." *Atlantic Monthly*, 156 (August 1935): 191.

22. Gertrude Stein, *The Autobiography of Alice B. Toklas*, p. 219.

23. Ernest Hemingway to Maxwell Perkins, 19 November 1926, *Selected Letters*, p. 229.

24. Ernest Hemingway, "The True Story of My Break with Gertrude Stein," *The New Yorker*, 3 (12 February 1927): 23.

25. Michael S. Reynolds, *Hemingway: The American Homecoming* (New York: Blackwell, 1992), p. 84.

26. Ernest Hemingway to F. Scott Fitzgerald, 9 October 1928, *Selected Letters*, p. 287.

27. Gertrude Stein, *The Autobiography of Alice B. Toklas*, p. 219.

28. For an overview of Hemingway's unpublished responses to Stein, including "The Autobiography of Alice B. Hemingway," see my essay, "'In the Temps de Gertrude': Hemingway, Stein, and the Scene of Instruction at 27, rue de Fleurus," in *French Connections: Hemingway and Fitzgerald Abroad*, edited by J. Gerald Kennedy and Jackson R. Bryer (New York: St. Martin's Press, 1998), pp. 121–140.

29. Interestingly, Pound's Hailey birthplace is less than fifteen miles from the Ketchum, Idaho, home where Hemingway committed suicide in 1961.

30. Ezra Pound, "Hugh Selwyn Mauberly (Life and Contacts)," in his *Selected Poems of Ezra Pound* (New York: New Directions, 1957), pp. 61–65.

31. James R. Mellow, *Hemingway: A Life Without Consequences,* p. 159.

32. A section of "Hugh Selwyn Mauberly" reads: "The 'age demanded' chiefly a mould in plaster / Made with no loss of time. / A prose kinema, not, not assuredly, alabaster / Or the 'sculpture' of rhyme." In Hemingway's poem, the demands have less to do with art than with moral corruption and hypocrisy. Nevertheless, "The Age Demanded" is equally gloomy about the prospects for literature in the 1920s: "In the end the age was handed," Hemingway writes, "the sort of shit that it demanded." See *88 Poems,* edited by Nicholas Gerogiannis (New York: Harcourt Brace Jovanovich / Bruccoli Clark, 1979), p. 53.

33. Ezra Pound, *Cantos,* in his *Selected Poems of Ezra Pound* (New York: New Directions, 1957), p. 108.

34. Julian Symons, *Makers of the New: The Revolution in Literature, 1912–1939* (New York: Random House, 1987), p. 220.

35. Ernest Hemingway to Arnold Gingrich, 13 March 1933, *Selected Letters,* p. 383.

36. Ernest Hemingway to Archibald MacLeish, 10 August 1943, Ibid., p. 548.

37. Ernest Hemingway to Ezra Pound, 26 June 1958, Ibid., p. 883.

38. Independent publishing firms often found it too expensive to trim the folded leaves of paper along the right-hand margin of a book, thus requiring readers to cut them with a letter opener before they could turn a page.

39. See Carlos Baker, *Hemingway: The Writer as Artist* (Princeton: Princeton University Press, 1952; revised, 1972), pp. 87–88.

40. Michael S. Reynolds, *The Paris Years,* p. 202.

41. Ernest Hemingway, "Conrad, Optimist and Moralist," in *By-Line: Ernest Hemingway: Selected Articles and Dispatches of Four Decades,* edited by William Wiser (New York: Scribners, 1967), p. 133.

42. In at least one 1920 letter, Hadley encourages Ernest to emulate the "vital throb of youth" in *Paradise.* Quoted in Michael S. Reynolds, *Young Hemingway,* p. 241.

43. F. Scott Fitzgerald to Thomas Boyd, May 1924, *A Life in Letters,* edited by Matthew J. Bruccoli (New York: Touchstone, 1994), p. 69.

44. F. Scott Fitzgerald, *The Great Gatsby* (New York: Scribners, 1925; republished, Cambridge: Cambridge University Press, 1991), p. 141.

45. F. Scott Fitzgerald to Maxwell Perkins, ca. 10 October 1924, *A Life in Letters,* p. 82.

46. Ernest Hemingway to Maxwell Perkins, 9 June 1925, *Selected Letters,* pp. 162–163.

47. Item 202c. Unpublished manuscript, in The Ernest Hemingway Collection, John F. Kennedy Library, Boston.

48. Ernest Hemingway, "The Art of the Short Story," in *New Critical Approaches to the Short Stories of Ernest Hemingway,* edited by Jackson J. Benson (Durham, N.C.: Duke University Press, 1991), p. 4.

49. F. Scott Fitzgerald to Ernest Hemingway, June 1926, *A Life in Letters,* pp. 142–144.

50. F. Scott Fitzgerald to Ernest Hemingway, June 1929, Ibid., p. 165.

51. F. Scott Fitzgerald to Zelda Fitzgerald, 26 October 1940. Quoted in Matthew J. Bruccoli, *Fitzgerald and Hemingway: A Dangerous Friendship* (New York: Carroll & Graf, 1994), p. 202.

52. F. Scott Fitzgerald, "Pasting It Together," in his *The Crack-Up,* edited by Edmund Wilson (New York: New Directions, 1945), p. 79.

53. Quoted in Matthew J. Bruccoli, *Fitzgerald and Hemingway: A Dangerous Friendship*, p. 228.

54. Ibid., p. 192. Bruccoli identifies several Hemingway allusions, both overt and subtle, to Fitzgerald. In the first draft of *Green Hills of Africa*, Hemingway referred to Fitzgerald as a "coward of great charm." Although he cut this particular reference before the publication of *Green Hills of Africa*, other attacks are evident in the text, including mention of "two good writers" who "cannot write because they have lost confidence through reading critics. . . . The critics have made them impotent." See *Green Hills of Africa* (New York: Scribners, 1935), pp. 23–24.

55. F. Scott Fitzgerald to Maxwell Perkins, 19 September 1936, *A Life in Letters*, p. 308.

56. F. Scott Fitzgerald to Ludlow Fowler, August 1924, *A Life in Letters*, p. 78.

57. Ernest Hemingway to F. Scott Fitzgerald, 28 May 1934, *Selected Letters*, p. 408.

58. Ernest Hemingway to Gerald Murphy, 27 April 1934, in *Letters from the Lost Generation*, edited by Linda Patterson Miller (Rutgers, N.J.: Rutgers University Press, 1991, p. 83.

59. Ernest Hemingway to Maxwell Perkins, 30 April 1934, in *The Only Thing That Counts: The Ernest Hemingway/Maxwell Perkins Correspondence, 1925–1947*, edited by Matthew J. Bruccoli (New York: Scribners, 1996), p. 209.

60. Ernest Hemingway to Maxwell Perkins, 25 March 1939, in *Selected Letters*, p. 483.

61. See Bruccoli, *Fitzgerald and Hemingway: A Dangerous Friendship*, pp. 218–222; Michael S. Reynolds, *Hemingway: The Final Years* (New York: Norton, 1999), pp. 51–52.

62. Ernest Hemingway, *The Torrents of Spring* (New York: Scribner, 1926), p. 68.

63. John Dos Passos, *Nineteen-Nineteen* (New York: Harcourt, Brace, 1932); republished in *U.S.A.* (Boston: Houghton Mifflin, 1960), p. 407.

64. John Dos Passos, "A Lost Generation," in his *John Dos Passos: The Major Nonfiction Prose*, edited by Donald Pizer (Detroit: Wayne State University Press, 1988), p. 93.

65. Ernest Hemingway to John Dos Passos, 26 March 1932, *Selected Letters*, p. 354.

66. John Dos Passos to Ernest Hemingway, February 1932, in *The Fourteenth Chronicle: Letters and Diaries of John Dos Passos*, edited by Townsend Ludington (Boston: Gambit, 1973), pp. 402–403.

67. Quoted in Michael S. Reynolds, *Hemingway: The 1930s* (New York: Norton, 1996), p. 86.

68. Hemingway did not excuse himself from ridicule while writing *To Have and Have Not*. As Reynolds notes, in one moment eventually excised from the published version of the book, Gordon refers "to an overweight writer who . . . has betrayed his promise, letting down a whole generation of young writers who once admired him. After that one great novel, nothing followed. All he was writing now was tripe for *Esquire.* . . . " See *Hemingway: The 1930s*, p. 237.

69. Ernest Hemingway to Edmund Wilson, 8 November 1952, in *Selected Letters*, p. 793.

THE LITERARY RELEVANCE OF
EXPATRIATE MODERNISM

In a 1924 letter Hemingway explains the peculiar organization of his first short-story collection, *In Our Time* (1925). The arrangement of the book juxtaposes full-length fictions such as "My Old Man" and "Big Two-Hearted River" with more compressed "interchapters" from the Paris edition of the 1924 *in our time* that offer brief but graphic glimpses of war, revolution, and bullfighting. These smaller vignettes, Hemingway writes, "give the picture of the whole between examining it in detail" in the longer stories. The effect is "like looking with your eyes at something, say a passing coast, and then looking at it with 15X binoculars."[1] Reading the one- to two-paragraph episodes provides an overview of the thematic focus of the collection, which is the prevalence of violence in the modern age. That idea is then magnified and explored in greater depth in the longer pieces. The result is the readers' shifting sense of proximity to the action. On one page audiences view the drama from a distance; on the next, they are immersed in its intensity.

Hemingway's binoculars offer a valuable image for describing how to view the relevance of a literary movement or genre (type of literature)—the reasons it remains popular with audiences—whether students, scholars, or the general public. When discussing the contribution of expatriate modernists to literary history, critics typically measure their achievement according to two broad criteria: the *synchronic* appeal of the movement—its ability to remain meaningful to readers despite its having occurred eighty years ago; and its *diachronic* import—what it can teach audiences about the specific historical and sociological context of the 1920s. Like an observation of Hemingway's passing coast with the naked eye, the synchronic view offers a broad "picture of the whole," while the diachronic looks in more detail at what Hemingway and other modernists reveal about life in their time.

A less technical way of describing these qualities is to distinguish between "universal" and "particular" characteristics. *Universal* is a problematic word, however, for it assumes that certain values and beliefs are ingrained in the human condition regardless of time and place—an assumption that soon proves impossible to substantiate. Synchronic relevance means something different. The term refers to the readers' capacity to relate to literature written in other historical periods. Rather than argue that a piece of writing expresses a timeless truth, critics say that audiences make it relevant, by identifying either with its characters or with the themes, conflicts, and dilemmas pertinent to their lives. Either way, they assume what is called a "synoptic" view, meaning they perform a sort of survey or overview of the subject under study. In doing so, they detach it from history. Readers may decide, for example, that they relate to a Hemingway text because it dramatizes the anxiety of feeling uprooted or displaced; and because they were able to glean that point from the work, they might conclude that such a fear is commonplace, then as well as now. Such an assumption is appropriate as long as one recognizes that the causes and consequences of that fear will vary from era to era. Assuming a synchronic perspective is thus a good introductory method for interpreting literature, for it allows scholars to compare works from different periods and speak in abstract terms of common human feelings and motives.

The following diagram sketches the relevance of expatriate modernism from a synchronic and diachronic point of view.

QUESTIONS	THE SYNCHRONIC VIEW	THE DIACHRONIC VIEW
How does expatriation enable writers' work and careers?	Expatriation affords the isolation and detachment from one's homeland necessary to establish an individual perspective; it is thus vital for avoiding conformity and creating a literary statement. It also offers writers an archetypal theme—the loss of home, often dramatized through allusions to the Garden of Eden story.	Expatriates in Paris in the 1920s were not writing in isolation as much as they were establishing an alternative publishing community. Through little magazines and small, independently owned presses, they produced experimental works that did not fit into the American mainstream.

QUESTIONS	THE SYNCHRONIC VIEW	THE DIACHRONIC VIEW
In terms of American literature in particular, what does expatriation reveal about the differences distinguishing American and European identity?	American writers living abroad depict Europe as a rite of passage for Americans that dramatizes their fall from innocence to experience.	Unlike nineteenth-century expatriates, however, modernists do not portray Americans overseas as naive and innocent. Their characters travel to Europe searching for an atmosphere as cynical and pessimistic as they believe themselves to be.
What does the expatriate tradition in nineteenth- and twentieth-century American literature suggest about the prospects for creating great art in American settings?	The steady exodus of artists to Europe suggests that America lacks the depth of history and tradition needed to create a national literature. Writers as varied as Washington Irving, Henry James, and T. S. Eliot look to Europe to provide the artistic models and forms, as well as the cultural backdrop, for their writing.	While many modernists idealized Europe, they also identified with the chaos and disorder rampant in England, France, and Italy at the turn of the century. Instead of seeing the Continent as a source of stability and tradition, they felt that Europe was in a state of decline and that this decline reflected the crumbling of Western civilization. By contrast, America, still believing in the myth of cultural progress, seemed incapable of acknowledging the upheavals of modernity.
Finally, what does expatriation reveal about the status of the writer in America?	From Irving to James to Eliot, American writers have traditionally felt alienated from mainstream American culture. Insisting that the American work ethic denigrates art as an unproductive indulgence, artists flock to Europe in search of a realm where literature is esteemed and recognized for its contribution to culture.	Nineteenth-century expatriates—Henry James and Edith Wharton most obviously—view the literary life as an aristocratic tradition; they see it as an avocation for the upperclass gentleman and lady whose tastes were cultivated and refined. Most modernists, by contrast, tended to adopt a more bohemian lifestyle, imagining their artistic experiments as an extension of their revolt against middle-class mores. Rather than preserving cultural traditions, they view themselves as inventing new, radical ones.

According to legend, the two key ingredients of expatriate literary life at Paris cafés such as the Dôme (pictured here in 1925) were liquor and conversation.

From a synchronic perspective, the most general reason critics deem expatriate modernism worthy of study is that it represents a recent manifestation of an age-old tradition. In *The Republic*, Plato argued that poets would be unwelcome in the ideal society because they cause longing and dissent among the populace. Since then, writers have been judged detrimental to the smooth workings of governments, and a great many writers have been banished from their homelands. Others who felt their temperaments out of place with that of their culture have chosen to relocate to a foreign milieu. The sheer array of artists who—voluntarily or not—have lived in lands not their own leads critics to view *exile* as an expression of the individuality necessary for creating great art. In his influential essay "Literature and Exile" (1961), Harry Levin surveys a range of classical and modern authors, arguing that isolation from their homeland was a vital catalyst to their creativity. Whether the Roman poet Ovid, expelled from Rome by Emperor Augustus in 8 A.D., or Vladimir Nabokov, whose family fled Russia after the 1917 Communist revolution, many great writers have suffered *une patria perdue* (a lost country). However personally tragic the loss, their alienation is essential to their art. As Levin explains, "isolation need not mean sheer withdrawal, but that detachment of the one from the many which is the necessary precondition of all original thought. The relation between the poet and the multitude . . . is perpetual ostracism. That is a hard lot . . . yet it is not a disheartening one, since exile has often proved to be a vocation, reinforcing other gifts with courage and looking forward to a final triumph of independence over conformity."[2] Levin insists that exile or expatriation is a professional prerequisite for the artist. Only by abandoning their native lands can writers stand apart from the crowd to express unpopular points of view.

Closely related to this notion is an issue critics call the "psychology of exile." While Levin argues that expatriation is a triumph of individuality over conformity, other commentators explore how it allows writers to inhabit the imagination so they can better tap into their creativity and originality. Living in another country, artists detach themselves from the external, social world and turn their focus inward to the less inhibited realm of the mind. Gertrude Stein's "An American and France" (1936) offers a good example of how expatriate isolation enhances creativity. As Stein argues, Paris was an ideal place for expatriates because "it let you alone." Writers relocated there because the city provided the freedom "not to be connected with anything happening." For Stein, art is an expression of "what is in" the writer, which has "nothing to do with what is necessarily existing outside of them." Artists thus need two homelands—the one from which they come and the one that allows them to live in isolation: "It is very natural that every one who makes anything inside themselves . . . does naturally have to have two civilizations. They have to have the civilization that makes them and the civilization that has nothing to do with them." Only through this extreme detachment can artistic expression occur, for "if you are you in your own civilization you are apt to mix yourself up too much with your civilization but when it is another civilization . . . you have freedom inside yourself."[3]

Still other synchronic critics offer mythological explanations for the relevance of expatriate literature. These commentators suggest that stories of exile are appealing because they dramatize the fear of homelessness, the anxiety of being dispossessed from one's roots. To convey the mythic significance of their feelings of displacement, for example, modernists such as James Joyce, T. S. Eliot, and Ezra Pound drew their allusions (literary references) from classical Greek literature. Other authors have borrowed from the Bible, equating exile with the loss of Eden. "What is the topic of literature?" asks Somali author

SINCLAIR LEWIS ON 1920S' EXPATRIATES

One of the most contemptuous portraits of expatriate life in Paris is Sinclair Lewis's "Self-Conscious America": "These self-conscious American aesthetes sit around the Dôme and the Rotonde interminably talking art and never producing any.... Precious little highbrows they are, talking about Joyce and Picasso and thinking themselves very advanced and superior."

Sinclair Lewis, "Self-Conscious America." *The American Mercury*, 6 (October 1925): 130.

The essay was inspired by the insults that Lewis suffered at the hands of the Montparnasse crowd when he toured France in the mid 1920s. Autobiographies such as Robert McAlmon's *Being Geniuses Together* and Samuel Putnam's *Paris Was Our Mistress* describe how poorly the best-selling author of *Babbitt* was received when he appeared in the Paris cafés. In one notorious incident at the Dôme, an inebriated Lewis loudly compared himself to Gustave Flaubert, author of *Madame Bovary*, prompting one expatriate to reply, "Sit down. You're just a best seller."

Not surprisingly, Hemingway delighted in bashing Lewis back as well. Many critics argue that a brief passage on an anonymous bar patron in *Across the River and into the Trees* alludes to Lewis, whose face was disfigured by skin cancer treatments late in life: "He had a strange face," Hemingway writes, "like an over-enlarged, disappointed weasel or ferret. It looked as pock-marked and as blemished as the mountains of the moon seen through a cheap telescope."

Ernest Hemingway, *Across the River and into the Trees* (New York: Scribners, 1950), p. 11.

Nuruddin Farah, a longtime expatriate resident of Europe. "It began with the expulsion of Adam from paradise. What . . . writers do is to play around either with the myth of creation or the myth of return. And in between, in parentheses, there is that promise, the promise of return. . . . It's a return to innocence, to childhood, to our sources."[4] Not surprisingly, images of paradise lost abound in expatriate modernism. The title of Hemingway's *The Garden of Eden* (1986) is an obvious example. Eliot's *The Waste Land* (1922) concludes with an allusion to the Fisher King, an archetypal figure whose duty, according to myth, is to return his drought-plagued kingdom to its Edenic past. Because the fisherman is a traditional symbol of both Christ and fertility, many scholars compare the fishing scenes in "Big Two-Hearted River" and *The Sun Also Rises* to the scenes of *The Waste Land,* noting that both express a longing to renew the stability and order of yesteryear.

In general terms, these three topics—the artistic, the psychological, and the mythic—allow synchronic critics to relate the experience of expatriation to the larger human drama of balancing individuality and community, separation and belonging. Artists need the freedom of distance to perfect their craft, but they must also maintain some attachment to home, lest the world of the imagination stray so far from its origin that it becomes irrelevant to it. Looking at isolation through the diachronic lenses of Hemingway's binoculars, though, reveals a need to qualify it and determine what it meant in the day-to-day context of expatriate life in Paris. Few writers in Paris disassociated themselves from American culture. Most lived in neighborhoods populated by other expatriates, situating themselves within walking distance of the sidewalk cafés along the Boulevard du Montparnasse. Living abroad did not mean they forsook the amenities to which America had accustomed them. In fact, Hemingway in 1922–1923 was unusual in his willingness to reside in an apartment where the facilities consisted only of a communal "Turkish" toilet—a hole in the floor with a footrest on either side.

More typically, expatriates imported consumer luxuries from home. Malcolm Cowley notes how their inability to do without certain goods made them ambassadors of American enterprise: "The exiles of art were also trade missionaries. Involuntarily they increased the foreign demand for fountain pens, silk stockings, grapefruit and portable typewriters. They drew after them an invading army of tourists, thus swelling the profits of steamship lines and travel agencies. Everything fitted into the business picture." What from a distance appears as alienation from American culture thus looks upon closer inspection like an extension of it. As Cowley admits, his fellow expatriates sincerely believed they were rebelling against middle-class American culture. Nevertheless, they carried that lifestyle overseas and helped create in Europe "a demand for all sorts of products—modern furniture, beach pajamas, cosmetics, colored bathrooms with toilet paper to match."[5]

Nor did isolation in Paris mean one worked without instruction or support from fellow Americans. Rather, the city was home to an alternative publishing industry that rose in response to the conservatism of mainstream American imprints. Expatriate publications included both literary journals and small-press books. The journals, referred to as "little magazines," included the *transatlantic review* (which Hemingway helped edit), *This Quarter* (which published "Big Two-Hearted River"), the *Little Review* (which began in Chicago in 1914 but relocated overseas in 1923).[6] They were often fly-by-night affairs, suffering from poor financing that doomed them to short life spans. Their editors, since they were literary types, often were temperamentally unsuited to managing their business affairs. Unlike mass-circulation magazines such as *The Saturday Evening Post* and *Red Book,* which demanded strict adherence to their fiction formulas, these outlets encouraged experimentation and originality. A representative issue suggests their importance to modernist literature. The April 1924 *transatlantic review* features selections from Stein's *The Making of Americans* (written 1906–1908, published 1925), Joyce's *Work in Progress* (later known as *Finnegans Wake*), Hemingway's "Indian Camp," as well as short stories by John Dos Passos and Djuna Barnes. This concentration of talent is by no means unusual. Unfortunately, little magazines also printed what Julian Symons calls the "genuine phoneys," untalented writers who "might be called victims of modernism" because they imitated the experiments of better writers "without at all understanding the implications or purpose of what they were trying to do."[7] Nevertheless, modernist literature probably could not have pushed the boundaries of experimentation to such extremes had it lacked little magazines that emphasized innovation over profits.

Several alternative presses also operated in Paris, allowing expatriates to publish full-length novels and story and poetry collections. Hemingway's *Three Stories and Ten Poems* and the original *in our time* appeared under the auspices of Robert McAlmon's Contact Press and William Bird's Three Mountains Press respectively. McAlmon was a flamboyant bisexual who funded his venture through an allowance from the family of his wife, Winifred Bryher Ellerman. He produced several noteworthy modernist works—including the first edition of Stein's *The Making of Americans,* H.D.'s *Palimpsest* (1926), and Djuna Barnes's *Ladies Almanack* (1928), as well as his own writings. Bird was an American

Sylvia Beach with James Joyce at her Shakespeare and Company bookstore, early 1920s. Beach was in the process of publishing Joyce's *Ulysses* when she met Hemingway in early 1922.

journalist who in 1922 purchased an antique handpress as a hobby. Through Hemingway he engaged Pound in editing a series of limited-edition books that Pound described as an "inquest" into "the present state of contemporary English prose." According to Hugh Ford, Pound secured commitments from well-known writers such as William Carlos Williams and Ford Madox Ford by insisting "that private limited editions encouraged one to be 'more intimate,' and, if more intimate, perhaps 'really interesting. . . .' Instead of writing for the public, Pound advised them, write as though talking to one's friends."[8] During its short existence, Three Mountains Press published Williams's *The Great American Novel* (1923) and a selection of Pound's *Cantos* (1925) in addition to *in our time*. Its demise was typical of such endeavors: it petered out in 1928 when Bird lost interest and sold his handpress to British expatriate Nancy Cunard, who founded her own amateur publishing house, the Hours Press.

Of other publishers in Paris, among the most important were Sylvia Beach, who in addition to running her Shakespeare and Company bookstore produced the first edition of Joyce's *Ulysses* (1922); Harry and Caresse Crosby, whose Black Sun Press printed editions of the works of Joyce, D. H. Lawrence, and Hart Crane, as well the couple's own occult poetry; and Jack Kahane, whose Guardian Obelisk published Henry Miller's *Tropic of Cancer* (1934). Even Gertrude Stein and her companion Alice B. Toklas established themselves as publishers at one point. Frustrated by the indifference of American publishers to Stein's work, the couple sold a prized Picasso painting titled *Woman with a Fan* in the early 1930s and printed four Stein volumes under the Plain Edition imprint.[9] The venture probably would have continued had the popularity of Stein's *The Autobiography of Alice B. Toklas,* a Literary Guild selection in the mid 1930s, not won her the interest of the New York publishers she long coveted. When Random House agreed to bring out one Stein book per year for the rest of her life, Plain Edition was promptly retired.

The commitment of Random House to an avant-garde author such as Stein suggests how the little magazines and small presses in Paris ultimately liberated publishers from their conservatism and transformed the American mainstream. Stanley Coben notes that several upstart publishing firms established in the mid 1920s scoured independent Paris presses for authors with artistic rather than commercial promise: "Among such new publishers, Alfred A. Knopf, Horace Liveright, Albert and Charles Boni, . . . Bennet Cerf's Random House (started in 1925), and Simon and Schuster (begun in 1923) . . . not only sought fresh authors but also welcomed dissident thought in the manuscripts they published."[10] In this way, the small presses in Paris exerted an influence in publishing disproportionate to their operations. By providing writers a proving ground, they offered novice authors an opportunity to cultivate their own voices and styles without concern for meeting sales expectations. And by daring to print more experimental writers such as Stein and Joyce, these independent publishers eventually helped rewrite the rules regarding what was acceptable in American literature.

Another issue critics discuss in determining the relevance of expatriate modernism is how these writers compare to expatriates from previous eras. Hemingway, Stein, Pound, and others were but one generation of Americans who relocated to Europe. Artists as diverse as Washington Irving (1783–1859), Nathaniel Hawthorne (1804–1864), Henry James (1843–1916), and Edith Wharton (1862–1937) also journeyed overseas at various points in their lives. The tradition of expatriation in American literature raises several questions that can be analyzed from a

THE APPEAL OF PARIS

In his essay "The European Capitals of American Literature," Alex Zwerdling notes how expatriates of the 1920s self-consciously distanced themselves from French culture, unlike Henry James's generation, which sought acceptance for American writers in Europe: "When a friend warned Hemingway that 'if we are going to stay here it means really we have to become Frenchmen,' he replied with a shrug, 'Who would want to stay?' The bohemian life was nomadic. 'I hate a room without an open suitcase in it,' Zelda Fitzgerald said, 'it seems so permanent.' Most of the expatriates in Paris never secured entry into French literary culture.... And despite their change in residence, the Americans remained recognizable representatives of the country, even patriotic in their way. Sylvia Beach boasted that she had the largest American flag in Paris, which she draped over the bookcases during parties at her shop both to protect and advertise her merchandise....

"This indifference to or exclusion from French literary life, however, struck other American expatriate writers as the essential problem in choosing Paris. Henry James had spent his first year abroad in the French capital, and though he came to know some of the leading writers there—Turgenev, Flaubert, Zola, and Daudet among them—he soon understood that he had made a mistake: 'I remember how Paris had, in a hundred ways, come to wear and displease me; I couldn't get out of the detestable American Paris,' he wrote in his journals. 'I saw, moreover, that I should be an eternal outsider.' What was the point of leaving your country behind only to reconstitute it on a foreign shore?... After a year James impulsively packed his bags and moved to London...."

Alex Zwerdling, "The European Capitals of American Literature." *Wilson Quarterly*, 17 (Winter 1993): 131.

synchronic and diachronic perspective: What values distinguish the American from the European? Is America capable of producing an original body of literature that reflects these values, or do its writers merely look to Europe to supply artistic forms and techniques? And does the nation accord the literary writer a significant social status, or does its democratic, Puritan-influenced mind-set render imaginative writing irrelevant to the majority of the population?

Of these concerns, the critical consensus is strongest on what expatriation reveals about American identity. According to Ernest Earnest, that "one of the enduring themes in the literature of the United States is the conflict between American and European values" suggests a desire to define the specific traits that distinguish the national character from its British antecedents.[11] As Malcolm Bradbury adds, writers defining these traits view Europe as an all-purpose antithesis, a convenient opposite against which ideals peculiar to the new nation can be articulated: "Europe has always been a deep metaphor in American writing, and more: it has been an alternative perception on life, a contrasting notion of culture."[12]

In this contrast Europe is aristocratic, while America is democratic; the Old World represents history and tradition, while the New World symbolizes a radical break with the past. Europe stands for sophistication and civilization; America, for naiveté and provincialism. If these dichotomies appear to idealize Europe at the expense of America, America also evokes optimism and progress, while Europe is associated with deterioration and corruption. These conflicting values are typically lumped under the much broader headings of innocence and experience. Philip Rahv explains how these terms allow American writers to dramatize the conflict between American and European identities as it relates to art and culture: "In the American novel the 'innocent abroad' appears in a dual role. His actions take on a positive meaning when he goes forth to battle the old evils of history encountered on 'Europe's lighted and decorated stage'; but in another mood this same 'innocent abroad' ceases to be a crusader and becomes a philistine, shallow, complacent, and vulgarly insensitive to the splendor and glory of the past."[13] In other words, the American abroad may be an ingenue corrupted by the Old World, or he or she may be a crude upstart oblivious to European standards of class and taste. Many expatriate novels, whether James's *Daisy Miller* (1878) or Wharton's *Madame de Treymes* (1907), ground their drama in this unresolved question, suggesting the mixed feelings of American writers toward their cultural heritage.

There is less agreement about what expatriation signifies in regard to the originality of American literature and the social status of its authors. In the first case, critics credit the exodus to Europe to artists' belief that America lacks the materials required to produce imaginative literature. In the nineteenth century in particular, writers criticized the American scene for its insufficiently inspiring environment. In one of the first expatriate works, *The Sketch Book of Geoffrey Crayon, Gent.* (published serially 1819–1820, in book form, 1820), Washington Irving's fictional narrator Geoffrey Crayon explains his motives for traveling abroad through an extended contrast between the American and European landscapes:

> I visited various parts of my own country, and had I been merely a lover of fine scenery, I should have felt little desire to seek elsewhere its gratification, for on no country have the charms of nature been more prodigally lavished. . . . But Europe held forth the charms of storied and poetical association. There were to be seen the masterpieces of art, the refinements of highly-civilized society, the quaint peculiarities of ancient and local custom. My native country was full of youthful promise; Europe was rich in the accumulated treasures of age. Her very ruins told the history of times gone by, and every mouldering stone was a chronicle.[14]

Irving was thirty-two and attempting to launch his literary career when he began a seventeen-year stay on the Continent in 1815. Nathaniel Hawthorne was much older, almost fifty, when he moved to Liverpool in 1853 as a federal employee and then to Rome five years later. Having produced a trio of celebrated novels—*The Scarlet Letter* (1850), *The House of the Seven Gables* (1851), and *The Blithedale Romance* (1852)—his reputation as the leading literary emissary of America was already more than secure. While previous novels and tales drew their inspiration from the rich Puritan history surrounding Salem, Massachusetts, his hometown, he began *The Marble Faun* with a preface that, much like Irving's, questioned the ability of America to stimulate the creative faculty: "No author can conceive the difficulty of writing a Romance about a country where there is no shadow, no antiquity, no mystery, no picturesque and gloomy wrong, nor anything but a commonplace prosperity, in broad and simple daylight, as is happily the case with my dear native land."[15] In his 1879 biography of Hawthorne, Henry James echoed the author of *The Marble Faun* by offering yet another "some such list . . . of the absent things in American life" that inhibited the production of great art: "No sovereign, no count, no personal loyalty, no aristocracy, no church, no clergy, no army, no diplomatic service, no country gentlemen, no palaces, no castles, nor manors, nor old country houses, nor parsonages, nor thatched cottages, nor ivied ruins. . . . "[16] Nor did detailed lists of American deficiencies end with the advent of modernism. Several twentieth-century intellectuals, from Van Wyck Brooks to Harold Stearns to William Carlos Williams, offered their own reasons the native soil was infertile for cultivating art.[17]

Alan Holder describes these sorts of lists as evidence of artists' "quarrel with America." But while expatriates attempted to compensate for the lack of literary tradition in their native country by schooling themselves in foreign arts, they also discovered that Europe could be as uninspiring as the world from which they fled. Although "expatriates were often severe on the America they could not live in, they came to be quite as unsparing of the Europe that had promised them refuge," Holder writes. "In effect, much of their work depicts their discovery of the Old World's inability to provide the kind of milieu that these writers sought."[18] In a similar vein, Eugene Bagger in 1928 cautioned writers embarking for Europe against absorbing Old World literary traditions. Expatriation could be an artistically invigorating experience, he noted. Yet, maintaining contact with native traditions was also important, for in the modern age, America, since it was so new and unbound to the past, possessed material suited to expressing the spirit of the times:

> It is principally through the moral freedom of its atmosphere and the perspective depth and associative riches of its scene that European life quickens the mind of the American expatriate engaged in some form or other of creative work. On the other hand, I believe that the tonic value which the hopeful young American looking forward to his spiritual rebirth attaches, in anticipation, to whatever is included under the mystic term "contact with European literary currents" is mainly illusory. . . . There is today in America . . . a ferment which in contrast to the late afternoon moods of Old World literature appears like the burst of a new day. . . . There is in the United States that surplus of faith and energy from which in the past the great arts have sprung. Against this resplendent springtime fulness, the mellow perfections of European culture shine with

the sadness of finished things, with the melancholy radiance of autumn decline toward winter.[19]

Still another issue raised by the expatriate tradition has to do with the role—or lack of one—reserved for literary authors in America. Just as writers lamented the failure of the country to provide the raw materials for art, they complained that it was indifferent to artists' contributions to culture. Europe, they insisted, holds its authors in high esteem because it regards literature as a crucible of human achievement. At home, by contrast, the American work ethic looks down upon literary pursuits as a lazy indulgence, an endeavor without practical or pragmatic value. This statement is a gross exaggeration, of course. As many European writers have felt alienated from their native culture as Americans have. Nevertheless, since the American Revolution, a pervasive myth has existed that the artists of new nations suffer perpetual inattention. Two years before departing for Europe, Irving described America as a country in which "literary leisure is confounded with idleness" and "the man of letters is almost an insulated being, with few to understand, less to value, and scarcely any to encourage his pursuits."[20]

Hawthorne expressed similar frustration in "The Custom House," his preface to *The Scarlet Letter,* when he imagined the horror of his Puritan ancestors upon learning of his literary endeavors: "A writer of storybooks! What kind of a business in life—what mode of glorifying God, or being serviceable to mankind in his day and generation—may that be? Why, the degenerate fellow might as well have been a fiddler!"[21] Such complaints raged as well in the 1920s. Harold Stearns blamed "the emergence of articulate mediocrity" and a "fear of excellence" for destroying any hope of the populace giving literature its due respect:

> The standardization processes [of industrialism] were at work with a speed and mercilessness unknown before in the history of mankind. . . . Everywhere there were short cuts to culture, whereby it was possible to know all about an author or a subject and never to have read through one of his books or a single book on a subject. . . . The arts became the "lively" arts, as if they must jazz it up too with the spirit of the age; and everywhere was this appalling spread of literacy so that the charlatans had a bigger and wider field to work on. Aristocratic ways of thought and life became "high hat" and taboo.[22]

Because these concerns over identity and the place of literature in America are prevalent throughout modernist writing, for synchronic critics to compare expatriates of various eras to each other is not uncommon. However, as many diachronic distinctions separate nineteenth- and twentieth-century expatriates as synchronic similarities bind them together. First and foremost, Europe symbolized something very different for Hemingway's generation than it did for authors such as Irving, Haw-

Gertrude Stein with collaborator Virgil Thomson in 1927, working on their opera *Four Saints in Three Acts.*

thorne, or James. Bradbury notes that a "change in the spirit of American expatriation" occurred during the 1890s as living abroad represented "a movement not toward the social and historical past but toward the present and future-oriented *avant-garde*." Instead of revering the established social and artistic traditions of Europe, Americans overseas began to identify with a spirit of radical experimentation emerging in painting, poetry, and fiction. This spirit was not confined to artistic endeavors. Many expatriates aspired to innovation in their lifestyles. Seeking escape from the confines of marriage, monogamy, and (in some cases) sobriety, they found in Europe a thriving subculture that prized indulgence and impulsiveness as creative stimulants. Some expatriates such as Edith Wharton continued to look to the Continent to supply the aristocratic codes of conduct that America lacked, but these became the exception rather than the rule. As Bradbury suggests, "It was now less toward high society than to bohemia that expatriates began to be drawn."[23]

Bohemia was not a late-nineteenth-century invention. The struggling artist who rebels against the middle class through decadence (deviancy) had been a figure in French popular culture for at least half a century. The international popularity of Henri Murger's *Scènes de la Vie Bohème* (*Scenes from the Bohemian Life*, 1851) exported the image of the artistic rebel to America, where colorful figures such as Walt Whitman delighted in offending middle-class sensibilities by celebrating hedonism as self-expression. Despite Whitman's example, however, most leading writers before the turn of the century derided the bohemian ideal. Not until the advent of modernity was the term widely accepted among artists who envisioned that their duty was to liberate the arts from Victorian rules against unseemly subject matter and impolite habits of expression. Soon there were attempts to import the bohemians' Parisian café society to isolated American outposts such as Greenwich Village, which became a haven for revolutionaries eager to challenge the public's idea of art as refined and uplifting.

To become a full-fledged fad, bohemia also needed the help of the mass media, which began ridiculing expatriates and villagers as a dangerous counterculture undermining American morals. In *Exile's Return* (1934) Cowley describes the battle of words between middle-class periodicals such as *The Saturday Evening Post* and the modernist rebels that commenced in the early 1900s: "Here, apparently, was a symbolic struggle: on the one side, the great megaphone of middle-class America; on the other, the American disciples of art and artistic living. Here, in its latest incarnation, was the eternal warfare of bohemian against bourgeois, poet against propriety."[24] By the 1920s, the conflict raged so loudly that subtleties of opinion on both sides were drowned out. Any author who relocated to Paris was a bohemian, and any commentator who stayed behind was a hopeless Philistine.

Hemingway is a good example of a writer identified as bohemian by association. Throughout his life, he professed disgust with the supposed rebelliousness of Greenwich Village types who treated expatriation as an excuse for doing just about everything *except* settling down to the hard work of writing. In a 1922 *Toronto Star* dispatch titled "American Bohemians in Paris," he described how "the scum of Greenwich Village, New York, has been skimmed off and deposited in large ladlesful on that section of Paris adjacent to the Café Rotonde." What most offended Hemingway was the idea that these idlers were artists: "You can find anything you are looking for at the Rotonde—except serious artists. . . . They are nearly all loafers expending the energy that an artist puts into his creative work in talking about what they are going to do and condemning the work of all artists who have gained any degree of recognition."[25]

Despite such attempts to distinguish himself from the bohemian stereotype, Hemingway did adopt certain aspects of its ethos. Biographers have noted how, within months of arriving in Paris, he grew a moustache, let his uncut hair fall over the back of his collar, and sported a beret. He also took up the quintessential bohemian pastime: "Without visible means of support and his collar as open as Ezra's or Walt Whitman's," Michael Reynolds writes, Hemingway could often be found "sitting in Paris cafés, nursing his drink and conspicuously writing."[26] However he might believe himself distinct from the poseurs at the Dôme and Rotonde, his earliest press clippings associated him with that crowd. A 1928 book titled *Bohemian Life in Paris* mentions him several times, including a derogatory review of *The Sun Also Rises,* which is condemned for focusing on the "squalid side of Montparnasse" instead of celebrating its spirit of artistic freedom.[27] A 1928 *Harper's Magazine* piece titled "Babes in the Bois" blames Hemingway for luring young people to Europe with the promise of "promiscuous dissipation." Because devotees of *The Sun Also Rises* were "stubbornly committed to an elegant sterility," they embraced its author as a "great divinity of barrenness and futility": "'You are all a doomed generation,' quoth Gertrude Stein once [he gets the line slightly wrong], and straightaway everyone under twenty who considered himself oppressed and misunderstood fell violently in love with the words of the prophetess. They long to be doomed; if destruction threatens to be tardy, they'll rush to meet it halfway by committing suicide."[28] "Babes in the Bois" is a fascinating record of how artistic expatriation was viewed in the 1920s as a bohemian debauch. As commentators such as Richmond Barrett informed middle America, young people no longer prized going abroad as an education but as an opportunity to break rules and taboos.

The economic rationale for residing overseas also distinguishes Hemingway's generation from previous expatriate waves. Nearly every article about the Paris colony in the 1920s credits its expanding population to the inexpensive cost of life in France. *The Literary Review* noted in 1928 that "the average 'exile' of today . . . is living in France, or elsewhere in Europe, because he can live there, live till he has had time to look about him, to think a little. . . . In short, till he has had the time to live a poem or a book before sitting down to write it and without the necessity of rushing into incessant hack work in order to pay his board and room."[29] As Harold Stearns added, life on the cheap was not glamorous, but as long as all one wanted was "enough to eat well, sleep comfortably, buy a book or two, and be able to move about," it was bearable because "more than that is of little value."[30] By contrast, the typical nineteenth-century expatriate, unless a government or business employee, was more likely to belong to an affluent family. Of course, there were expatriates in the 1920s who were upper-class scions (Natalie Barney and Harry Crosby, whose uncle was J. P. Morgan). But by and large, the deflated French economy allowed a new class of Americans to experience Europe.

Beyond their finances, expatriates of various eras also differed in their attitudes toward leisure. James's era was driven by what is called a "production ethos," a belief that the main purpose of life was to be productive and frugal. But the early twentieth century witnessed the rise of consumerism, which dismissed this attitude in favor of entertainment and fun. Accordingly, while expatriates in the nineteenth century were expected to study culture, refining their appreciation of it, later generations viewed living abroad as an extended vacation. Bagger notes that a primary inducement to leaving America in the 1920s was freedom from responsibility:

> The irresponsibility that goes with the status of outsider constitutes, no doubt, one of the subtlest charms of exile. . . . The expatriate need not concern himself . . . with injustice and stupidity in public life, with the incapacity and corruption of officials, the struggles of class and party, the callousness of rulers, the sheepishness of the ruled, the boobishness of the boobs, with all the symptoms of decay and degradation exhibited by democracy. What in one's own country would cut into one's flesh becomes abroad a mere spectacle, to be viewed from a box seat.[31]

HARRY CROSBY'S REASONS FOR EXPATRIATING

In 1928, the Paris-based little magazine *Transition* asked several Americans living in postwar Paris to explain why they chose to live abroad. Poet and publisher Harry Crosby responded with a sometimes cryptic list of reasons:

I prefer to live outside America

1. because in America the *stars* were all suffocated inside
2. because I do not wish to devote myself to perpetual hypocrisy
3. because outside America there is nothing to remind me of my childhood
4. because I prefer perihelion to aphelion
5. because I love flagons of wine
6. because I am an enemy of society and here I can hunt with other enemies of society
7. because I want to be in at the death (of Europe)
8. because I like tumults and chances better than security
9. because I prefer transitional orgasms to atlantic monthlies
10. because I am not coprophagous
11. because I would rather be an eagle gathering sun than a spider gathering poison
12. because by living outside of America New York can still remain for me the City of a Thousand and One Nights
13. because the Rivers of Suicide are more inviting than the Prairies of Prosperity
14. because I prefer explosions to whimperings.

Reprinted in *Altogether Elsewhere: Writers on Exile,* edited by Marc Robinson (Boston: Faber & Faber, 1994), p. 208.

Instead of an embrace of European culture, expatriation in the 1920s was an escape from the American work ethic, which regarded leisure as indolence.

The issues discussed above suggest how important it is while reading works by Hemingway and the Lost Generation to balance their similarities to expatriates of other eras with their differences. Generalizing about the ways that living in exile affects the writer's creativity and imagination can reveal how certain issues such as artistic individuality and the fear of homelessness transcend time. At the same time, locating those broad themes in the context of *les années folles* (the crazy years)— as the 1920s were known in France—demonstrates the ways that expatriate modernism was peculiar to its time. Just as Hemingway recommended that readers view the contents of *In Our Time* with the naked eye and through binoculars, the reader will benefit from looking at this body of literature both from a distance and up close.

NOTES

1. Ernest Hemingway to Edmund Wilson, 18 October 1924, in *Ernest Hemingway: Selected Letters, 1917–1961,* edited by Carlos Baker (New York: Scribners, 1981), p. 128.

2. Harry Levin, "Literature and Exile," in his *Refractions: Essays in Comparative Literature* (New York: Oxford University Press, 1966), p. 81.

3. Gertrude Stein, "An American and Paris," in her *What Are Masterpieces,* edited by Robert Bartlett Haas (New York: Pitman, 1970), pp. 62–63. Elsewhere, Stein elaborates a similar fantasy of isolation: "Everybody who writes is interested in living inside themselves in order to tell what is inside themselves. That is why writers have to have two countries, the one where they belong and the one in which they live really. The second one is romantic, it is separate from themselves, it is not real but it is really there." See *Paris France* (London: Batsford, 1940), p. 2.

4. Quoted in *Literature in Exile,* edited by John Glad (Durham, N.C.: Duke University Press, 1990), p. 4.

5. Malcolm Cowley, *Exile's Return: A Narrative of Ideas* (New York, 1934); revised and enlarged as *Exile's Return: A Literary Odyssey of the 1920s* (New York: Viking, 1951), pp. 62–63.

6. The most influential little magazines included *Broom* (1921–1924); *The Double Dealer* (1921–1926), which was published in New Orleans; *Exile* (1927), edited by Ezra Pound; *The Little Review* (1914–1929); *Poetry* (1912–); *Der Querschnitt* (*The Cross Section,* 1920–1930), published in Germany; *This Quarter* (1925–1932); *transatlantic review* (1924); and *Transition* (1927–1938).

7. Julian Symons, *Makers of the New: The Revolution in Literature, 1912–1939* (New York: Random House, 1987), p. 210.

8. Hugh Ford, *Published in Paris: American and British Writers, Printers, and Publishers in Paris, 1920–1939* (New York: Macmillan, 1975), p. 99.

9. Those four works were the novel *Lucy Church Amiably* (1931); *Before the Flowers of Friendship Faded* (poetry; 1931); *How to Write* (essays; 1931); and *Operas and Plays* (closet dramas; 1932).

10. Stanley Coben, *Rebellion Against Victorianism: The Impetus for Cultural Change in 1920s America* (New York: Oxford University Press, 1991), pp. 52–53.

11. Ernest Earnest, *Expatriates and Patriots: American Artists, Scholars, and Writers in Europe* (Durham, N.C.: Duke University Press, 1968), p. 1.

12. Malcolm Bradbury, *The Expatriate Tradition in American Literature* (Durham, U.K.: BAAS Pamphlets in American Studies, 1982), p 5.

13. Philip Rahv, introduction to *Discovery of Europe: The Story of American Experience in the Old World,* edited by Rahv (Boston: Houghton Mifflin, 1947), p. xiv.

14. Washington Irving, "The Author's Preface," in his *The Sketch Book of Geoffrey Crayon, Gent.*, Volume 8 of *The Complete Works of Washington Irving*, 30 volumes, edited by Richard Dilworth Rust and others (Boston: Twayne, 1978–1989), p. 9.

15. Nathaniel Hawthorne, *The Marble Faun*, Volume 4 of *The Centenary Edition of the Works of Nathaniel Hawthorne*, 16 volumes, edited by William Charvat and others (Columbus: Ohio State University Press, 1962–1985), p. 3.

16. Henry James, *Hawthorne*, in his *The Art of Criticism: Henry James on the Theory and Practice of Criticism,* edited by William Veeder and Susan M. Griffin (Chicago: University of Chicago Press, 1986), p. 109.

17. For a good example of a modernist expatriate's list of dissatisfactions with America, see Harold Stearns, "Apologia of an Expatriate," *Scribner's Magazine*, 85 (March 1929): 338–341.

18. Alan Holder, *Three Voyagers in Search of Europe: A Study of Henry James, Ezra Pound, and T. S. Eliot* (Philadelphia: University of Pennsylvania Press, 1966), p. 268.

19. Eugene Bagger, "Uprooted Americans," *Harper's*, 159 (September 1929): 482.

20. Washington Irving, in Volume 28 of *The Complete Works of Washington Irving*, p. 52.

21. Nathaniel Hawthorne, "The Custom House," in his *The Scarlet Letter,* Volume 1 of *The Centenary Edition of the Works of Nathaniel Hawthorne*, p. 10.

22. Harold Stearns, "Apologia of an Expatriate," p. 339.

23. Malcolm Bradbury, *The Expatriate Tradition in American Literature*, p. 24.

24. Malcolm Cowley, *Exile's Return*, p. 53. Two examples of antibohemian propaganda in *The Saturday Evening Post* offer evidence of the war between artists and the middle class that Cowley describes. One 1913 parody recounts a poetry reading at the Dôme in which a pretentious French poet "salutes" American poetry with nonsense verse, only to be greeted with an actual excerpt from Stein's "Portrait of Mabel Dodge." The futurist disciple performing the piece inspires the American-obsessed French audience to scream "Cheese it!" before storming the lectern. See Samuel Blythe's "The Grand Fête Amèricaine," *The Saturday Evening Post* (22 March 1913): 10–11. A 1925 essay, meanwhile, suggests that the same rebels who complain of artists' economic exploitation in America flock to France because they "couldn't live half so comfortably at home on the same amount of money. . . . They couldn't even get one servant for the price of three here." See Maude Parker Child, "Expatriated Americans," *The Saturday Evening Post* (13 June 1925): 22.

25. Ernest Hemingway, "American Bohemians in Paris," in his *By-Line: Ernest Hemingway: Selected Articles and Dispatches of Four Decades,* edited by William Wiser (New York: Scribners, 1967), pp. 23–25.

26. Michael Reynolds, *Hemingway: The Paris Years* (New York: Blackwell, 1989), p. 25.

27. Sisley Huddleston, *Bohemian Literary and Social Life in Paris: Salons, Cafés, Studios* (London: Harrap, 1928), p. 146.

28. Richmond Barrett, "Babes in the Bois," *Harper's,* 156 (May 1928): 736.

29. "Whom America Has Failed," *The Literary Digest* (26 May 1928): 23–24.

30. Harold Stearns, "Apologia of an Expatriate," p. 341.

31. Eugene Bagger, "Uprooted Americans," *Harper's,* 159 (September 1929): 483.

HEMINGWAY WRITINGS ON THE EXPATRIATE EXPERIENCE

A quick glance at Hemingway's most celebrated works reveals an obvious commonality: *The Sun Also Rises, A Farewell to Arms,* "The Snows of Kilimanjaro," and *A Moveable Feast* all focus on characters struggling to maintain their morality while living abroad. Why did the author locate his fictions in foreign settings? In essence, expatriation provided him a powerful metaphor for exploring the challenge of surviving the modern, postwar world. As John W. Aldridge has suggested, "In introducing us literally to the life of foreignness, Hemingway at the same time created the illusion that *every* element of life is in fact foreign, hence new and without precedent in the known experience of the past."[1] Eluding dissipation and despair amidst this startling newness proves difficult for the majority of his characters. Tempted by unfamiliar freedoms to compromise and betray their values, they must accept their fallibility and lost innocence. Resilient protagonists persevere by exhibiting grace under the pressure. The weaker, more tragic ones give in to self-destruction. In the author's words, they "go to hell completely."[2]

This chapter offers an overview of Hemingway's basic story lines, main character types, central themes, and major images and symbols. Because this study is intended as an introduction to expatriate modernism, the discussion is restricted to texts about Americans overseas. As a consequence, Hemingway classics such as "Indian Camp" (1924), "The Killers" (1927), and *The Old Man and the Sea* (1952) go unmentioned. "Big Two-Hearted River" (1925) is discussed, however, for two reasons: Hemingway was in Paris when he wrote this story of a fishing expedition in the upper peninsula of Michigan, and it has long been interpreted as an expression of the postwar disillusionment that drove the lost generation abroad.

PLOTS

Great writers can become unfairly linked in readers' minds with a specific story line. Audiences familiar with Henry James's many novels

Hemingway (second from left) in Milan, 1918, recuperating from the mortar-shell blast that almost killed him.

and stories about the cultural differences between America and Europe may be surprised to discover that he also composed several ghost tales, including the classic *The Turn of the Screw* (1898). Similarly, while John Updike has written extensively about the suburban angst of contemporary New England communities, from time to time he uses an unusual setting such as Africa or Brazil to generate a quite different sort of plot. Hemingway is another author whose diverse interests are not always given their just due. Unknowledgeable readers may even presume they can summarize what happens in his works with four words: *war, bullfighting, drinking,* and *sex.* Such a presumption is not only off target but also vastly minimizes the significance of what he has to say about those topics. Hemingway's expatriate texts include many different kinds of plots, ranging from adventure to romance to tragedy. For the sake of convenience, they can be grouped into three main categories: war, marriage, and sports.

I. WAR STORIES: In a 1925 letter to F. Scott Fitzgerald, Hemingway lists the best subjects for authors to tackle. Love, money, greed, and murder are all proper topics, he admits, but for a truly great writer, nothing compares to war. "War is the best subject of all," he insists, because "it groups the maximum of material and speeds up the action and brings out all sorts of stuff that normally you have to wait a lifetime to get."[3] One might say that Hemingway spent a lifetime clarifying just what those "sorts of stuff" are, for he returned repeatedly to battle-torn settings in his writing to explore the damage suffered by soldiers, nurses, and civilians caught in the crossfire. Hemingway's July 1918 wounding in a trench along the Piave River outside Fossalta, Italy, offers an obvious biographical justification for this fascination. Indeed, psychoanalytic critics such as Philip Young interpret the anguish and conflict in *all* Hemingway's writing as a response to the trauma of his wounding. Hemingway rejected this idea, insisting that the experience inspired the empathy necessary to render others' injuries with accuracy.[4] The truth perhaps rests somewhere in between. In some texts—*A Farewell to Arms* is an obvious example— he transformed the circumstances of his early exposure to war into fiction. In other cases, he assembled his plots from events witnessed and stories overheard at fronts he toured as a journalist, whether the Spanish Civil War in *For Whom the Bell Tolls* or World War II in *Across the River and into the Trees* (1950).

Hemingway first drew from his military service after returning from Italy in January 1919. Early, unpublished efforts such as "The Woppian Way" and "The Mercenaries" were written in the slick, commercial style popularized by *The Saturday Evening Post*. Rather than examine the anguish of battle, they glamorize heroism and treat war as if it were a boyhood adventure.[5] Once abroad in Paris, however, Hemingway developed a starker, more graphic style that conveys the horrors of armed conflict with a coldly detached, observational tone. The initial result was a series of one-paragraph vignettes, published in the *Little Review* in 1923 and subsequently placed between longer stories in *In Our Time* (1925) as "interchapters." By narrating these scenes of brutality in an unemotional manner, he projected a sense of detachment that implies his narrators are unable to comprehend the absurdity of the violence they have witnessed. Thus, the eleven-sentence episode titled "Chapter IV" describes soldiers firing on enemies climbing a wrought-iron grating used to barricade one end of a bridge: "It was simply priceless," the narrator reports. "They tried to get over it, and we potted them from forty yards. They rushed it, and officers came out alone and worked on it. It was an absolutely perfect obstacle."[6] There is no effort to justify the carnage. He simply reports events with cool efficiency, his laconic tone ("simply priceless") suggesting that the spectacle of German soldiers trying to scale the grating while avoiding bullets was, in a bizarre way, entertaining.

Another paragraph-long scene, "Chapter VII," is intriguing since it is set in the trenches outside Fossalta, the site of Hemingway's wounding. A terrified witness to an enemy bombardment—whether the protagonist is a soldier or an ambulance driver is not clear—begs Jesus to spare his life. "I'll tell everyone in the world that you are the only one that matters," he promises. After the shelling stops, however, his fear subsides, and he forgets his pledge. "The next night back . . . he did not tell the girl he went upstairs with at the Villa Rossa about Jesus," the paragraph concludes. "And he never told anybody" (109). The conclusion reveals this character's inability to sustain his faith; rather than survive war by trusting in Christ, he seeks escape from its danger in sensual indulgences. (The Villa Rossa is a brothel; the girl, a prostitute.) His silence about his fear may arise from the shame of being afraid, or he simply may not believe he was saved by divine intervention. Either way, the vignette dramatizes the powerlessness of religion in the face of modern warfare.

The plot of "Chapter VII" might be classified as an "initiation story," a phrase in literary studies describing the loss of innocence suffered when a young person gains knowledge of human frailty and sin. Commonly, Hemingway's war stories initiate their heroes into an awareness of the essential indifference of nature. In "Now I Lay Me" (1927) Nick Adams—a recurring character in Hemingway's stories, often described as his fictional alter ego—tries to soothe his insomnia in a barn not far from the Italian front by recalling scenes from home. He remembers the trout streams he fished as a boy, his family's house, and even the foods and street names of his native Chicago. But these recollections are far from comforting, for he realizes that each is tainted by violence. Thinking of his family, Nick remembers how his mother once cleaned the house by burning a pile of his father's belongings in the front yard. That image of domestic aggression complements the haunting sound of silkworms devouring the mulberry leaves outside the barn; both suggest to Nick that there is no respite, whether at home or in nature, from all-consuming conflict.

Another Nick story, "A Way You'll Never Be" (1933), documents the psychological damage that witnessing the violence of war causes. Although he is returning to the front a few months after his wounding, Nick suffers hallucinations and is prone to outbursts on the futility of the war. Because of these spells, he has, in his words, been "certified nutty" by the authorities (310). Nick can no longer believe in the glory of military service; nor can he restrain himself from expressing his cynicism. His condition makes him woefully unfit for his new duty, which is to parade around the front in an American uniform to reassure Italian soldiers that American troops will join them. As he passes through a recently attacked village, Nick discovers corpses of Allied soldiers littering the roadway, their pockets pulled out, private memorabilia and photographs left fluttering around the piles of bodies. "These were new dead and no one had bothered with anything but their pockets," Nick realizes. "They showed, by their positions, the manner and the skill of the [Austrian] attack. The hot weather had swollen them all alike regardless of nationality" (307). The sight heightens his sense of despair, triggering a relapse of emotional instability that makes him a liability on the battle lines. Speaking to one soldier he is supposed to comfort, he compares the color of his American uniform to the brown bodies of locusts, implying that American forces are not saviors of the war effort but harbingers of another plague of battles and massacres. Recognizing Nick's disillusioning influence on his battalion, the Italian commander asks him to leave. Angry, Nick confronts the officer: "Why don't they bury the dead? I've seen them now. I don't care about seeing them again. They can bury them any time as far as I'm concerned and it would be much better for you" (314). Nick's inability to envision any purpose in continued fighting suggests the despair and loss of hope soldiers suffer. The curious title of the story implies that Hemingway is telling readers that they will never understand Nick's crisis of belief unless they have experienced similar conditions. Even survivors such as Nick, the story informs readers, are casualties.

A Farewell to Arms (1929) also examines the soldier's struggle to survive the violence inherent in war and nature. A partial fictionalization of Hemingway's wounding at Fossalta and his love affair with Agnes von Kurowsky, the Red Cross nurse he met during his recuperation in Milan, the novel questions whether love and war can coexist. The hero, Frederic Henry, an American lieutenant in the Italian army ambulance corps, witnesses both the grim conditions and the pessimism rampant at the front. After nearly dying in a trench, he is sent to the Red Cross hospital in Milan, where he falls in love with Catherine Barkley. The idyllic months they spend together away from the war revive his belief in the power of love to redeem violence and despair. Henry is subsequently called back to the front, where he witnesses the panic and hysteria of Italian soldiers and civilians fleeing from the city of Caporetto, where Austrian forces have broken through the front. When he learns that Italian *carabinieri* (the military police) are executing officers for allowing the retreat, Frederic deserts his post and returns to Catherine. Together, they escape the war by illegally entering Switzerland, where Catherine discovers she is pregnant from their affair in Milan. Their hope for happiness proves illusory, though, since Catherine and the baby die in childbirth. By linking battlefield brutality to the pain and danger of birth, *A Farewell to Arms* insists that violence is an essential fact of existence. Frederic realizes this point when, during Catherine's ordeal, he recalls watching ants swarm on a burning log: "Some got out, their bodies burnt and flattened, and went off not knowing where they were going. But most of them went toward the fire and then back toward the end and swarmed on the cool end and finally fell off into the fire."[7] In this memory, Henry understands the futility of his and Catherine's desire to flee the war; they have escaped it only to suffer another form of brutality.

In other war stories Hemingway focuses less on the shock of initiation than on the struggle to recover from and cope with violence. In "Chapter VI" of *In Our Time,* Nick waits for a stretcher shortly after being wounded in the spine. Nearby, another soldier lies facedown in the rubble. "You and me we've made a separate peace," Nick tells the man. "Not patriots" (105). By "separate peace," Nick suggests that ideals such as duty and valor are not enough to settle the terror of taking a bullet. Each man will have to measure the significance of his brush with death individually, for in the heat of battle, notions of honor and glory are meaningless, and one is left only with the instinct to survive. Many Hemingway stories explore the soldier's effort to make peace with the private fears that war creates and return to a normal, everyday life.

In "Soldier's Home" (1924) Harold Krebs discovers his family is incapable of appreciating how military service has hardened him. After participating in the battles of World War I, his only ambition is to avoid conflict so he can "live along without consequences" (113). According to his parents, a month away from battle is sufficient time for rehabilitation. They insist that Harold find a job and settle down to a career. In the climax of the story, Krebs tries to convey his anguish by telling his pious mother he no longer loves her. But when she breaks down in tears, he realizes he cannot articulate the deadening effect of war: "It wasn't any good. He couldn't tell her, he couldn't make her see it" (116). To stop his mother's crying, Krebs consents to pray with her, but giving in to her demands makes him realize that he can "keep his life from being complicated" (116) only by abandoning his family. The title of the story captures Krebs's dilemma through a clever play on words. A "soldier's home" in the postwar era was a convalescence center for recuperating soldiers. Yet, as Hemingway makes clear, home is not a safe haven. Finding "separate peace" is not possible at home if families remain oblivious to the horrors their children have experienced.

Another story of recuperation, "In Another Country" (1927), foreshadows *A Farewell to Arms* by asking whether love can supply soldiers the peace they so desire. It begins with one of Hemingway's most memorable lines: "In the fall the war was always there, but we did not go to it anymore" (206). Living at a safe remove from the conflict, however, proves ironic as a group of maimed soldiers at the Red Cross hospital in Milan struggle through various stages of physical therapy. The narrator, an unnamed American (many argue that he is Nick Adams), works on a new mechanical bicycle designed to help his shattered knee bend. Another character wears a handkerchief across his face to hide his missing nose. A third, a major once known as the best fencer in Italy, struggles to regain use of his crippled hand. The major warns the narrator not to get married because a man "should not place himself in a position to lose. He should find things he cannot lose" (208). The narrator cannot understand this negativity toward marriage until he learns that the major's wife has died of pneumonia. To encourage the man's recovery, the doctors have placed pictures of rehabilitated hands around his machine. But after returning from his wife's funeral, the major stares out the window, no longer caring about his therapy. Despite the promise of restoration that the machines offer, Hemingway shows how wounds afflicting the spirit and soul are as incapacitating as any bodily injury.

Other stories offer discipline and self-control as remedies for these emotional wounds. On the surface, "Big Two-Hearted River" seems a world away from the ravaged landscapes of the *In Our Time* vignettes or "In Another Country." Set in northern Michigan, the story follows Nick Adams through a long hike into the woods, where he pitches a tent, cooks his meals, and fishes for trout. Such a summary makes the plot sound uneventful, but the seeming lack of drama is deceptive. Nick is so intent on executing each step of his adventure with precision that the reader soon realizes that Nick's trip is an effort to restore order and balance in his life. However mundane, every action requires deliberation, for it is a therapeutic ritual by which he can derive the maximum meaning and pleasure from activity. Whether eating his dinner slowly (so as not to burn his tongue) or reeling in his fishing line with patience (so the trout's resistance will not snap the leader, allowing it to escape), Nick must weigh the consequences of what he does. At the end of the story, after catching and cleaning two trout, he decides he is not ready yet to enter the swamp downstream: "He was going back to camp. . . . There were plenty of days coming when he could fish the swamp" (180). Nick's awareness that he is not prepared for the deeper waters and ominous currents of the swamp further confirms that this trip is part of a process of learning discipline.

Just what has happened to Nick to require this trip? The story itself is frustratingly silent on the matter. Early on, readers learn that entering the woods has allowed Nick to leave "everything behind, the need for thinking, the need to write, other needs" (164). But Hemingway does not explain why these needs must be left behind. Because other stories in *In Our Time* show Nick wounded in the war, critics often infer that "Big Two-Hearted River" is about a returning veteran hoping to reconnect with nature in order to overcome his trauma. Only in *A Moveable Feast* (1964) did Hemingway confirm this interpretation; he described the story as "about coming back from the war but there was no mention of the war in it."[8] Ultimately, whether it is specifically about recovering from war is left to the reader to decide; what is certain is that Nick's cure for his troubles—self-control—is the remedy prescribed in all Hemingway writings.

The Sun Also Rises, too, can be interpreted as a story of recuperation. Once an airman flying on the Italian front, Jake Barnes was wounded in such a way that he is incapable of sexual intercourse, although he retains his sexual desire. His disability is a physical corollary to the emotional traumas suffered by Brett Ashley. A former nurse whose fiancé had died of dysentery in the war, she subsequently married a British aristocrat whose military service also left him unhinged. (He sleeps with a loaded revolver by his side.) Now, as an expatriate in Paris, she has descended into a self-destructive cycle of alcoholism and promiscuity. Jake and Brett's respective injuries doom their love, for he is incapable of consummating his passion for her, and her romantic tragedies have eroded her belief in monogamy. The couple's inability to heal each other's wounds proves mutually destructive when they travel to the bullfights in Pamplona, Spain. While aggrieved by Brett's casual love affairs, Jake nevertheless facilitates her seduction of the promising young bullfighter Pedro Romero. Her reliance on Jake costs him his friendship with the bullfighting locals who consider him an aficionado, someone who, unlike other tourists flocking to Pamplona, is knowledgeable and passionate about the traditions of the sport. The novel concludes with Jake and Brett riding in a Madrid taxicab, wondering how their lives might have been had the war not robbed them of the capacity to love. "We could have had such a damned good time together," Brett says, to which Jake responds, "Isn't it pretty to think so?"[9]

II. MARRIAGE TALES: While novice readers may approach Hemingway's work with some foreknowledge of his interest in war, they may not know that his plots just as often address marital problems. There is a superficial reason for this topic. Wed four times, Hemingway was ambivalent about domesticity. While he depended on his wives for emotional support, he saw domestic responsibilities as a burden that interfered with art. His marriage tales can be divided into three groups that loosely parallel his private life. *In Our Time*–era stories, written during his first marriage, to Hadley Richardson (1921–1926), feature husbands who lament that matrimony entails the loss of male camaraderie and wives who find their spouses remote and unloving. The second group dates roughly from Hemingway's adulterous affair with Pauline Pfeiffer in early 1926 (they were married the following year) to the bitter dissolution of that relationship in the late 1930s. It includes stories that convey the guilt and self-pity Hemingway felt over his divorce from Hadley ("A Canary for One") as well as gloomy explorations of the communication problems that drive couples apart ("Hills Like White Elephants"). Later efforts from this era ("The Short Happy Life of Francis Macomber" and "The Snows of Kilimanjaro" [both 1936]) explore the resentment, verbal abuse, and adultery characteristic of domestic discontent. Finally, Hemingway's fourth marriage, to Mary Welsh (1946–1961), corresponds to a period of nostalgia for young romance. (During his 1940–1945 marriage to Martha Gellhorn, Hemingway did not write fiction, concentrating instead on journalism.) Both *A Moveable Feast* and *The Garden of Eden* (1986) describe how protagonists' youthful unions are doomed by the temptation and rootlessness of expatriate life. The romantic perils associated with living abroad are a unifying motif throughout these different periods. In Hemingway's love stories, expatriation symbolizes the alienation that leads to marital estrangement.

"Out of Season" (1923) offers an early example of this instability. Hemingway claimed the story was a "literal translation" of a fight with Hadley over fishing: "Your ear is always more acute when you have been upset by a row," he insisted, "and when I came in from the unproductive fishing trip I wrote that story right off on the typewriter without punctuation."[10] Set in Italy, "Out of Season" describes a young couple badgered by a guide who insists on escorting them to the local fishing grounds, even though, as the title suggests, the season has passed. The couple has already bickered over

THE LITERARY INFLUENCE OF HEMINGWAY'S WIVES

"The image of Hadley...appears throughout his work. He found her stoic, smart, devoted, romantic, and wounded. These qualities also belong to the heroines of his three major novels.... What's more, the romances in these books follow the same pattern as Ernest and Hadley's. The couples meet and immediately fall in love, but the relationships are doomed."

Gioia Diliberto, *Hadley* (New York: Ticknor & Fields, 1992), p. xiii.

"Many . . . fragments [from *A Moveable Feast*]enlarge upon Ernest's regret for the breakup of his first marriage, his anger at Pauline for precipitating it, and bitter memories of his own misery. But there are other deleted passages that express a much different point of view about Pauline, one that implicitly supports Ernest's remark to his brother and others that she may have been the best wife after all."

Bernice Kert, *The Hemingway Women* (New York: Norton, 1983), p. 484.

"As writers and lovers, Martha Gellhorn and Hemingway were never closer [in 1939].... She admired the new novel [*For Whom the Bell Tolls*], which she dedicated to her, and found it 'funny, wonderful, alive and exciting.' She also had reservations. Years later, she remembered severely criticizing it...."

Carl Rollyson, *Nothing Ever Happens to the Brave: The Story of Martha Gellhorn* (New York: St. Martin's Press, 1990), p. 137.

"When they met in 1944 Mary ... gave Hemingway almost everything he wanted and failed to get from Martha.... Mary, lively and uninhibited ... adored him.... In contrast to the willful and independent Martha, Mary understood his emotional needs and made a conscious effort to please him."

Jeffrey Meyers, Hemingway: *A Life* (New York: Harper & Row, 1985), p. 393.

some unspecified problem; the guide's drunken disregard for local gamekeeping laws leads to another argument. "Of course you haven't got the guts to just go back," the wife complains when the husband worries about getting arrested. "Of course you have to go on" (137). After she returns to their hotel, the man and the guide briefly fish without interruption. When the guide suggests that they meet again the next day for another excursion, however, the American hesitates, perhaps wishing to avoid yet another spat. "Out of Season" exemplifies Hemingway's early approach to drama: the subject of the couple's conflict is not revealed. Some critics argue that she is pregnant, while others point to various verbal clues that imply the sterility of their relationship. Yet the cause of the couple's discontent does not really matter. Readers recognize that they have problems that they are not able to resolve. "It doesn't make any difference. . . . None of it makes any difference," the wife keeps insisting, but the unresolved conclusion of the story reveals that their inability to confront their troubles guarantees future conflict.

Another story set in Italy, "Cat in the Rain" (first published in *In Our Time*, 1925), also involves an uprooted, alienated couple. Spying a cat trapped under a sidewalk table during a rainstorm, an American woman rushes from her hotel room to save it. When the cat is nowhere to be found, her disappointment leads her to recite for her husband all the things their marriage lacks: "I want to have a kitty to sit on my lap and purr when I stroke her. . . . And I want to eat at a table with my own silver and I want candles. And I want it to be spring and I want to brush my hair out in front of a mirror and I want a kitty and I want some new clothes." The husband's response is not encouraging: "Oh, shut up and get something to read" (131), he tells her. The wife's wish list suggests her desire for the couple to have a home of their own; the wish for a cat may even represent a desire for a child. The husband, however, seems perfectly content reading his newspaper. Again, Hemingway refrains from revealing any information about the pair. The final paragraph, in which the woman is overjoyed when the hotel maid delivers a cat to her, confirms again the disparity of their desires and foreshadows the inevitability of subsequent arguments.

"Mr. and Mrs. Elliot" (1924) exaggerates marital alienation in order to ridicule the priggishness of an expatriate couple who desire a child but who dislike sex. The premise is a bawdy joke at the Elliots' expense, for the wife's inability to conceive obliges them to attempt conception again and again, much to their mutual distaste. Sterility is a metaphor for the barrenness of their relationship. In the end, Hubert and Cornelia each discover a distraction to avoid the intimacy that they dread. She insists on bringing to Europe a female friend to whom she devotes all her time, while he begins writing poetry. As in "Cat in the Rain," expatriation also conveys the emptiness of their marriage. Drifting from Paris to other European tourist traps, the Elliots use incessant traveling as an excuse to avoid dealing with their marital misery. In the end, the liberal atmosphere of expatriate life provides an unconventional solution to their aversion to sex, one by which they can remain together and yet apart. As Cornelia begins sharing a bed with her American girlfriend, Honey, Hubert moves into his own room where he can write and drink white wine in peace. "They were all quite happy," reads the ironic conclusion of the story (125).

Other stories explore men's ambivalence toward marriage by examining their fears of losing their freedom and male friendships. "Cross-Country Snow" describes a skiing adventure in Switzerland that proves less carefree than it appears. At first Nick and his buddy George (based on Hemingway's friend George O'Neil) revel in the euphoric sense of flight and movement that the slopes provide. "Don't you wish we could just bum together?" George asks. "Take our skis . . . and not give a damn about school or anything" (145). That fantasy is unlikely to materialize, for Nick admits what George suspects: Nick's wife, Helen, is pregnant, and the pair are planning to return to America. "Maybe we'll never go skiing again" (145), George complains. Nick assures him they will but stops short of promising it; he simply does not know how his life will change once he becomes a father. Intriguingly, the original ending of "Big Two-Hearted River" also explored the anxiety of being cut off from male camaraderie. Titled "On Writing" when published for the first time in *The Nick Adams Stories* (1972), the fragment reveals that Nick is preoccupied, not by his service in the war but by the friends who faded from his life after he and Helen were wed: "When he married he lost Bill Smith, Odgar, the Ghee, all the old gang. He lost them because he admitted by marrying that something was more important than fishing."[11]

Hemingway's second period suggests a growing pessimism toward the possibility of domestic content. "A Canary for One" (1927), based on Hemingway's last trip with Hadley before their August 1926 separation, exemplifies the irony with which he treated ideals of marital bliss. On a Paris-bound train, a chatty American shows off a canary she has purchased for her daughter. The gift is the mother's apology for interfering in the girl's courtship by a Swiss man. "Americans make the best husbands," (260) the mother insists to a young American wife traveling with her expatriate husband. The mother confesses that she cannot abide the thought of her child married to a foreigner. The couple had honeymooned, as it turns out, in the same Swiss town where the daughter met her suitor. The two women share fond memories of the sights of the city, but as the train arrives in Paris, the husband-narrator admits, "We were returning to Paris to set up separate residences" (261). Although the story does not mention the reason for the couple's breakup, the surprise revelation casts doubt on the older woman's insistence that "American men are the only men in the world to marry" (260).

"Hills Like White Elephants" (1927) is Hemingway's most famous portrait of a doomed relationship. Set in a train station in Spain's Ebro valley, the plot involves a subtly rendered dialogue between an expatriate couple, the subject of which can only be inferred. Whether they are married or not is unspecified, but the emptiness and indirection of their relationship clearly upsets Jig, the woman. Because the word "abortion" is never spoken, many first-time readers fail to understand the significance of the man's encouraging her to undergo "an awfully simple operation," one that is "not really an operation at all" (212). Jig recognizes that regardless of whether she consents or not, their relationship has lost its romantic innocence, for their conversation reveals his selfishness and lack of commitment to her. "I don't want you to do it if you don't want to," the man insists. "I'm perfectly willing to go through with it if it means anything to you." As Jig recognizes, the unborn child does not mean anything to him. The genius of the story rests in the patterning of the dialogue, which reveals Jig's efforts to draw from her companion a straightforward confession of his feelings. His effort to convince her that *she* wants the abortion suggests his unwillingness to confront the problem directly and assume responsibility. The story ends in frustration, with Jig demanding that they stop talking about it because "there's nothing wrong with me. I feel fine" (214). As with so many of Hemingway's marriage tales, the conflict is far from resolved, and the characters are trapped within their conflicts.

"A Canary for One" and "Hills Like White Elephants" both sympathize with women whose mates are indifferent to their need for commitment. Stories of the later 1930s such as "The Short Happy Life of Francis Macomber" and "The Snows of Kilimanjaro" are controversial because they depict wives as threats to their husbands' masculinity. "The Short Happy Life of Francis Macomber" is the more overt of the two in its unflattering portrait of women. As the story opens, the titular hero has just acted cowardly while hunting a lion during a safari in Africa. His guide, Robert Wilson, is inclined to forgive him, but Macomber's wife, Margaret, ridicules his cowardice and weakness. Wilson is stunned by her "American female cruelty"; she is "the hardest [type of woman] in the world; the hardest, the cruelest, the most predatory and the most attractive," the sort whose men "have softened or gone to pieces nervously as they have hardened" (9). To further humiliate her husband, Margaret sleeps with Wilson. During the hunt the next day, Macomber's anger transforms into a strange sort of bravery, and he regains his honor during a hunt for buffalo. But just as he is about to reestablish his masculinity by not "bolting" from a charging buffalo, a bullet from his wife's gun strikes him in the back of the head. The story declines to specify whether the shooting is intentional or not, but even if Margaret hits him by mistake, the symbolism of his sudden demise remains the same. She has robbed him of the opportunity to assert his manhood. In death as well as in life, Macomber is a victim of his wife's killer instinct.

Expatriate publisher Robert McAlmon (left) with Hemingway in a Spanish bullfighting ring, 1923. McAlmon published Hemingway's first book, *Three Stories and Ten Poems.*

"The Snows of Kilimanjaro" is less violent but equally vicious in its estimation of marriage. An American writer infected with gangrene during a safari lashes out at his wife, denouncing her as a "rich bitch" and a "kindly caretaker and destroyer of his talent" (45). Unlike Margaret, however, Helen is not malicious. She is a symbol rather of her husband's self-loathing. Attributing his failures as an artist to the security and comfort her money has provided him is less a condemnation of her than of his corruption. "You don't have to destroy me. Do you?" she demands during a barrage of verbal abuse. "I'm only a middle-aged woman who loves you and wants to do what you want to do" (46). Harry, though, believes that he must destroy her, because renouncing the materialism that she represents is the only way he can make peace with the stories he never found time to write. Passing in and out of consciousness while stretched out on his cot, he recounts the experiences he assumed would some day be turned into his fiction. Among them, he remembers the arguments and infidelities that ruined his first marriage. "Why had they always quarreled when he was feeling best?" (49) Harry asks himself. The question implies that for Harry art and marriage are irreconcilable; as his other memories suggest, the writer must be an objective observer, standing apart from events to record them. Domesticity compromises that stance, making him a participant rather than a witness. In the end, Harry loses on both scores. Not only is Helen's love incapable of comforting his bitterness, but he must die with the knowledge that he never realized his artistic promise.

Harry's memories of his first marriage foreshadow the final phase of Hemingway's domestic fiction, which draws from his early romance with Hadley a mixture of nostalgia and regret. In "The Snows of Kilimanjaro," Harry remembers how "with the woman that he loved he had quarreled so much they had finally, always, with the corrosion of the quarreling, killed what they had together" (48). Both *A Moveable Feast* and *The Garden of Eden* document this corrosive process, attributing it to their protagonists' failure to withstand the temptations of expatriation. Throughout most of *A Moveable Feast,* the young expatriate and his wife (known as "Hem" and "Tatie") live an idyllic if impoverished existence in Paris. Hadley is portrayed as an ideal mate: she not only supports her husband's literary career, encouraging him to follow his artistic instincts and avoid the fakery of Montparnasse Americans, but she is also eager to follow Hem on various European jaunts. She never complains about their poverty, and she listens attentively as her mate tries to make sense of Gertrude Stein's convoluted advice about art and sex. Yet, these scenes of domestic bliss are also filled with a sense of doom; shortly after discovering Shakespeare and Company, the couple plan a romantic evening of reading and making love. "We're lucky that you found the place," Hadley remarks, to which her husband responds, "We're always lucky." Hemingway the narrator comments on their naiveté: "Like a fool I did not knock on wood. There was wood everywhere in that apartment too" (38).

The Garden of Eden represents Hemingway's most tangled exploration of the relationship between writing and marriage. The book remains controversial for two reasons. First, the abridged version published in 1986 represents only a small portion of the 1,700 manuscript pages that Hemingway intermittently struggled with between 1946 and his death. More problematic for some readers, the novel seems to imply that the discipline an artist needs to be productive requires the support of a mate who is self-sacrificing if not outright servile. Set in the Camargue region of southern France, with excursions to resort towns in North Spain, *The Garden of Eden* centers on a recently married expatriate couple, David and Catherine Bourne, who, at the wife's insistence, embark on a program of gender-bending experiments. Catherine repeatedly cuts her hair like a boy's, wears slacks (thus shocking the locals), and even cultivates an alter ego she calls Peter. David passively participates in her fantasies. But while he adopts her unisex haircut and briefly consents to the erotic role reversals she concocts, he views her intrigue with androgyny as an ominous sign of her emotional instability—something he fears will interfere with his rigorously maintained writing schedule. The Bournes' conflict becomes more complicated when they meet Marita, a bisexual who begins affairs with both Catherine and David. While the relationship between the women exacerbates Catherine's emotional problems, Marita provides David the sympathetic audience for his fiction that his wife does not. Catherine proves so jealous of both his writing and Marita that she burns his manuscripts. As the novel ends, Catherine recognizes that David needs Marita more than he needs her, and she obligingly departs. David is thus free to begin rewriting his story, his new lover (cured of her lesbianism) sleeping at his side. However belligerent in its equation of heterosexuality with emotional and artistic stability, *The Garden of Eden* is one of the few Hemingway works in which the hero overcomes the dangers of expatriation with his talents intact.

III. SPORTSMANSHIP STORIES: Because Hemingway was a sports enthusiast, he was drawn to local athletic endeavors while living abroad in Europe, often incorporating them into his fiction. The best known of these sports is bullfighting, which Hemingway helped introduce to Americans through *The Sun Also Rises* (1926) and *Death in the Afternoon* (1932), a full-length study of the ancient Spanish spectacle. He was also an avid fisherman, as "Big Two-Hearted River" demonstrates, and he enjoyed skiing the slopes of Schruns, Austria. Additional interests he drew upon include horse racing, boxing, bicycle racing, and hunting. As Delmore Schwartz asserts, the sporting life is fundamental to Hemingway because it indexes an individual's moral character: "The most sensitive human beings feel a passionate devotion to sport because they find a fulfillment in it which they cannot attain. . . . Skiing and activities like it give the self a sense of intense individuality, mastery, and freedom." Sports are a test, a "trial of the self" governed by rules that "require honesty, sincerity, self-control, skill, and above all, personal courage. To be admirable is to play fairly and well; and to be a good loser when one has lost, acknowledging the victor and accepting defeat in silence."[12] As the title of Hemingway's 1933 short-story collection *Winner Take Nothing* suggests, the difference between victory and defeat is minimal. Nevertheless, sportsmanlike conduct is an ethical imperative for his protagonists.

The struggle to maintain self-control and discipline in a world of relative values is perhaps best rendered in the Pamplona scenes in *The Sun Also Rises*. Unlike other Americans who frequent the Spanish village each July for the festival of San Fermín, Jakes Barnes is an aficionado, someone "who is passionate about the bullfights." By passion, Hemingway does not mean the excitement that spectators feel when a bull rushes toward a matador. That visceral thrill can be attained without any knowledge of the history or tradition of the sport. An aficionado appreciates the ritualized moves by which matadors demonstrate their courage in the face of danger. He understands that the symbolic meaning of the contest between man and animal represents humanity's broader struggle to conquer nature. Jake displays his devotion to the sport in describing Pedro Romero's poise in the ring. While other bullfighters know how to impress a crowd with moves less dangerous than they appear, he inspires "real emotion," because he keeps "the absolute purity of line in his movements and always quietly and calmly let the horns pass him close each time. . . . Romero had the old thing, the holding of his purity of line through the maximum of exposure, while he dominated the bull by making him realize he was unattainable, while he prepared him for the killing" (172–173). Because he knows how to evaluate a bullfighter's skill, Jake is respected among the locals. Whenever he visits Pamplona, he is guaranteed a room at the Hotel Montoya, whose owner caters to aficionados.

Jake's tortured love for Brett Ashley, however, leads him to violate the values of an aficionado. Montoya insists on protecting bullfighters from tourists who will destroy them with cheap flattery and adulation. In one scene he asks Jake whether he should tell Romero that the American ambassador has requested an introduction; Jake agrees that associating with foreigners will corrupt the young bullfighter. Yet, when Brett demands to meet Romero, Jake assents, enabling her to seduce the boy when he should be concentrating on his sport. When the festival concludes and the Americans prepare to leave Pamplona, Montoya refuses to speak to Jake. He even has a maid deliver the bill. Jake recognizes the gesture means he is no longer welcome at the hotel and is no longer recognized as an aficionado.

The ritualistic significance of the bullfight is also the subject of "The Undefeated," the opening selection of *Men Without Women* (1927), Hemingway's second volume of stories. Instead of a promising young matador, the hero is an aging veteran of the *toredo* named Manuel Garcia, who is attempting to redeem his reputation after a recent wounding in the ring. Given a second-rate bull to fight, Garcia must also confront a hostile crowd that has witnessed too many poor exhibitions by unworthy matadors. Manuel acquits himself well, until the time comes to kill the animal. The ultimate test of a matador's skill is the ability to deliver an *estocade,* or sword thrust between the shoulder blades that severs the spinal cord. The death blow should ideally be made on the bull's first charge at the performer's *estoque* (sword) after the animal has been wearied. Garcia, however, can only deliver a *pinchar en el duro;* that is, his sword keeps striking bone, an occurrence that in and of itself should not arouse the crowd's animosity. Nevertheless, the spectators begin heckling him and throwing seat cushions into the ring. Then, as the bull charges again, Manuel trips on a cushion and is gored. Rather than go to the infirmary, he makes one final effort, finally placing his sword in the required spot. Despite the goring, Garcia remains undefeated in spirit because he performed to the best of his abilities. In Hemingway's world, that makes him heroic.

The precision and exactitude demanded by bullfighting are typical of every sport described in Hemingway's work. In "Big Two-Hearted River," every minute aspect associated with fishing, whether catching the grasshoppers used as bait or snapping the line taut to hook the trout, is treated with an intensity that elevates its significance from mere habit to ritual. In a revealing moment Nick wets his hand before attempting to touch a fish gliding along the surface of the water. A dry hand will infect the trout with a deadly fungus. Nick recalls how during previous expeditions he came upon dead fish "floating belly up in some pool," and he realizes how carelessly fellow enthusiasts treat nature: "Nick did not like to fish with other men on the river. Unless they were of your party, they spoiled it" (176). On the surface, this simple rule that is applicable to any sport—do not damage the environment—assumes a larger moral significance. If the story is interpreted as Nick's struggle to recuperate from the war, his attention to detail conveys his effort to reestablish the order and certitude of purpose destroyed by that gruesome conflict.

Hemingway's sporting plots, however, do not always involve morally conscientious people such as Nick. Indeed, his drama often pivots upon ethical failures and lapses of judgment that symbolize the ease with which otherwise good men and women can be corrupted. In "The Short Happy Life of Francis Macomber," the title character feels flushed with courage when a successful buffalo hunt redeems him from the fear felt the previous day while pursuing a lion. Yet, that courage has not been honorably earned, for the hunting party has chased its prey by car, and Macomber has even fired from within the vehicle—something a true hunter would never do. Wilson assures Francis that the kill is "sporting enough," but when pressed by Margaret, Wilson admits that his career as a hunting guide would be over if game authorities in Nairobi knew of the illegal chase. The bullet that Macomber takes to the back of the head symbolically reenacts his unsportsmanlike conduct. Even if one assumes that Margaret accidentally kills her husband, her firing while he stands in her line of sight displays the same lack of regard for the rules of the game as shooting at an animal from a car. In this way, Hemingway implies that those who show disrespect for the code of fair play are sure to be punished for it.

CHARACTERS

In a 1977 essay on *The Sun Also Rises,* David Zehr describes three sorts of "expatriate consciousnesses" distinguishing Americans in Paris. Most contemptible for Hemingway is the superficial tourist mentality that views Paris as "a vacation spot . . . a place to be 'amused' and 'have a good time.'" The tourists' limited attachment to the city means their attraction to it is short-lived, and they soon set out for fresh diversions. The second type are the decadents, who are "isolated from any regenerating activity" and suffer "ennui, lack of energy, and mental stupor" resulting from "uninvolved and purposeless activity" while abroad. They have given in to despair and are unable to find meaning in their lives. The final group are the "detached observers," those who bear witness to the spectacle of modern moral decay. This group corresponds to what other critics call the "Hemingway hero." The observer's job is both to assess the temptations of "the mythified idea of Paris as a dissipating playground" and to counteract that myth with "concrete, particularized descriptions" of the locale that reveal the hero's deeper attachment to his environment.[13] Zehr's categories are not applicable only to *The Sun Also Rises* and Paris; with some modification, they can be borrowed to characterize protagonists throughout Hemingway's work and their connection to other expatriate settings, whether Southern France, Spain, or Italy. For Hemingway, individuals' responses to their foreign milieu reveal how they handle the changing landscape of modernity.

I. THE TOURISTS: At first glance, Hemingway's tourists appear to be minor characters inconsequential to the core conflict. Their central function is to provide a contrast against which the dilemmas of the decadents and Hemingway heroes seem more complex and compelling. Passing through foreign vistas, tourists view the world as a romantic spectacle without recognizing the underlying despair and anxiety. Robert Cohn in *The Sun Also Rises* offers another example of this character type. Early in the novel, this expatriate writer begs Jake to accompany him on an excursion to South America. "I can't stand to think my life is going so fast and I'm not really living it," Cohn explains (18). Jake balks at the idea, recognizing that the compulsion to travel reflects Cohn's inability to settle down and commit himself to the responsibilities of a man his age. At thirty-four, Cohn is a divorced father of three who apparently has little contact with his children. He is in Paris searching for invigoration: "Don't you ever get the feeling that all your life is going by and you're not taking advantage of it?" he asks Jake. But taking advantage of life requires that he adopt and discard various stimuli, whether a setting or a woman. (Having grown bored with his mistress, Cohn is in the process of leaving her, too.) "You can't get away from yourself by moving from one place to another," Jake tells him, but Cohn is oblivious to the advice (19). As Jake understands, Cohn's desire for constant motion reflects an immature inability to accept that life is not necessarily glamorous and romantic.

Hemingway criticizes other tourists for their lack of direction and purpose. In *A Moveable Feast* he describes how unwanted visitors frequently interrupted writing sessions at his favorite Paris café, the Closerie des Lilas. In particular, an expatriate named Hal listed for Hem all the personal problems that prevented him from embarking on his masterpiece. "You shouldn't write if you can't write," Hem snaps. "What have you to cry about? Go home. Get a job. Hang yourself. Only don't talk about it. You could never write" (94). The outburst may seem harsh, but it is typical of Hemingway's insistence that poseurs were loitering in Paris. Their presence in the Montparnasse cafés marks their lack of artistic initiative. Unlike Hemingway, who always frequents these establishments with a notebook and pencil, expatriates such as Hal are there to chitchat, hobnob, and gossip—to do anything but sit down to work.

In still other works, Hemingway treats tourists with more empathy by exploring the disappointment they suffer when impulsive traveling does not satisfy the yearning for stimulation. In "Hills Like White Elephants" a brief glimpse of the many hotel labels on the couple's baggage suggests that they have been traveling for some time (214). Jig and her companion's inability to confront their problem directly implies a connection between their conversational and geographic rambling. Jig's pregnancy offers them the opportunity to put down roots, but the companion's insistence that she undergo an abortion reveals he is not ready to end their traveling. "That's all we do, isn't it," Jig complains in the midst of their conversation. "Look at things and try new drinks" (212). The lament succinctly captures the ultimate emptiness of the vagabond lifestyle. As Jig hints, the novelty of new settings and experiences fades at some point, leaving the tourist with a longing for attachment.

II. THE DECADENTS: These Hemingway types are not oblivious to tragedy but eager participants in it. Suffering deep emotional wounds, the decadents externalize their anguish through self-indulgence, self-pity, and self-destruction. As Hemingway described them, they are "burned out, hollow and smashed."[14] They represent the failure to pass the fundamental test of expatriation. Rather than impose order on the chaotic world in which they live, they perpetuate that upheaval by giving in to the narcotic pleasures of wreckage and recklessness. Proclaiming themselves powerless to change their behavior, Hemingway's decadents seem attractively larger than life with their dramatic indifference to the future. Beneath their defiant flamboyance, however, they reveal themselves as morally bankrupt; equally ominously, they have a talent for corrupting others.

Hemingway's most famous decadents are Mike Campbell and Brett Ashley in *The Sun Also Rises.* Mike is an alcoholic bankrupt; forever "stony" (low on funds), he relies on his friends to pick up the tab. He even shocks Jake at one point by borrowing money from the hotel owner Montoya, a violation of the code of the aficionado. "One never gets anywhere by discussing finances," Mike decides when his situation looks particularly grim (234). That indifference is symbolic of his larger irresponsibility, which figures most prominently in his behavior while drinking. Of the intoxicated revelers in *The Sun Also Rises,* Mike is by far the most obnoxious. Like Jake, he is powerless to stop Brett (his fiancée) from roving from lover to lover, but whereas Jake stoically suffers her infidelities, Mike loses control when drunk, allowing his bitterness to burst forth. He lashes out at Robert Cohn, comparing him to the steers (castrated bulls) of the fiesta. Later, after Brett's affair with Pedro Romero, Mike starts a public row over the bullfighter, tipping over a table full of beer bottles and shrimp. Simply put, Mike is a "bad drunk," and in Hemingway's world, failure to hold one's liquor is one of the surest signs of an undisciplined approach to life.

Brett's decadence is more complicated. Superficial readers often condemn her for her promiscuity, sometimes labeling her a nymphomaniac. That judgment is too harsh, however, for Hemingway supplies enough background information to convey how deeply Brett has been wounded by the war. Because she has lost one love to dysentery and her husband to insanity, her descent into self-destruction is understandable, though not excusable. Her behavior is also a response to the limitations imposed upon her sex. With her bobbed hair and bare legs, Brett represents the "new woman" of the 1920s, a heroine who gained social freedom by eschewing traditional adult female prerogatives such as marriage, motherhood, and monogamy. And yet with that freedom came new confines. The sleek, angular body and boyish hairstyles associated with the female flappers of the era conveyed not just androgyny but willful prepubescence. Eluding conventional female roles required maintaining a facade of perpetual youth that precluded any behavior that might mark her as mature. Intriguingly, Brett makes Pedro Romero leave her in Madrid when he tries to transform her into a conventional woman. He wants her to grow her hair longer and dress more demurely. Fifteen years his senior, Brett will begin showing her age if forced to be "more womanly." Hemingway's original draft of the scene made the conflict clear. Originally, Brett was to have explained the end of the affair by telling Jake, "In Paris you can't tell whether a boy is with his wife or his mother. . . . I'm not going to be that way."[15] In the published text, only a hint of this dilemma remains: "I'm thirty-four, you know. I'm not going to be one of these bitches that ruins children" (247). As Brett implies, she is trapped in the expatriate lifestyle of heavy drinking and casual sex because it allows her to see herself as young and free of responsibility. In another way, this lifestyle contains the damage she might commit. By remaining with Mike and Jake, she only hurts those who have already been so wounded that they are numb to the pain.

In *A Moveable Feast,* Hemingway also offers a maliciously skewed depiction of F. Scott Fitzgerald as self-destructive and undisciplined. Recalling the most intense period of their friendship in the mid 1920s, he ascribes to his fellow writer every weakness of character he associated with corrupt protagonists. Fitzgerald is forever broke, fails to hold his liquor, and finds excuses for not working. Indeed, as Hemingway recounts a disastrous trip the two took to Lyon in 1925, he paints a portrait of Fitzgerald as unreliable. On the morning of their departure from Paris, Fitzgerald fails to show up at the train station: "I had never heard, then, of a grown man missing a

OTHER HEMINGWAY WORKS ABOUT EXPATRIATION

"The Capital of the World" (1936). Set in Madrid, the story follows a young boy named Paco whose fascination with bullfighting proves fatal.

"Che Ti Die La Patria?" (1927). First published as an autobiographical essay in *The New Republic* but reprinted as fiction in *Men Without Women,* this story describes two Americans' brief trip through Italy, during which time they gauge the effects of Mussolini and fascism on the country.

"A Day's Wait" (1933). A young boy with the flu believes he will die because his temperature is 102 degrees and he was told that no one can live with a fever of more than 44 degrees. Only later does he learn from his father the difference between Fahrenheit and centigrade.

"Get a Seeing-Eyed Dog" (1957). One of the two final short stories Hemingway published in his lifetime (the other is "A Man of the World"), this tale, set in Venice, describes a writer's fear that his recent blindness will make him dependent on his wife.

"Homage to Switzerland" (1933). An experimental story in which Hemingway tells three separate stories about men simultaneously waiting in Switzerland for a train to Paris, it is notable for its derogatory references to F. Scott Fitzgerald.

"Old Man at the Bridge" (1938). One of Hemingway's Spanish Civil War stories, it concerns a soldier who comes across an elderly man too fatigued from walking from his village to worry about an imminent fascist attack.

"On the Quai at Smyrna" (1930). An intense vignette composed to introduce the 1930 Scribner's reissue of *In Our Time,* this story is drawn from Hemingway's experience covering the Greco-Turkish war in the early 1920s. It catalogues the different types of violence and brutality witnessed at a harbor dock.

train," Hemingway complains. "But on this trip I was to learn many new things" (157). Among them are Fitzgerald's prodigality and hypochondria. Unaccustomed to luxury, Hemingway was uncomfortable staying in a fancy hotel and eating the elaborate meals that Fitzgerald ordered. He was also unprepared for his friend's ill-health; on the trip home, Hemingway had to nurse Fitzgerald, who announced his imminent death from pneumonia and demanded that his temperature be taken. And while Fitzgerald promised to pay for the trip, Hemingway ended up covering the tab with funds he and Hadley had saved for their annual Spanish vacation. "I was getting tired of the literary life, if this was the literary life that I was leading," Hemingway declares. "Already I missed not working and I felt the death loneliness that comes at the end of every day that is wasted in your life" (165–166).

Hemingway's insistence that Fitzgerald wasted his talent proves his most devastating accusation. As an admirer of *The Great Gatsby* (published in 1925 shortly before the writers met), Hemingway describes how he encouraged his friend to abandon commercial fiction and expand upon the artistic breakthrough that the novel marked. Fitzgerald balked at the advice, arguing he could not make a living unless he catered to the popular marketplace: "I must write stories and they have to be stories that will sell" (182), he complained. Hemingway suggests that while he and Hadley were perfectly content in their poverty, Fitzgerald and his wife, Zelda, were incapable of scaling back their needs to economize. Nor could Fitzgerald resist the distractions of expatriate life and work regularly. Hemingway blames Zelda for this problem; whenever Scott tried to stop carousing in the

Paris nightspots to concentrate on his next novel after *The Great Gatsby,* she would call him a "kill-joy" and "spoilsport." The first time he and Hadley visited the Fitzgeralds' apartment, Hemingway remembers, Zelda smiled as her husband drank more and more wine during lunch: "I learned to know that smile very well," he reports. "It meant she knew Scott would not be able to write." Her efforts to interfere with his writing formed a pattern that exhausted their friends' patience: "Scott would resolve not to go on all-night drinking parties and to get some exercise each day and work regularly. He would start to work and as soon as he was working well Zelda would begin complaining about how bored she was and get him off on another drunken party" (180–181). To distinguish his dedicated work ethic from Fitzgerald's, Hemingway uses a geographic contrast. While he found Paris the "town best organized for a writer to write in that there is" (182), Fitzgerald was drawn to the French Riviera, where the whirlwind expatriate life was even wilder and more outrageous. The emphasis placed on Fitzgerald's lack of productivity signals Hemingway's overarching criticism of the expatriate decadent. Without discipline or self-control, he insists, expatriates are bound to fall into a dissolute life.

III. THE HEMINGWAY HERO: In marked distinction to the tourists and decadents is a character type that critics have come to call the "Hemingway hero." Protagonists such as Jake Barnes, Frederic Henry, Robert Jordan, Nick Adams, and even Hemingway himself in his nonfiction display the virtues necessary to withstand the moral confusion of modern life. These heroes are by no means perfect people; Jake's loss of his status as an aficionado is a good example of how they are apt to compromise their principles. Nevertheless, unlike other expatriates, these main characters subscribe to a code of conduct. According to Philip Young, this code "is made of the controls of honor and courage which in a life of tension and pain make a man a man and distinguish him from the people who follow random impulses, let down their hair, and are generally messy, perhaps cowardly, and without inviolable rules for how to live holding tight."[16] The "make a man a man" phrase may suggest that only those possessing a Y chromosome are capable of courage and endurance; yet, several female characters—for example, Catherine Barkley in *A Farewell to Arms* and the Spanish guerilla Pilar in *For Whom the Bell Tolls* (1940)—also possess the courage of their convictions. Male or female, Hemingway heroes are besieged and embattled by violence and absurdity. In the end, they may be beaten; yet, they remain, as the title of bullfighter Manuel Garcia's story proclaims, undefeated.

Jake Barnes's story reveals how the experience of expatriation creates ethical problems for the Hemingway hero. Other Americans view Europe as an immense playground, but Jake is in Paris to work as a journalist. Brett, Mike, and Robert Cohn all finance their indulgent lifestyle through alimony, allowances, or the largesse of fellow revelers. Jake, by contrast, limits himself only to luxuries he can afford. In one early scene he balances his checkbook, discovering that he has saved nearly $2,000 by living overseas. The detail seems unimportant until one recognizes that monetary metaphors dramatize Jake's awareness that there is a cost for one's actions. "You paid some way for everything that was any good," he realizes. "Either you paid by learning about them, or by experience, or by taking chances, or by money. Enjoying living was learning to get your money's worth and knowing when you had it. You could get your money's worth." Frugality and responsibility are thus important values for him; unlike Mike and Brett, he realizes that there is no "getting something for nothing" and that "the bill always came" (152).

Drinking is another behavior through which Jake demonstrates the effort required to uphold the code. While he enjoys his liquor, he is a connoisseur, not a drunk. Early in the novel Brett shows up unannounced at his apartment. Jake treats her to brandy but declines her invitation to join her for a champagne breakfast, courtesy of a wealthy Greek expatriate named Count Mippipopolous. "I have to work in the morning" (66), he tells her. His discipline is confirmed again when a disappointed Brett departs and, rather than drink alone, Jake pours the contents of his half-empty glass down the sink. Not "getting tight" by himself suggests he views drinking as a social act or communal ritual, not a means of escape—a point confirmed by the many scenes in Paris cafés in which Jake demonstrates control. This behavior does not mean he remains sober throughout the story. Far from it. But when he is intoxicated in Pamplona, it is because he has *chosen* to get drunk to blunt the pain of his love for Brett. As John W. Crowley suggests, "In his drinking, as in the rest of his life, Jake tries to display manly courage without ever becoming 'messy.' But when he does get drunk, as when he yields to Brett's seduction, Jake loses control of himself and thus dishonors the ideal of discipline."[17] What separates Jake from Mike and Brett is that he understands the importance of *trying* to maintain self-control. While his decadent compatriots claim they are powerless to rectify their behavior, by the end of the story he decides he is "through with fiestas for awhile" (236).

Like Jake's, Nick Adams's experiences abroad test his commitment to the code. Critics disagree about how many short stories center upon this alter ego, for several Hemingway texts feature unnamed protagonists who may or may not be Nick. There is little debate, however, over what this recurring character represents. Nick is Hemingway's portrait of the artist as a young man, a fictional self who in each story undergoes an experience that challenges his moral and artistic resolve. Readers need not be familiar with the autobiographical parallels to the author's life to appreciate the Nick stories, for their drama encompasses a universal range of human experience, tracing Nick's development from childhood exposure to the pain and evil in the world through more personal adult anxieties over marriage and parenthood. "Big Two-Hearted River" offers the best stylistic representation of Nick's psychic struggle to maintain poise in an unbalanced environment. As simple an act as cooking a campfire meal demands a self-conscious commitment to doing things the right way. As Nick prepares to eat his spaghetti-and-bean dinner, he is careful not to rush for fear of ruining the experience: "He was not going to spoil it all by burning his tongue. For years he had never enjoyed fried bananas because he had never been able to wait for them to cool" (168). Nick's purposefulness displays the intent necessary to realize self-control. As Joseph Flora writes, "We are told exactly how he performs each act and why he does it as he does" because the "steady detail mirrors the values that Nick is seeking in life—order, neatness, purpose."[18] Other Nick stories, such as "Now I Lay Me" and "A Way You'll Never Be," include less extensive but equally important passages revealing this struggle to establish mental order and discipline.

Many readers note that Frederic Henry in *A Farewell to Arms* and Robert Jordan in *For Whom the Bell Tolls* face the same test: how to love in the midst of war. When Frederic first meets Catherine, he does not love her. He tries to seduce her, but their initial flirtation is just a "game, like bridge, in which you said things instead of playing cards." Kissing her, he decides, is "better than going every evening to the house for officers where the girls climbed all over you and put your cap on backward as a sign of affection between their trips upstairs with brother officers" (31–32). Upon glimpsing her again after his wounding, though, Frederic declares deeper feelings for her: "God knows I had not wanted to fall in love with her. I had not wanted to fall in love with any one. But God knows I had and . . . I felt wonderful" (100). Before the blast that landed him in the hospital, he was hardened by the war, but his near-death experience makes him vulnerable, suggesting he realizes (even if he cannot articulate it) that love is the only possible countervailing force against mortality. Yet, that belief ultimately proves naive as Frederic is subjected to the inescapable violence of the natural world. As Catherine suffers the agony of a difficult labor, delivering a stillborn child in Switzerland, he learns that the hostility of nature renders love impotent: "That was what you did. You died. You did not know what it was about. You never had time to learn. They threw you in and told you the rules and the first time they caught you off base they killed you. . . . They killed you in the end" (350). When Catherine subsequently expires from a hemorrhage, Frederic must accept that, however redemptive, love is no match for the inevitability of death.

Robert Jordan comes to a different conclusion. Rather than lose love to the cruelty of nature, he learns it can transcend the violence of war through personal sacrifice. Joining a band of Spanish guerillas to destroy an enemy bridge, Jordan falls in love with Maria, a young girl brutally gang-raped by fascists who executed her parents. Maria embodies the beauty of nature that must withstand the "mechanized doom" of human warfare.[19] At several points Jordan contemplates the absurdity of loving someone in the middle of a military mission, but making love with Maria at night gains him a previously unknown feeling of belonging and acceptance. Jordan describes a sense of "integration" (a key word in the novel) that love inspires: "One only one, there is no other one but one now . . . one and one is one" (379). As the guerillas make their escape after destroying their target, a stumbling horse falls on Jordan, crushing both his leg and his hopes of taking Maria back to America after the war. Realizing he must stay behind so the others can survive, he insists that as long as Maria lives, their love will not be destroyed: "If thou goest then I go, too. Do you not see how it is? Which one there is, is both?" (463). For Jordan, the couple's spiritual union is powerful enough to withstand their physical separation.

The most controversial Hemingway hero is Hemingway himself. In the 1930s he turned to nonfiction, publishing *Death in the Afternoon,* a study of bullfighting, and *Green Hills of Africa,* an account of a 1934 safari in Tanzania in East Africa. (In this period he briefly served as a columnist for *Esquire;* the posthumous collection *By-Line: Ernest Hemingway* [1967] includes these contributions as well as his earlier *Toronto Star* dispatches.) Conventionally, critics argue that these first-person works are so belligerent in articulating the code that the Hemingway hero comes across more as a braggart and bully than as an empathetic protagonist. As Edmund Wilson wrote in a review of *Green Hills of Africa,* Hemingway was "his own worst-drawn character" and "his own worst commentator" because he seemed more interested in his "publicity legend" than in the "irreducible hazards and pains of life and the code of honor which one must evolve to live among them."[20] Such judgments are pervasive among critics—so much so that they deserve reconsideration. Hemingway's intent was not to boast or show off but to demonstrate how the "code of honor" applies to all aspects of the artist's life, his pastimes as well as professional pursuits.

Foremost among the values that Hemingway's artists must embody is honesty. Just as bullfighters and hunters cheat their confrontation with death to appear heroic, writers adopt phony techniques intended to enhance the importance of their art. In *Death in the Afternoon,* Hemingway criticizes those who mistake "overwritten" prose for significance: "If a man writes clearly enough any one can see he fakes. If he mystifies to avoid a straight statement . . . there is no mystery . . . only the necessity to fake to cover lack of knowledge or the inability to state clearly."[21] Straightforward writing for Hemingway is the same as confronting life's unpleasantries without being evasive—it expresses the artist's commitment to truth. *Green Hills of Africa* likewise insists that writers must possess an "absolute conscience as unchanging as the standard meter in Paris to prevent faking."[22] The book details several ways that writers succumb to artificiality. They may overwrite, or they may fall prey to critics' flattery and grow self-conscious about producing books that will be celebrated as masterpieces. They may even make money and then they "have to write to keep up their establishments, their wives, and so on, and they write slop" (23). Honesty is vital, for it is the only value a writer can rely upon when detractors begin to denounce one's efforts: "When you write well and truly of something and know impersonally you have written in that way . . . those who are paid to read it and report on it [will] not like it so they say it all is a fake" (148–149). Only by trusting one's instincts, Hemingway asserts, can the artist protect him- or herself from the slings and arrows of outrageous criticism. Not surprisingly, because *Death in the Afternoon* and *Green Hills of Africa* depict critics as detrimental to writers, reviewers were hostile to Hemingway's opinions and questioned why he was so defensive and sensitive.

A Moveable Feast also demonstrates the principles a writer must maintain to remain honest. In recounting his early expatriate years, Hemingway insists that what set him apart from most writers in Paris was discipline. A chapter titled "Hunger Was Good Discipline" employs the metaphor of appetite to describe the self-control he needed to perfect his craft. As he wanders Paris, Hemingway must avoid the culinary temptations of the city so he will not overeat and dull his senses. Feeling "belly-empty, hollow-hungry" heightens his powers of perception so he can better study the Cézanne paintings that inspire his prose. Hunger can also be deceptive, though, for the unfulfilled feeling it creates encourages self-pity. Hemingway must remind himself of the importance of moderation, a lesson he learns when he discovers a small check waiting for him at Sylvia Beach's bookshop. The money, earned by selling a short story, allows him to stop at a nearby *brasserie* called Lipp's for a frankfurter, potato salad, and beer, which calm his nerves and soothe doubts about whether or not he can become a great writer in Paris. "It is necessary to handle yourself better when you have to cut down on food so you will not get too much hunger-thinking," he insists. "Hunger is good discipline and you learn from it" (75). This lesson also applies to his artistic appetites. As he works on his short stories, he must recognize that they are like his snack—they prepare him to write a longer novel. As the chapter concludes, a content, productive Hemingway works on "Big Two-Hearted River," a story, not coincidentally, in which the main character must also learn to control his hunger. Throughout *A Moveable Feast*, Hemingway exaggerates his poverty; he and Hadley drew a comfortable annual income of roughly $2,000 from interest generated by her trust funds. Nevertheless, the link between eating and writing in his memoirs demonstrates how the Hemingway hero must exert rigorous discipline in all actions in order to maintain order and control.

THEMES

Constructing a list of major themes from any author's corpus courts oversimplification. Nevertheless, Hemingway's novels and stories about expatriation suggest a recurring concern with identity, respect for foreign rituals and customs, and the lessons of experience. Hemingway was a literary ethicist, and from *In Our Time* through *A Moveable Feast*, the beloved vistas of France, Spain, and Italy provide a backdrop against which he can measure the moral fiber of his characters. Accordingly, in text after text he insists that surviving modernity depends upon establishing the boundaries of proper behavior—whether in war, love, or writing. Fitzgerald recognized the concern with setting down the right way of living when he called *The Sun Also Rises* a "romance and guidebook."[23] The second term suggests that Hemingway views art as a means of guiding readers, not by demanding that they subscribe to a fixed set of behavioral regulations but by outlining the process by which the individual distinguishes truth from falsity. The five basic themes described below all arise from his belief that living abroad is either an opportunity or a pitfall, depending on how well the expatriate responds to its moral challenges.

1. *At its simplest, expatriation is an initiation experience that enables the construction of a new identity; whether this transformation of self is exhilarating or debilitating depends upon the individual's ability to channel the process into some productive outcome and not end up "burned out, hollow*

and smashed." "We live by accidents of terrain," Hemingway writes in *Across the River and into the Trees.*[24] The phrase suggests that *who* people are is somehow tied to *where* they are. Setting shapes one's sense of identity, with various locations drawing out different aspects of personality. Hemingway knew intimately how expatriation encouraged experiments in self-definition. Raised by strict, conservative parents, he sought refuge from their overbearing devotion to decorum and propriety in Paris, where promiscuity and intoxication were as commonplace as church socials. According to J. Gerald Kennedy, as Hemingway adopted several bohemian affectations, including his beret and whisky flask, his "Oak Park stiffness gave way to . . . a curiosity about the sexual negotiations occurring in the cafés, and then to a preoccupation with innuendo, body language, glances, clothing."[25] Despite his intrigue with expatriate decadence, he never lost the reverence for work, moderation, and discipline with which his parents imbued him. The result was an enduring tension between temptation and restraint. His characters are often drawn into the expatriate world of excess only to discover their regret when they sample its forbidden fruits.

Life abroad posed several types of temptation for Hemingway. *The Sun Also Rises* and *The Garden of Eden* explore how androgyny, the blurring of masculine and feminine characteristics, can be liberating and yet confusing for Brett Ashley and Catherine Bourne. "The Sea Change" (1931) further examines how bisexuality affects identity. In a Paris bar, a couple argue about the woman's attraction to a lesbian affair. The man, Phil, condemns her desire as "vice" and "perversion," but she insists she is merely acting upon an unrealized part of her identity. "We're made up of all sorts of things," (303) she explains. Phil relents only when the woman promises to return to him after her adventure; after she leaves, he announces how the experience has transformed him. "I'm a different man," he tells the bartender. "You see in me quite a different man" (304). Although characters such as Phil seem to lose their sense of self, Hemingway does not necessarily argue that strict conformity to traditional sex roles prevents such crises. Catherine's emotional instability in *The Garden of Eden* is not the fault of the male alter ego she creates; rather, her inability to be female in the conventional way that her husband wants causes her problems. "I broke myself in pieces trying to be a girl and all it did was break me in pieces,"[26] she realizes. Nor is the loss of self always the result of gender bending. In "The Snows of Kilimanjaro" and *A Moveable Feast*, Hemingway shows how heterosexual adultery corrupts one's moral ideals, leading one to a betrayal of artistic standards. Affluence is yet another negative influence. "The Snows of Kilimanjaro" and *A Moveable Feast* link their protagonists' personal and artistic failures to money. As Harry confesses in "The Snows of Kilimanjaro," "Each day . . . of comfort, of being that which he despised, dulled his ability and softened his will to work so that, finally, he did no work at all" (44). *Green Hills of Africa* also cautions repeatedly against luxuries that blunt artistic perception.

2. *Although expatriation can lead to identity crises, it also introduces the individual to foreign rituals that can supply the sacramental significance needed to give meaning to modern life.* Hemingway's work lavishes attention upon the local customs and cuisine of France, Spain, Italy, and Austria. Often interpolated into his fiction are what seem step-by-step instructions for appreciating bullfights, fishing, and refreshments. For some readers, these passages function as the literary equivalent of a *Fodor's Guide:* they create the flavor of a place while highlighting the regional peculiarities that make it unusual. (American tourists often travel to Paris, Pamplona, and other sites with Hemingway novels in hand.) These descriptive moments, however, amount to more than mere travel writing. In documenting foreign rites and rituals, Hemingway offers these customs as substitutes for traditions that have fallen away in the modern age. He wants readers to recognize that Pedro Romero's moves in the bullring and the African natives' approach to hunting in *Green Hills of Africa* provide models of morality that can guide them through the perils of changing times.

The second Mrs. Hemingway, Pauline Pfeiffer, with her future husband in 1926. Her family wealth enabled Hemingway to indulge in expensive travels and sporting activities which provided new material for his writings.

Several examples of such instructional passages have already been discussed. Jake's explanation of the bullfight pageantry in *The Sun Also Rises,* Nick's conscientiousness in his camping and fishing in "Big Two-Hearted River," the rules for tracking lions and buffalo in "The Short Happy Life of Francis Macomber"—all evince Hemingway's belief that conduct determines one's responses to experience. His belief that there is a right way to deal with complexity and conflict is perhaps best dramatized in the countless eating scenes found throughout his fiction. Readers will immediately recognize that Hemingway's expatriate world is rich in gastronomy. Eating is important in his writing because of its ritualistic associations; as "Big Two-Hearted River" and the chapter titled "Hunger Was Good Discipline" in *A Moveable Feast* demonstrate, how protagonists eat reveals how they control their other appetites.

In other cases, eating symbolizes the establishment of community. Both *A Farewell to Arms* and *For Whom the Bell Tolls* include several descriptions of soldiers and guerillas eating. Feasting in a war zone might seem out of place, but for Hemingway the gesture reveals how his characters' futures are tied up with one another, how (to quote the John Donne poem that introduces the latter novel) "no man is an island / entire of itself." In *A Farewell to Arms,* shortly before his wounding, Frederic Henry insists that soldiers eat while waiting for an attack to begin. Although the mobile kitchen feeding them has been lost, Henry scrounges up a tin of cold macaroni and a cheese block. As each soldier dips his fingers into the macaroni, their shared meal becomes a primitive form of communion that demonstrates their solidarity in the face of death. (A moment later a shell explodes among them, killing two and almost claiming Frederic's life.) Similarly, at the end of the novel, as Catherine is dying, Henry attempts to eat a plate of ham and eggs at a café. He is not hungry, but he makes himself consume the food to preserve his strength. He does not eat for pleasure; the act is a routine intended to impose order upon the uncertainty of experience.

3. *Expatriation for Hemingway either represents a vital engagement with life or an escape from it. While living abroad exposes the Hemingway hero to the harshness of existence, other expatriates view it as an opportunity to hide from reality.* Throughout Hemingway's novels and stories, one can trace a persistent contrast between the lessons his heroes learn from their experiences abroad and other exiles' denial of the lessons. While his protagonists realize the importance of upholding values such as courage and integrity, secondary characters do whatever is necessary to avoid that recognition. Thus, Jake Barnes must come to grips with violating the values of the aficionado, but Robert Cohn, after the disastrous week in Pamplona, remains the same naive romantic who poetically pined for Brett's love. Jig's retreat into silence at the end of "Hills Like White Elephants" marks her awareness that there is no point in trying to communicate with her companion; his anxious desire to board the arriving train and set off for a new destination implies a superficial belief that they can leave their problems behind in the Ebro Valley. In "The Snows of Kilimanjaro," Harry recalls witnessing the bloodshed of the 1922 Greco-Turkish War, only to return to Paris to find an "American poet with a pile of saucers in

front of him . . . talking about the Dada movement [deliberately absurd works that suggested that modern life was meaningless] with a Rouma-nian who said his name was Tristan Tzara, who always wore a monocle and had a headache." By suggesting that Tzara and this "potato-faced" poet (Malcolm Cowley) are oblivious to violence in Europe, Hemingway calls attention to the frivolousness of expatriate *artistes*. Observing the fighting, Harry "had seen the things that he could never think of"; these writers' understanding of the world, by contrast, is as shallow as the sau-cers they stack before them (49). *A Moveable Feast* includes this contrast as well, with Hemingway comparing his own awareness of violence and war to the wilful ignorance of Stein and others, whose motto is "never the real, never the bad" (25).

4. *A key aspect of engagement for Hemingway is acknowledging the brutality and treachery of nature; Europe is an important setting for him because, unlike in America, violence is an elemental fact of life.* In titling his first book of short stories, Hemingway drew a phrase from the English *Book of Common Prayer* that read "Give us peace in our time, O Lord." In the context of his fiction, the plea is ironic, for he constantly exposes readers to scenes of bloodshed and devastation in the belief that, as he writes in *Death in the Afternoon,* "all stories, if continued far enough, end in death, and he is no true story-teller who would keep that from you" (122). As the site where Hemingway first witnessed death, Europe became associated in his mind with the carnage endemic to the twentieth century, something that America, with its optimism and geographic isola-tion, failed to fathom. In one of his most graphic stories, "A Natural History of the Dead" (1932), Hemingway parodies nature writers such as W. H. Hudson and Gilbert White, who focus on the beauty of nature and turn blind eyes to the brutality of dying. Cataloguing the various types of gruesome death the author witnessed in Italy in 1918, the story insists that "most men die like animals, not men" and that any attempts by writers to obscure this fact is tantamount to lying. At one point Hem-ingway even hopes to witness "the actual death of members of [the 'deco-rous'] literary sect and watch the noble exits that they make": "I hope to see the finish of a few, and speculate how worms will try [their] long pre-served sterility; with their quaint pamphlets gone to bust and into foot-notes all their lust" (338). Authors who shy away from violence do not understand that they, too, are doomed to suffer its indignity. "A Natural History of the Dead" is one of Hemingway's goriest writings, illustrating his belief that honesty obliges the writer to expose readers to the hostility and strife that festers beneath the calm exterior of nature.

5. *Finally, expatriation for Hemingway is a necessary form of individualism. By living overseas, the writer strips himself of familiar beliefs and outlooks in order to achieve a clarity of vision impossible in his native land. This purging is vital because without it he can never be sure of the authenticity of what he experiences.* In Hemingway's world, travel is a form both of sensory stimulation and of deprivation. At the same time that it overwhelms the senses with exotic new experiences, it also strips one of acculturated habits and behaviors that allow one to avoid "living full up." What Hemingway says of writing conveys his attitude about individual perception—the way each person looks at the world. As he writes in *Death in the Afternoon*, gauging reality (acknowledging its brutality while not succumbing to despair) is a matter for him of "knowing truly what you really felt, rather than what you were supposed to feel, and were taught to feel." Achieving this aim involves an active breakdown of experience to discover "what the actual things were which produced the emotion that you experienced." Expatriation cleanses the palate, much as wine tasters must to appreciate the quality of what they sample. Defamiliarization and disassociation allow one to discover "the real thing, the sequence of motion and fact which made the emotion and which would be as valid in a year or in ten years" (2).

The Hemingway character who best illustrates this theme is Robert Jordan in *For Whom the Bell Tolls*. As Jordan prepares to carry out his mission to destroy an important fascist bridge, he must reconcile his political loyalties with his individual motives for fighting in the Spanish Civil War. At the beginning of the novel, he thinks of himself as an "instrument to do your duty" (43), as a tool of a larger cause that must

HEMINGWAY ON AMERICA

Hemingway wrote so frequently and in such depth about the locales he traveled that his interest in the symbolic power of geography and landscape raises an obvious question: What did he think of America? Unfortunately, unlike Henry James or even his former mentor Gertrude Stein, he rarely attempted to define the overall significance and character of his native country. One exception is a passage in *Green Hills of Africa*, in which Hemingway suggests that he would prefer to live in the unspoiled African wilderness rather than return to America, where there are no more opportunities for living close to nature:

"I would come back to Africa but not to make a living from it. I could do that with two pencils and a few hundred sheets of the cheapest paper. But I would come back to where it pleased me to live; to really live. Not just let my life pass. Our people went to America because that was the place to go then. It had been a good country and we had made a bloody mess of it and I would go, now, somewhere else as we had always had the right to go somewhere else and as we had always gone. You could always come back. Let the others come to America who did not know that they had come too late. Our people had seen it at its best and fought for it when it was well worth fighting for. Now I would go somewhere else. We always went in the old days and there were still good places to go."

Green Hills of Africa (New York: Scribners, 1935), p. 285.

not be questioned. Yet, he grows increasingly aware that his comrades are as capable of inhumanity as the enemy. In one chapter, the guerillas' mother figure, Pilar, recounts how Pedro, their leader, executed fascist sympathizers in a village. The men were forced to run a gauntlet of loyalists armed with flails and pitchforks that ended with a three-hundred-foot drop into a river. As Pilar observes, the experience of killing changed the men, hardening them: "The people of this town are as kind as they can be cruel and they have a natural sense of justice and a desire to do that which is right. But cruelty had entered into the lines" (116). As such stories raise doubts about the morality of the cause, Jordan attempts to separate himself from politics and contemplate his mission strictly in individual terms: he is a soldier intent on honoring himself in the tradition of his grandfather, who fought in the American Civil War. Only by not allowing himself to recognize the moral complexities of war can Jordan find satisfaction in the knowledge that he serves the ideal of honor well, even when it demands the ultimate sacrifice—his death. The assurance that he has done as he believed right is Jordan's payment for his service.

SYMBOLS

The prose style Hemingway developed in Paris in the 1920s has proved one of the most original and innovative of this century—not to mention one of the most imitated. At a time when the majority of expatriate artists equated literary experimentation with complexity, he believed in simplification through omission and compression (suggesting meaning through a symbol or image). Hemingway's best-remembered sentences avoid adverbs and adjectives, which he dismissed as "ornament and scrollwork" (12) in *A Moveable Feast*. They also display the author's preference for simple grammatical structures over the complex, convoluted ones associated with Joyce and Faulkner. The result is a deceptively straightforward style that is arresting in its clarity and urgency. Fellow modernist Wallace Stevens once complimented Hemingway for conveying "extraordinary actuality"—meaning the power of his writing arises from its immediacy. In *Death in the Afternoon*, Hemingway described why he believed in cutting sentences to the bone: "If a writer of prose knows enough about what he is writing about he may omit things that he knows and the reader, if the writer is writing truly enough, will have a feeling of those things as strongly as though the writer had stated them. The dignity of movement of an iceberg is due to only one-eighth of it being above water" (192). Because this "iceberg principle" insists that seven-eighths of the drama floats unseen beneath the surface, readers must infer the central conflict by searching for clues that hint at the meaning.

Symbols are a vital tool in this interpretive process. Although Hemingway denied that he consciously inserted them into his work, his habit of omission inevitably places symbolic weight on those elements not cut. Three major categories illustrate the range of symbols he employed: *geographic symbols,* or the use of specific places and landmarks to imply emotional conflict; *landscape and climate symbols,* the use of terrain and weather to dramatize mood; and *dialogue,* the use of conversational patterns to reveal characters' compulsions. This last group requires some explanation, for students are apt to think of symbols strictly as physical objects signifying abstract emotions or ideas. Yet, actions and events are symbolic inasmuch as they also stand for complex attitudes and beliefs. Just as writers imbue a protagonist with a physical trait that signifies an inner attribute, so too they devise peculiar speech patterns representative of the character's unspoken motives and feelings. A cursory glance at Hemingway's writing reveals how extensively he relied on the symbolic uses of dialogue: much of his work is constructed out of it. Consequently, the way that characters verbally interact provides a vital tool for analyzing their behavior.

I. GEOGRAPHIC SYMBOLS: Hemingway sets the expatriate world of his writing in the actual restaurants, streets, and neighborhoods he frequented during his various journeys. Insistent that his work accurately reflect the environs he visited, he included in his fiction an amazing amount of geographic detail. It serves to give readers the impression that they have traveled to locales such as Paris, Milan, and the Serengeti Plain. Inevitably, these sites function as symbols that reveal the mind-sets of Hemingway's characters. Paris is an obvious example. Many critics ask what it reveals about Jake and his compatriots in *The Sun Also Rises* that they are regular customers at specific cafés such as the Sélect, or why they live in certain areas of the city. J. Gerald Kennedy finds it significant that Jake resides just *outside* of Montparnasse instead of *in* that bohemian enclave. His address is a sign of his ambivalence toward this area, whose amorality he condemns even as he roams through it night after night. As Kennedy suggests, by "liv[ing] on the periphery . . . and on the fringes of its excitement," Jake reveals that "he is caught between desire and disdain, perversely attracted by that which sickens him."[27] Readers therefore recognize an understated aspect of Jake's character—his belief that he can live amid decadence without being corrupted by it, an assumption that proves untrue.

Some critics have an unfortunate tendency to oversimplify the values that Hemingway associated with different cities and countries that he loved. Because Paris was the setting for stories of dissipation and self-destruction, critics describe it as Hemingway's wasteland, a realm of spiritual emptiness and despair. Spain, meanwhile, because the works set there tend to be rustic rather than urban, is described as a refuge or site of redemption. Rather than perpetuate this notion, readers should recognize that different locales evoke conflicting emotions for Hemingway, symbolizing the attitudes of different characters. While Paris might convey the decadence of the expatriate crowd in *The Sun Also Rises,* it also exemplifies the hard work and professionalism to which Hemingway subscribes in *A Moveable Feast:* "To have come on all this new world of writing, with time to read in a city such as Paris where there was a way of living well and working, no matter how poor you were, was like having a great treasure given to you" (134). Similarly, while the Spanish countryside outside Pamplona provides a pastoral respite for Jake and Bill, the barren terrain in "Hills Like White Elephants" reflects the emptiness of its vagabond couple's relationship.

The same range of values applies to Hemingway's varying depictions of Italy in *A Farewell to Arms* and *Across the River and into the Trees.* *A Farewell to Arms* builds its contrast between war and love by juxtaposing the surreal life in rural villages along the front with the faraway world of Milan, where the fighting is known only through news reports. In Gorizia and Caporetto, soldiers and townspeople attempt to ignore the rubble of homes and streets, trying to live ordinary, sane lives in the midst of shelling raids. But even stranger is the life Frederic Henry enjoys with Catherine in Milan, where they ride in carriages and attend the horse races, as though the war no longer exists for them. As Hemingway shows, the romance that Milan embodies is illusory—violence and pain will follow the lovers wherever they run for cover.

In *Across the River and into the Trees,* Hemingway uses the changing landscape of Venice to symbolize Colonel Cantwell's awareness of his approaching death. Cantwell fought his first world war near Venice; the vistas of the city evoke alternating images of him as a young idealist in 1918 and a more somber soldier in the 1940s. Reconciling the discrepancy between these two visions is the major drama of the novel. The colonel must accept the inevitable transformations in both the city and himself if he is to die with dignity. A flashback early in the novel reveals that he has recently driven through Fossalta, where he (like Hemingway) was wounded in 1918. Cantwell is amazed that, while the landscape has changed in the intervening thirty years, the scars are still faintly detectable: "Where the heavy machine gun post had been, the crater was smoothly grassed. It had been cropped, by sheep or goats, until it looked like a designed depression in a golf course." The sight briefly relieves the colonel of the anxieties brought on by his ill health and aging, for he recognizes that the passing of time has not obliterated his youthful sacrifice. Indeed, he understands that his blood has enriched the soil: "It's fine now," he decides, gazing over the once decimated area. "Look how that grass grows; and the iron's in the earth along with Gino's leg, both of Randolfo's legs, and my right kneecap" (18–19). That assurance allows Cantwell to reconcile himself to his own imminent passing; he knows now that even while history moves forward, the earth shelters its past.

II. LANDSCAPE AND CLIMATE: Hemingway readers recognize instantly his commitment to depicting the landscape accurately. With a naturalist's eye for detail, he describes the mountain ranges, valleys, plains, and flora and fauna that define a particular region. The famous opening paragraph of *A Farewell to Arms* is a masterpiece of landscape writing: "In the late summer of that year we lived in a house in a village that looked across the river and the plain to the mountains. In the bed of the river there were pebbles and boulders, dry and white in the sun, and the water was clear and swiftly moving and blue in the channels. Troops went by the house and down the road and the dust they raised powdered the leaves of the trees. The trunks of the trees too were dusty and the leaves fell early that year and we saw troops marching along the road and the dust rising and the leaves, stirred by the breeze, falling and the soldiers marching and afterward the road bare and white except for the leaves" (3). Because Hemingway so intently studies the effect of human presence in the environment, his references to the elements of nature assume symbolic importance.

Mountains are a recurring image in Hemingway's novels and stories. Carlos Baker in the 1950s was one of the first critics to note their importance, arguing that they evoke several metaphoric associations: "with the man of God and his homeland; with clear dry cold and snow, with polite and kindly people, with hospitality, and with natural beauty." Opposing these images are those of the plain, with its "lowland obscenities . . . cheap cafés, one-night prostitutes, drunkenness, destruction, and war."[28] Thus, in *A Farewell to Arms* mountains briefly shelter Frederic and Catherine—both in Gorizia, where they meet, and later in Switzerland, where they escape the war. And yet in

For Whom the Bell Tolls, the Spanish mountains of Sierra de Guadarrama trap Robert Jordan and his gypsy loyalists and heighten their sense of the futility of war. The argument over the abortion in "Hills Like White Elephants" is prompted by Jig's comparing the hills flanking the Ebro Valley to slumbering beasts; the simile of the title of the story not only conveys her rich, imaginative perspective—to which her companion is oblivious—but also the landscape itself suggests the different paths their lives will take, depending upon whether she consents to the abortion. On the one hand, before them are the dry, sterile hills; on the other hand, rich green fields that suggest fertility.

Mountains make another appearance in "Wine of Wyoming" (1931), a story about the different attitudes toward family and community that distinguish Europeans and Americans. An American couple vacationing in the West break a dinner engagement with a French family that has immigrated to the United States. As the couple departs from their disappointed friends, the narrator remarks on the similarities between European and American mountains. The comparison is ironic, for the mountains are actually quite distinct. Overlooking the differences seems a denial of the disparate values of each culture; in standing up the Fontans, the narrator and his wife reveal their lack of respect for their friends' hospitality—a fault they fail to recognize, just as they do not recognize the differences in landscape. But the most powerful use of the mountain is in "The Snows of Kilimanjaro." On the one hand, the African peak represents Harry's dying vision of his ascent into the afterlife. (The western slope of the mountain is called "The House of God" by locals.) On the other hand, because this image is a dream—Harry dies in his tent, not on the airplane sent to evacuate him—its symbolic import is ironic. The heights of Mt. Kilimanjaro also mark the summit of literary success that the writer failed to reach. Like the leopard whose frozen carcass rests on the western side of the mountain, Harry dies without completing his life's journey.

Hemingway also uses climate to add symbolic atmosphere to his narratives. Rain is a persistent motif for dramatizing feelings of dreariness and saturation with life. Early in *A Farewell to Arms,* Frederic Henry's reference to the coming of "permanent rain" (4) suggests the soldiers' ever-dampening morale. The steady rainstorm that Frederic must walk through after Catherine's death parallels his feelings of sadness and loss. Similarly, rain confines the couple in "Cat in the Rain" to their hotel room and thus heightens the conflicts undermining their relationship. When the padrone of the hotel insists that the woman should not be out in the rain trying to rescue the cat, he implies that she ought to be protected from the elements—something her companion is not going out of his way to do. Marriage, the story suggests, should provide shelter from the storminess of life; yet, more often, it exposes people to the tempestuousness of nature.

Snow is another recurring element. In some cases cold weather conveys the hardening of humanity, its capacity for brutality. "An Alpine Idyll" (1927) offers a horrific example. During a skiing vacation in the Austrian Alps, a pair of American skiers overhear a gruesome tale about a peasant who has just buried his wife. The woman died months earlier, but because of the heavy snow her husband, Olz, was unable to carry her to the village for a proper burial. To keep the corpse from decomposing, he stored it in an outdoor shed. At night when he chopped firewood in the shed, he would hang his lantern from his wife's open, frozen jaw. The story shocks both the Austrian innkeeper and the sexton who buried her. They demand an explanation from the peasant, who shrugs and departs for somewhere he can drink without reproach. For the Austrian locals, Olz's actions reflect the harshness of mountain life where people live in isolation. Although he claims to have loved his wife, the long winters have frozen his heart. For the Americans, the peasant's story is a foreign peculiarity without relation to their lives. After hearing the tale, one turns to the other and announces he is ready for dinner. "All right" (266), the narrator replies, and the story abruptly ends.

Elsewhere, snow represents deception. In *For Whom the Bell Tolls*, Robert Jordan describes how the whiteness of snow dulls the senses with its illusory purity: "In a snowstorm it always seemed, for a time, as though there were no enemies. In a snowstorm the wind could blow a gale; but it blew a white cleanness and the air was full of a driving whiteness and all things were changed" (182). Snow then becomes ominous when a sudden storm dooms Jordan and his guerilla band. In *Across the River and into the Trees*, snow and ice symbolize the death that winter brings. Recalling in flashbacks his physical decline and the end of his love affair with the much younger Renata (through whom he hoped he could regain his youth), Colonel Cantwell is duck shooting in a frozen Venetian lagoon. The ice and cold make him realize that he is "no longer of any real use" (306), either to the army or to his lover.

In other stories, cold is purifying; the chill, a metaphor for clarity and the dispassionate attitude necessary to cast a realist's eye on experience. The opening description of Milan in "In Another Country" includes a subtle reference to snow: "There was much game hanging outside the shops, and the snow powdered in the fur of the foxes and the

SLINGING THE BULL: HEMINGWAY'S PARODISTS

Parodies of a writer are a sure sign that he or she is a literary original. Not surprisingly, Hemingway's themes and stylistic habits sparked countless lampoons, many of them focusing on his fascination with bullfighting and his use of dialogue. The following passage—as well as the Ralph Barton illustration on the facing page—reveals how readily satirists seized upon Hemingway's depiction of expatriate life to poke fun at him.

"...I was sitting at a table at the edge of the arena, sipping *Anis del Toro,* and Hemingway was in the centre of the ring, under the lights, fighting a bull. As he flung open his dialogue with both hands, the bull charged, tail up. Hemingway swung his plot clear and, as the bull recharged, brought around the dialogue in a half-circle that pulled the bull to his knees. We all applauded.

'Why he's a great bull-fighter,' the coffee-boy said.

'They're all trying to imitate him,' I said.

'He's all right,' said the waiter, resting his bottle on his hip. 'He's all right so long as he don't try to drive his point too deep.'

'Sure,' I said, 'maybe he wouldn't last very long in the big fights. But right now's he's got everything.'

'Huh,' said Hemingway, *'toro!'* He took up his dialogue, and the bull charged again. Hemingway side-stepped, swung his plot in back of him and pivoted, so the bull followed a swirl of dialogue and then was left with nothing, fixed by the plot. Ernest swung the dialogue under his nozzle with one hand, to show the fight was over, and waved his hand at us...."

John Riddell, "A Parody Interview with Mr. Hemingway," *Vanity Fair,* 29 (January 1928): 78.

wind blew their tails" (206). As with similar examples of Hemingway's ability to use description, the detail can seem gratuitous until one recognizes that the gathering snow in the dead animals' fur counteracts the illusion of life that the wind creates by fanning it. Only by noticing this minute sign does the narrator register the larger symbol of death that the creatures represent. And in "Cross-Country Snow," the blankness of the winter landscape is a metaphor for the carefree sporting fun that George and Nick must soon relinquish.

III. DIALOGUE: Another celebrated aspect of Hemingway's style is its reliance on dialogue. In his works, characters speak with only a minimal amount of the intrusive exposition or background information that most writers view as necessary to convey their points. For Hemingway, though, conversations between protagonists are the visible surface of the iceberg. Whatever emotion or motive floats below the surface must be inferred. In this way, dialogue functions as a symbolic indicator of the implied drama, every bit as important to decoding the conflict as the more concrete images of the European terrain and climate. Early Hemingway critics sometimes judged his use of dialogue as a gimmick that excused him from engaging his characters' deeper feelings. He himself resented reviewers' relentless interest in this device and even ridiculed their assumption that he was incapable of in-depth psychological analysis. "But, you say, there is very little conversation in this book," Hemingway writes in *Death in the Afternoon.* "Why isn't there more dialogue? What we want in a book by this citizen is people talking; that is all he knows how to do and now he doesn't do it" (120). Of course, Hemingway did know how to do more; nevertheless, dialogue is key to his depiction of the expatriate condition. By demonstrating how people talk around their subject, contorting their words to avoid confronting problems, he pictures a shell-shocked generation unable to articulate its feelings of confusion and loss.

BEAUTY AND THE BEAST
Mr. Ernest Hemingway, legendary hero of the bull-ring and the short story among all who eschew the salads and junkets of literature, is etched above by Mr. Ralph Barton while discussing technic with his *fidus Achates*, the bull

One of the best-known examples of Hemingway's use of dialogue is "Hills Like White Elephants," more than eighty percent of which is composed of tension-laden exchanges between Jig and her companion. Throughout the story, patterns in each character's conversation become obvious. Jig tends toward what are called "tag" questions, sentence-ending interrogatives such as "isn't it?" or "aren't we?" that obligate the companion to respond to her. He, meanwhile, uses repetition to convince her that the abortion is her decision. At least six times he declares, "If you don't want to you don't have to. I wouldn't have you do it if you didn't want to." The more he makes this declaration, the more Jig realizes that he is trying to convince her to take responsibility for this "really simple operation." As if tricking him into acknowledging that *his* desire is that she abort their child, she asks a series of questions that expose his selfishness:

> "If I do it, then it will be nice again if I say things are like white elephants, and you'll like it?"
>
> "I'll love it. I love it now but I just can't think about it. You know how I get when I worry."
>
> "If I do it you won't ever worry?"
>
> "I won't worry about that because it's perfectly simple."
>
> "Then I'll do it. Because I don't care about me." (213)

Of course, the American cannot allow the conversation to end with such a self-sacrificing announcement, so he again insists that he only wants what she does. Realizing he will never be honest and admit he does not want a child, Jig breaks off the exchange in a famous line: "Will you please please please please please please please stop talking?" In saying "please" seven times, she ridicules the companion's empty repetition, blaming it for preventing them from openly discussing their dilemma.

Not even this exaggerated pronouncement stops the man, however. When he tries one last time to persuade her he will accept whatever choice she makes, she tells him "I'll scream" (214). In the end, Jig is a woman without a language to communicate. Readers need not know whether Jig eventually agrees to the abortion, for the story reveals that this conversation marks the end of their relationship. The insincerity of his dialogue mirrors their alienation in the empty Spanish countryside.

The Sun Also Rises also includes several notable passages in which characters' conversation reveals their inability to confront the cause of their despair. Brett, for example, confesses her affair with Robert Cohn to Jake:

> "Don't you think it [the trip to Pamplona] will be a bit rough on him?"
>
> "Why should it?"
>
> "Who do you think I went to San Sebastian with?"
>
> "Congratulations," I said.
>
> We walked along.
>
> "What did you say that for?"
>
> "I don't know. What would you like me to say?"
>
> We walked along and turned a corner.
>
> "He behaved rather well, too. He gets a little dull."
>
> "Does he?"
>
> "I rather thought it would be good for him."
>
> "You might take up social service." (89)

Jake's sarcasm is an effort to convey the pain that Brett's promiscuity causes him. Why not just come out and express his anguish? Given his debilitating wound, it would do little good; Jake and Brett's love is a casualty of war that no amount of talk can reverse. Indeed, thinking about his emasculation only makes Jake feel sorry for himself. Not dealing with his condition becomes the only way he can cope with circumstances he is powerless to change. For better or worse, other characters share this belief. As a result, to find Hemingway's "wastelanders" cutting off the dialogue when the emotional stakes are too serious is not at all uncommon. "I've talked too ruddy much," Brett announces when Count Mippipopolous wonders why she would rather drink than converse. "I've talked myself all out to Jake" (65). Later, when Bill Gorton while fishing inquires into Jake's feelings for Brett, Jake responds haltingly: "I'd a hell of a lot rather not talk about it" (128). And when Mike angrily denounces Robert Cohn by informing him that Brett has had affairs with much better men, Brett says she would rather not acknowledge her aversion to fidelity: "It's all rot to talk about it. Michael and I understand each other" (148).

Perhaps the most revealing of these moments occurs toward the end of the novel as Jake rescues Brett in Madrid. She *wants* to tell him why she made Pedro Romero leave her, however painful the explanation is. "Oh, let's not talk about it," she says repeatedly. When Jake does not disagree with her, she continues her tale: "There were some funny things, though" (146). Such passages suggest that these characters are capable of analyzing their behavior—Brett would not have left Romero if she had not foreseen that she would ultimately corrupt him—but that they lack the resolve to change their lives. In this case Brett needs to explain herself to Jake, if only to try to understand her own actions.

Such moments encapsulate the essence of Hemingway's suggestive technique: whether through geographic symbols, images of the land and the weather, or dialogue, Hemingway refrains from explaining directly the meaning of his fiction. The result is a richer reading experience, for as audiences ponder the significance of his plots, characters, themes, and symbols, they immerse themselves in the hidden depths of his writing to perform the fundamental task of interpretation—determining the significance of a story.

NOTES

1. John W. Aldridge, "*The Sun Also Rises:* Sixty Years Later," in his *Classics and Contemporaries* (Columbia: University of Missouri Press, 1992), p. 43.

2. Ernest Hemingway to Maxwell Perkins, 16 November 1926, in *Ernest Hemingway: Selected Letters, 1917–1961,* edited by Carlos Baker (New York: Scribners, 1981), p. 224.

3. Ernest Hemingway to F. Scott Fitzgerald, 15 December 1925, Ibid., p. 176.

4. Hemingway was upset when Young's *Ernest Hemingway* was on the verge of publication in 1952. The book argued that Hemingway's 1918 experiences in Italy had permanently stamped his imagination, his wounding in particular becoming a recurring motif in his fiction. As Hemingway wrote to Young's editor: "A critic has a right to write anything he wishes about your work no matter how wrong he may be. I also hold that a critic has no right to write about your private life while you are alive." See Ernest Hemingway to Thomas Bledsoe, 17 and 31 January 1952, Ibid., p. 748. As for his empathy, see his unpublished comments about the effect of war on him: "For one thing that I had seen or that had happened to me I knew many hundreds of things that had happened to other people who had been in the war in all its phases. My own small experiences gave me a touchstone by which I could tell whether stories were true or false." See Item 179a-1, Unpublished manuscript. The Ernest Hemingway Collection, John F. Kennedy Library, Boston, Massachusetts.

5. Five of these early stories are republished in Peter Griffin's 1985 biography of Hemingway: "The Mercenaries," "Crossroads," "Portrait of the Idealist in Love," "The Ash Heel's Tendon," and "The Current." See *Along With Youth: Hemingway, the Early Years* (New York: Oxford University Press, 1985).

6. Ernest Hemingway, "Chapter IV," in his *The Complete Short Stories of Ernest Hemingway* (New York: Scribners, 1987), p. 83. Unless otherwise noted, subsequent references to Hemingway's short stories refer to this edition and are cited parenthetically in the text.

7. Ernest Hemingway, *A Farewell to Arms* (New York: Scribners, 1929), p. 350. Subsequent references are cited within the text.

8. Ernest Hemingway, *A Moveable Feast* (New York: Scribners, 1964), p. 76. Subsequent references are cited within the text.

9. Ernest Hemingway, *The Sun Also Rises* (New York: Scribners, 1926), p. 251. Subsequent references are cited within the text.

10. Ernest Hemingway to F. Scott Fitzgerald, 24 December 1925, *Selected Letters,* p. 180.

11. Ernest Hemingway, "On Writing," in his *The Nick Adams Stories,* edited by Philip Young (New York: Scribners, 1972), p. 234.

12. Delmore Schwartz, "The Hero as Good Sport," in *Readings on Ernest Hemingway,* edited by Katie de Koster (San Diego: Greenhaven Press, 1997), pp. 62–63.

13. David Morgan Zehr, "Paris and the Expatriate Mystique: Hemingway's *The Sun Also Rises,*" *Arizona Quarterly,* 33 (1977): 156–160.

14. Ernest Hemingway to Grace Hall Hemingway, 5 February 1927, *Selected Letters,* p. 243.

15. Ernest Hemingway, *The Sun Also Rises: A Facsimile Edition,* volume 2, edited by Matthew J. Bruccoli (Detroit: Omnigraphics, 1990), p. 212.

16. Philip Young, *Hemingway: A Revaluation* (University Park: Pennsylvania State University Press, 1966), p. 63.

17. John W. Crowley, *The White Logic: Alcoholism and Gender in American Modernist Fiction* (Amherst: University of Massachusetts Press, 1994), p. 51.

18. Joseph Flora, *Hemingway's Nick Adams* (Baton Rouge: Louisiana State University Press, 1982), p. 160.

19. Ernest Hemingway, *For Whom the Bell Tolls* (New York: Scribners, 1940), p. 87. Subsequent references are cited within the text.

20. Edmund Wilson, "Letter to the Russians about Hemingway," in *Hemingway: The Critical Heritage,* edited by Jeffrey Meyers (London: Routledge & Kegan Paul, 1982), pp. 218–219.

21. Ernest Hemingway, *Death in the Afternoon* (New York: Scribners, 1932), p. 54. Subsequent references are cited within the text.

22. Ernest Hemingway, *Green Hills of Africa* (New York: Scribners, 1935), p. 27. Subsequent references are cited within the text.

23. F. Scott Fitzgerald, *The Notebooks of F. Scott Fitzgerald,* edited by Matthew J. Bruccoli (New York: Harcourt Brace Jovanovich / Bruccoli Clark, 1978), p. 158.

24. Ernest Hemingway, *Across the River and into the Trees* (New York: Scribners, 1950), p. 123.

25. J. Gerald Kennedy, *Imagining Paris: Place, Writing, and American Identity* (New Haven, Conn.: Yale University Press, 1993), p. 87.

26. Ernest Hemingway, *The Garden of Eden* (New York: Scribners, 1986), p. 192. Subsequent references are cited within the text.

27. J. Gerald Kennedy, *Imagining Paris: Place, Writing, and American Identity*, p. 100.

28. Carlos Baker, *Hemingway: The Writer as Artist* (Princeton: Princeton University Press, 1952; revised and enlarged, 1972), p. 103.

CRITICAL RESPONSES

Of twentieth-century writers, Hemingway remains one of the most discussed and debated. While scholars analyze his themes and style, journalists continue, forty years after his death, to explore his personal mystique and adventurous life. Travel writers often journey to his various homes and hangouts, noting that Hemingway landmarks in Paris, Key West, Bimini, and Idaho remain major tourist attractions. His work is even popular among sportswriters, who refer to his bullfighting and hunting stories to illustrate the values of good sportsmanship. When the specific topic under discussion is expatriation and Hemingway's role in the modernist movement, critics tend to pose several interrelated questions: How do his novels and stories reflect the displacement and uncertainty felt in the early decades of the century? How does his treatment of life abroad compare to that of earlier expatriate writers, especially Henry James? And how did Hemingway transform his personal experiences overseas into fiction? The criticism excerpted below offers insights into these major concerns.

In Paris in the early 1920s the expatriate colony looked to one source for news and gossip about American writers—the *Paris Tribune.* As Shari Benstock notes, this subsidiary of the *Chicago Tribune* "created something of a 'community' identity for the Left Bank. It devoted columns to the activities of the Young Intellectuals, the titles of which reveal the journalistic perspective: 'La Vie de Bohème,' 'Rambles through Literary Paris,' 'Latin Quarter Notes,' 'What Writers Are Doing.'"[1] In addition, the *Tribune* reviewed the literary works of expatriate modernists while reflecting on the broader causes of expatriation and its effect on American literature. One of Hemingway's earliest mentions in the paper occurred in June 1924, when he had published only *Three Stories and Ten Poems, in our time,* and a smattering of stories in little magazines. Yet, correspondent Eugene Jolas's description demonstrates how, still in the midst of his Parisian

The Sélect, one of several Montparnasse Paris cafés frequented by American expatriates in the 1920s.

apprenticeship, Hemingway had crafted a virile, athletic persona. Jolas later founded *transition*—a little magazine with one of the largest circulations—in which Hemingway's "Hills Like White Elephants" first appeared.

From "Through Paris Bookland," by Eugene Jolas, in *The Left Bank Revisited: Selections from the Paris Tribune, 1917–1934,* edited by Hugh Ford (University Park: Pennsylvania State University Press, 1972), p. 92.

> We met in one day Miss Gertrude Stein, Mr. Ernest Hemingway, and Mr. Donald Ogden Stewart, recently. Mr. Hemingway explained to us his esthetic theories, although he is the least theoretical of writers. His *Three Stories* (of which "My Old Man" has just been republished in O'Brien's *Best Short Stories of 1923*) have a dynamic directness and go straight to life, without being "literary" at all. Watching him engage in a friendly boxing bout, as we did, gives a definite index as to his method. He told us he had never read Zola, and we were wondering how many writers still read the great experimenter of the scientific novel.

The ever-increasing American population in Paris in the mid 1920s intensified debate over the causes of expatriation. The *Tribune* often addressed this issue, noting how different types of Americans were drawn to Paris's different *quartiers* (quarters or neighborhoods). In late August 1926 Elliot H. Paul catalogued the various expatriate factions, focusing in particular on Montparnasse and the three major cafés—the Dôme, the Rotonde, and the Sélect—where artists congregated. Although Hemingway is not mentioned in this article, it is nevertheless useful for its portrait of Latin Quarter life in the Lost Generation's heyday. In addition to working for the *Tribune* for several years, Paul also wrote several novels, including *The Last Time I Saw Paris* (1942).

From "From a Litterateur's Notebook," by Elliot H. Paul, in *The Left Bank Revisited: Selections from the Paris Tribune, 1917–1934*, pp. 20–22.

The Americans in Paris, and they are becoming so numerous that I expect some political party in the States will soon start a movement to permit them to vote by mail, fall into various classes and each class receives its share of abuse.

Those who have money excite the envy of the native of low-exchange countries and the penniless have an especially hard time with the French creditors because of the current belief that all citizens of the land of the free are wealthy. If Americans talk, the sound of their voices drowns out the conversation of their more copiously be-vowelled neighbors, and if they keep silent they are suspected of plotting against European prosperity.

Those who know the French language have the disadvantage of being able to understand uncomplimentary remarks and those who do not are uncomfortable because they suspect such remarks are worse than they really are. If they are temperate or moral, it is called bigotry, and the other ninety percent are thought to be disorderly. To conform to American customs as to dress and deportment exposes one to the charge of being provincial, and if one wears a pinchback suit, a black necktie, and drinks sweet aperitifs, one is accused of aping the Latins.

The tourists, whose orbit swings with reference to the Opera by day and Montmartre by night, ride the big busses, tiptoe through cathedral aisles, stumble along the corridors of the more accessible museums, infest the shops, motor to the battlefields, and spend the balance of their time looking for ham and eggs and ice cream.

The hardy annuals who go in for society inhabit the Etoile district and are considered snobs by their countrymen and climbers by the remnants of the European aristocracy. The business and professional men have to prey largely upon the tourists, and while away their leisure hours during the closed season by listening to pep talks at the Chamber of Commerce or the American Club.

Visiting politicians entertain Paris journalists with their recollections of prohibition and prosperity in the States in exchange for hints as to what they shall tell the New York journalists about liquor and poverty in Europe, and divide the rest of their stay between the Folies-Bergère, the Embassy, the neighborhood florist, and the tomb of the Unknown Soldier.

The students occupy themselves in trying to find familiar books in the unindexed French libraries, in painting narrow streets in oils, bridges or gardens in water colors, making drawings and woodcuts of the hoboes on the Seine, or practicing Czerny's School of Velocity on a pension piano. On Sunday evenings, they gather at some American welfare organization to look at the street scenes, etc., on the walls, and hear one of their classmates play Rachmaninoff's "C-sharp-minor Prelude," ending with community singing of "Seeing Nellie Home" and "Sur le pont d'Avignon."

On both sides of the Atlantic, the ways and days of the aforementioned groups are known. They have their friends and admirers, all except the tourists, and the articles or books written at their expense or in their behalf are either avowedly humorous or humorously earnest.

There remains Montparnasse.

Montparnasse is more difficult to define and classify, and by its elusiveness commands either respect or vituperation.

The Montparnassians sleep in the morning and in the afternoon and spend the evening and the neo-evening, up to the rising hour of ashmen and concierges, upon the terrace of the Dôme, The Rotonde, The Sélect, and other neighboring cafés. They have dark circles under their eyes, have read parts of *Ulysses,* and are likely to be self-made Freudians. They speak most impressively when they are vague and most erratically when they seek to be specific. They hate to spend money for either food or clothes.

The fact that they lay themselves open to the conventional kind of ridicule leads me to suspect there is something profound about them, and while their positive qualities escape both quantitative and qualitative analysis, their negative ones are delightful.

First of all, they make no pretense to love work and they do nothing whatever which may be termed useful by any of the known standards, either practical or esthetic. Although they have a world-wide reputation for Aphrodisian drollaries, actually they are less interested in sex than the average graduating class of a Michigan high school. Prices are too high to admit of drunkenness.

For hours at a time, they sit on the terraces talking of Heaven knows what or staring into space. But why should they be abused? Why should successful magazine writers and wallpaper designers sniff at them, when they cannot understand them? If inscrutability is a virtue in La Joconde, Buddha, and the Sphinx, why not in a Montparnassian? If they have devised a mode of life which cannot be utilized even in this most efficient of civilizations, all honor to them. They are no funnier than the business men, the producing artists, or the politicians, and exist with much less exertion and gusto.

The notoriety of *The Sun Also Rises* in late 1926 and 1927 inspired concern over the morality of the expatriate lifestyle. Many fellow Americans in Paris objected to Hemingway's emphasis on the drunkenness and promiscuity of his characters, insisting that he had not adequately acknowledged the creativity of those living abroad. In "Some American Expatriates," published in *Vanity Fair* in April 1927, Ford Madox Ford defends artists in Paris—including Hemingway, George Antheil, and Ezra Pound—against the decadent, debauched image propagated by *The Sun Also Rises*. As Ford insists, "There is a great deal of tosh about this." The expatriate colony of the Left Bank, he notes, is far more productive than American white-collar workers living across the Seine—mainly because the Right Bankers are so busy invading Montparnasse "trying to improve the morals of their unfortunate artistic compatriots." Ford founded the short-lived but highly influential *transatlantic review,* for which Hemingway served as an assistant editor. A friend and associate of Pound, James Joyce, and Joseph Conrad, he was an important author in his own right. Both *The Good Soldier* (1915) and his novels of the 1920s, collectively known as *Parade's End,* remain influential modernist works.

From "Some American Expatriates: An English Novelist Explains Why Many of Our Artists Prefer to Live Abroad," by Ford Madox Ford, in *Vanity Fair* (1 April 1927): 64, 98.

Sir Henry Wotton, the inconveniently witty envoy of James I, incensed his royal master by stating that an ambassador was a man sent to lie abroad for the good of his country, and I am frequently reminded of his epigram when in this country I hear—as I constantly do—comments on those fortunates or unfortunates who go to Europe in order to live whilst they paint pictures, write books, compose music or do such other things as make Europe respect the United States. For Big Business may make the United States envied, or detested, or ignored, or avoided, by Europe in general and France in particular; respect it cannot earn. It is long since France discovered that a country's books are its best ambassadors.

But such Americans here as talk to me about the American artistic colony in Paris call them expatriates *coram publico* and have the air of secretly gloating over their supposed exploits with the bottle and other implements of bliss or of forgetfulness. I do not know that Mr. Ernest Hemingway's admirable novel *The Sun Also Rises* or the fame of the uproars that arise when Mr. George Antheil gives a public concert have not added to or confirmed these rumors of riotous lives led in the greyer and more mouldering streets of Paris. Now, as the gentleman says in *Major Barbara,* there is a great deal of tosh about all this and the last gentleman who leeringly interrogated me as to the habits of American-Parisian expatriates was considerably drunker than I have ever seen any of his compatriots across the water. Mr. Hemingway's book is certainly finely alcoholic and irregular, but it is not a balanced record of life in Paris, any more than the newspaper records of crime in New York give a balanced impression of the quiet metropolitan existence that life in New York really is. And when Mr. Antheil gives a concert, representatives of the French, Polish, Russian, Hungarian, Czech-Slovak and Lithuanian *jeunes*—but not too *jeunes*—attend and throw things, emit catcalls, wave their arms and demonstrate from the galleries of the concert hall. Then the music comes to a stop and Mr. Ezra Pound arises in his place and shouts "Dogs! *Canaille!* Unspeakable filth of the gutter!" and French enthusiasts for the music of Mr. Antheil exclaim with tired voices: *"Oh, Taisez-vous!"* and *"Laissez-vous écouter!"* and it is all very gay and revives the demonstrations that have always attended the births of new forms of Art in Paris. . . . But that does not make Mr. Antheil a riotous figure.

On the contrary, during these demonstrations, he sits at his piano on the platform and patiently grins at the footlights, waiting to go on with the *Ballet Mécanique* or a Symphony. And Mr. Pound is a patriot, championing American music, a very Ajax; and the rest of the Colony in their best bibs and tuckers modestly applaud the fulminant chords with a well-drilled unanimity and so the cause of American art is advanced in the most art-loving city of the world.

I select a concert of Mr. Antheil's, rather than any other festivity of the American Latin Quarter, for adumbration because these are the most riotous social functions that I ever there attend, and because they pretty well attest my text of the moment—that there is a good deal of tosh about these Paris-American legends.

And if you think it out for yourself you will see that that must be the case. Mr. Hemingway writes extremely delicate prose—perhaps the most delicate prose that is today being written; Mr. Antheil composes music that, besides being very advanced, is of an extremely—I had almost written excruciatingly—learned nature. I know this because not only have I studied his scores with attention, but I have turned over for him whilst he played, so that I have seen and heard the exact relation of the sounding music to the written page. And Mr. Antheil's eccentricities are of the sort that is born of knowledge; he is carrying the old music of tradition a stage further, not merely making an irresponsible row on tin canisters.

Now it is an extremely difficult thing to write delicate prose, and perhaps almost more difficult to write scholarly music that is also advanced. You as lay reader may not believe this. There is a tendency amongst members of the public to think that, if they turned their attention to it, they could easily write books as good as those of—oh, whoever is your favourite author; and that with a little attention they could write music as complicatedly beautiful as the four- or eight-part fugues of Bach. But they could not. Try it and see.

Well, you cannot write delicate and beautiful words, still less can you compose advanced and very complicated music, in what is here, I believe, called a state of hang-over. It cannot be done. Try it and see. Art—any art by which you may become famous—is a tiresome and laborious affair; if it were not, famous painters, musicians, and writers would grow on every blackberry bush. They do not. Then it is mere common sense to assume that the artist is not the candidate for *delirium tremens* or the other things that men fear. Of course there are gentlemen who take studios for purposes of debauchery—but it is done more often in New York than in Paris. There is more money in New York. And New York is much the more amusing city—for people who have such tastes. At any rate the South Side of Paris is less amusing than New York, for it is a place of hard work and precious little money. How it may be with Montmartre I do not know; the readers of this journal probably know better than I, for I have been here only twice in the last thirty years and then did not much like it.

The South Side—the Latin Quarter, I know very intimately and have known it all my life. I studied there as a boy and live there now. It is a region of professors, doctors, judges, lawyers, students, some artists, some musicians, some writers and except for a notorious *carre-four* rendered disagreeable by foreign tourists of all nations, it is about as quiet as the British Museum. To that crossroads the tourists of all nations go to make as near beasts of themselves as they dare, and other tourists of all nations who are less courageous go and play the rubberneck from cheap tourists' cars, their eyes sticking out of their heads, so attractive is "vice." But the resident American colony avoids those *parages*. It really does. So do I. One has to be at work at a decent hour of morning.

But the queer thing is that a constant warfare wages between the American colony of the North Bank and that of the Quarter—or rather, the American Colony of the *Quartier de l'Etoile* is constantly making raids on the Americans of the *Quartier Montparnasse*. Why Americans cannot let each other alone I could never understand. I do not know that my own countrymen in Paris are especially gay or attractive or interesting, but at least they never try to uplift *me*. But the resident Americans of Commerce, Industry, Finance and the rest are never easy but when they are trying to improve the morals of their unfortunate artistic compatriots on the South of the Seine. A little time ago they were seriously proposing—the serious proposal appeared in the local Press—to go in bands and, either by persuasion or by appeals to the police *de bonnes mœurs,* to make the South Side of Paris a little, if not brighter, then better, than they found it.

There is no end to these activities. The other day I was applied to to furnish a character for Mr. Antheil—not of course by Mr. Antheil himself, but by an American organization. Now I do not know Mr. Antheil so very well as all that—but if there were anything against his morals I should know, for though Paris is not as much of a whispering gallery as New York, it can do its bit in that way too. So I replied in words to that effect, adding that whenever I had been in his company on social occasions his conversations and behaviour had been of the most impeccable and that his music was wholly admirable. (I may make the note that the other day in Chicago I heard M. Darius Milhaud speak complimentarily of Mr. Antheil's music, and if you know anything at all about French composers, you know what *that* means.)

Now my "character" of Mr. Antheil was quite sufficient to secure for him the travelling scholarship or whatever it was that the American Organization desired to bestow on him. It was more than sufficient. But what happened? This: an ornament of sorts of the commercial resident American Colony, occupying some sort of minor official position, took it upon himself to write to that American Organization imploring them as they value the purity of America's daughters and the spotless folds of Old Glory—imploring them not to honour Mr. Antheil. And why? . . . Because Mr. Antheil was a friend of Mr. Pound! . . . Now I ask you!

As I have said, I do not know Mr. Antheil very well. But I meet him in drawing rooms where he would not be admitted if there were anything against him. That is enough for me and for any sensible human being. But Mr. Pound I know very well indeed—as well as it is possible for one man to know another. And I will vouch for it that no more sober, honest, industrious and wholly virtuous American is to be found on this, or the other side of the Atlantic. To know him is to know that—and to know him is an honour. That that minor American official does not know that, is due to the fact that Mr. Pound does not suffer fools gladly. That is perhaps a fault.

But I think the United States ought to do something to stop that sort of imbecility, which renders it ridiculous in foreign eyes. The American artistic colony of Paris—and, heaven knows, of New York too—do do a great deal to dignify the United States in the eyes of the world. Let the testimony of myself, a foreigner, bear witness to that. Then the non-artistic part of the United States should at least let them alone. The reason why large numbers of American artists live in Europe is almost entirely economic. They are very badly paid; they can live in Paris for almost nothing. There is no conspiracy against the United States, or even against hundred per cent Americanism. They are hundred percenters all right. They make me tired with it most times. And that any obscure and ignorant minor official commercially occupied, should have the power to interfere with the destinies of an artist whom the rest of the world considers to adorn this country . . . well, it makes the whole of Paris and the Russians and Czecho-Slovakians and Lithuanians and Spaniards and the Ruthenians and the Wallachians and Armenians, cackle.

I don't know exactly what is to be done about it—except that Americans should read the poems of Mr. Pound and see that the works of Mr. Antheil are performed often and with some applause. That is bound to come some day. It would be well if it came soon—for that would really be the New World redressing the balance of the Old.

Despite Ford's essay, attention remained fixed on expatriates' debauchery, not their artistry. In the following excerpt from *Harper's Magazine*, Richmond Barrett describes the effect of *The Sun Also Rises* on several young people he met during a transatlantic voyage to Paris. For Barrett, these postadolescents exemplify a new attitude of rebellion among twentieth-century youth, one ultimately more destructive than liberating. He does not blame Hemingway for promoting dissolution. Rather, these college-age readers are simply too immature to appreciate how *The Sun Also Rises* is a cautionary tale that illustrates the consequences of breaking moral boundaries.

From "Babes in the Bois," by Richmond Barrett, in *Harper's,* 156 (May 1928): 724–725, 729–730.

More than a year ago a novel was published which was destined to become the Bible of all the callow cynics who were old enough to shave the down off their chins but not old enough to vote. Men over twenty-one read the book and admired it; but the youngsters learned it by heart and, deserting their families and running away from college, immediately took ship for Paris to be the disciples of the new faith under the awnings of the Dôme and the Rotonde and the other sidewalk cafés. The book, needless to say, was *The Sun Also Rises;* and Ernest Hemingway, that brilliant black sheep from the Middle West, suddenly found himself the reluctant leader of a modern Children's Crusade. Upon the banner that these adolescents carried so proudly aloft there was written, not "Excelsior," but the braver, bitterer word, "Futility." Poor Hemingway! He wrote a hard-boiled muscular book and was hailed as prophet by a crowd of sentimental puppies who went about proclaiming that they weren't appreciated in the land of their birth, that they were eternal rebels, martyred Shelleys, and what not.

In unbiased moments I can still appreciate the stark merits of *The Sun Also Rises;* many a time, however, in the six months after it was issued I grew profoundly bored at the very mention of it. Particularly during a trip abroad in the early spring I cursed the day on which Hemingway was born. All the boys and girls who used to pore dutifully over *Lorna Doone* on shipboard were re-reading marked copies of *The Sun Also Rises,* discussing it furiously over drinks in the bar, quoting it at length, and probably sleeping with it under their pillows—if they ever went to bed!

We sailed at eleven in the morning; by three o'clock in the afternoon the bar was crowded and everybody over fifteen, it seemed, had drunk enough to be argumentative. The sudden haphazard, illogical friendships of an ocean voyage were being formed. Some of these alliances probably led to elopements; others were snapped off abruptly before dinner that very night; one came to a tragic conclusion of murder and suicide just eight days later in the forest of Fontainebleau.

There were five men at my table in the bar. We all looked about the same age. In these days males from twenty to thirty-five differ from one another only in height and weight and coloring. The actual years we have struggled through leave no visible impress upon us. Our particular group had drifted together by a sort of magnetism. Four of us wrote, and the fifth was an artist.

"Have you read *The Sun Also Rises?*" That query was not long in coming. As a starting-point for polite conversation it had run neck-and-neck all winter in New York with "Have you seen 'The Captive'?" and was beginning to have a slight edge on its rival.

"I've read it three times," the man on my right announced.

"I'm reading it now for the third time," my left-hand neighbor chimed in.

At once a deathless friendship sprang up between those two and, forgetting my existence, they began to exchange deep philosophical thoughts across me. The rest of us—the poor wretch who didn't know Hemingway at all and the two whose acquaintance with him was so absurdly superficial—turned to the more humdrum topics of the day.

"I see you've got a Phi Beta Kappa key—what college?"

"Yale, 1918."

"I'm Yale, too, 1916."

"I'm University of Washington, 1917."

And then, of course, at the mention of those years during which the whole civilized world had blown up like a volcano, we got started on our war records. I was leaning over the table now, and the Hemingway lovers were chanting behind me about their doomed generation.

Suddenly one of them—the handsome blond youth to my right—deigned to enter our dull discussion. "They'd never have got me to fight," he told us with superb hauteur. "*I'd* have gone to Leavenworth with Debs."

"Didn't they try to get you?" I asked.

"I was six in 1914," he said, "and nine in 1917."

"I was eight in 1914 and eleven in 1917," the other member of the new Damon-Pythias combination sang out.

"My father tried to thrash me into being a patriot—but he couldn't." This with the air of a professional martyr!

So this explained why the five of us couldn't find a common meeting-ground for more than two consecutive minutes. Three of us had already slumped into middle-age, were as hopelessly out of date as Grand Army veterans; the other two were incandescent youths, mere children; and naturally, like Marchbanks in "Candida," they considered themselves as old as the world and were determined to be bored, bored, bored by everything their elders stood for. They were not only bored but positively outraged at the thought that they were sitting at the table with three men who had been graduated from college. The blond cherub had suffered the ignominy of a single term at one of our most dignified Eastern universities; the dark one, demanding freedom, decrying academic bondage, had refused to matriculate anywhere. As for a Phi Beta Kappa key—that was a badge of shame.

"I may make a mess of my life," quoth Damon. It was obvious that he rather hoped that he would—a glorious, passionate kind of mess. "But at least I won't be ready-made, the sort that's turned out by hundreds."

"I intend to make my own mistakes—not my father's mistakes over and over again," Pythias backed him up. "Come on—let's take a walk around the deck. It's stifling in here."

And off they went, brothers in arms against collegiate mediocrity. . . .

I was curious to find out their views on the subject of their careers. Suddenly I remembered that Damon and Pythias had announced on the first day out that they wrote. Coming upon Damon in the act of reading a novel of mine (I must confess that I had lent it to him; it had never achieved sufficient popularity to push its way into the library of an ocean liner!) I opened fire on him.

"By the way, what sort of thing do you write?" I began.

"Poems—in the modern manner," he returned grandly. "I haven't any patience with most of the fiction that's turned out today," and drooped a languid eyelid in the general direction of my poor effort.

"Have you ever had anything published?" I pursued pleasantly, with veiled malice.

"No—I've never tried." He was lying, of course. I used to make the same excuse myself in my first discouraging year at college, when printed rejections filled my mail-box. "I write only for myself. It's all question of mood; and usually, when the mood has gone by, I tear up what I've done."

"Do you have regular hours for writing?" I led him on.

"Good God, no!" He was indignant at the suggestion. "The middle of the night—when I'm fried—is when I do my best work. How about you?"

"I work every morning from eight-thirty to twelve," I confessed.

He looked once more at my book. "You would!" his expression eloquently conveyed.

"Do you ever expect to finish anything?" I asked.

"No."

Long pause.

"Tom's writing a novel," he brought out at last. (Pythias had been christened "Thomas," by the way.)

I looked properly shocked, as who should say, "What right has he to drag his Muse down to such unspeakable degradation?"

"Oh, not the conventional novel," he hastened to add. "A combination of D. H. Lawrence and Hemingway."

"How far has he got?" I was interested.

"He's finished the three big scenes. He read them to me the other day. I tell you, they're tremendous."

"Is that all?" I inquired politely.

"A chap like Tom is so highly wrought that—well, he's too big for anything *but* the big scenes," I was informed in weighty accents. "I'm afraid he'll never get down to filling in the other parts. It's inspiration or nothing—with us."

He tossed my book aside and picked up something by Jean Cocteau. In other words, I was being dismissed.

Inspiration or nothing! The world will wait many, many years, I fear, before the divine visitation of Tom's novel is vouchsafed it. And that's a pity; for those two youngsters have brains. If only they could have awakened to their infantile silliness some day they might have done brilliant work. Having encountered them again, five months later, on the Left Bank in Paris, I'm inclined to think it's too late now. They're stubbornly committed to an elegant sterility. Strangely enough, they dote on inexhaustible robust forces like Isadora Duncan and the unfortunate Hem-

Hemingway at Shakespeare and Company shortly after arriving in Paris, early 1920s.

ingway; but they consider these fecund divinities of theirs as the great apostles of barrenness and futility. "You are all a doomed generation," quoth Gertrude Stein once; and straightway everyone under twenty who considered himself oppressed and misunderstood fell violently in love with the words of the prophetess. They long to be doomed; if destruction threatens to be tardy, they'll rush to meet it half-way by committing suicide.

Meanwhile they go in for promiscuous dissipation. Very few of them enjoy it; but they're too cowardly to admit that. They stage loud orgies, drink a lot, and stagger around in circles because they have interpreted that sort of nonsense to be their exalted duty. . . .

In 1934 Malcolm Cowley published *Exile's Return*. Part memoir, part literary sociology, the book marked one of the earliest efforts to describe expatriation in 1920s Paris as indicative of a generational mind-set. In the following passages, Cowley compares his own tenure as an ambulance driver in World War I to the adventures of characters in writings by Hemingway, John Dos Passos, and E. E. Cummings. As Cowley claims, for his generation war was more a spectacle than a cause, with young Americans experiencing it as observers rather than participants. The legacy of the global conflict was what Cowley calls a "spectatorial attitude," a sense of looking upon life with detached indifference.

From *Exile's Return: A Narrative of Ideas,* by Malcolm Cowley (New York, 1934); revised and enlarged as *Exile's Return: A Literary Odyssey of the 1920s* (New York: Viking, 1951), pp. 41–47.

. . . our service was, in its own fashion, almost ideal. It provided us with fairly good food, a congenial occupation, furloughs to Paris and uniforms that admitted us to the best hotels. It permitted us to enjoy the once-in-a-lifetime spectacle of the Western

Front. Being attached to the French army, it freed us from the severe and stupid forms of discipline then imposed on American shavetails and buck privates. It confronted us with hardships, but not more of them than it was exhilarating for young men to endure, and with danger, but not too much of it: seldom were there more than two or three serious casualties in a section during the year—and that was really the burden of our complaint. We didn't want to be slackers, *embusqués*. The war created in young men a thirst for abstract danger, not suffered for a cause but courted for itself; if later they believed in the cause, it was partly in recognition of the danger it conferred on them. Danger was a relief from boredom, a stimulus to the emotions, a color mixed with all others to make them brighter. There were moments in France when the senses were immeasurably sharpened by the thought of dying next day, or possibly next week. The trees were green, not like ordinary trees, but like trees in the still moment before a hurricane; the sky was a special and ineffable blue; the grass smelled of life itself; the image of death at twenty, the image of love, mingled together into a keen, precarious delight. And this perhaps was the greatest of the lessons that the war taught to young writers. It revivified the subjects that had seemed forbidden because they were soiled by many hands and robbed of meaning; danger made it possible to write once more about love, adventure, death. Most of my

HEMINGWAY AND COWLEY

Considered the preeminent social historian of the Lost Generation due to *Exile's Return,* Malcolm Cowley also played an important role in establishing Hemingway's academic reputation. As Michael Reynolds notes, Cowley "brought Hemingway's work into a clearer focus for general readers and young college instructors.... Cowley, seeing the [thematic and symbolic] patterns emerge, linked Hemingway to 'the haunted and nocturnal [American] writers, the men who dealt in images that were symbols of an inner world.' That there was an inner world to Hemingway, a world beneath the surface of his fiction, that one needed to read all of his stories to see it—these suggestions moved Hemingway's work out of the category of popular fiction and up to the level of American classics."

But while Cowley saw Hemingway as one of his generation's leading literary lights, the question of how Hemingway regarded Cowley is more complicated.

In a 1932 letter Hemingway calls Cowley a "twirp," and "The Snows of Kilimanjaro" includes a line about a "potato-faced poet" at the Café du Dôme widely presumed to be a veiled slight at the reviewer who had confessed his ambivalence to *Death in the Afternoon* and *Green Hills of Africa.* Beginning in 1944, however, after Cowley edited *The Portable Hemingway,* the writers began a long-running correspondence. Hemingway appreciated Cowley's eagerness to resuscitate his reputation after the beating it had taken in the previous decade, and he helped facilitate (though not without second thoughts) a short biography called "Portrait of Mr. Papa" that Cowley wrote for *Life* in 1949. Yet, while Hemingway on occasion professed fondness for his fellow writer, the relationship between the two never grew beyond its initial businesslike cordiality.

friends were preparing to follow danger into other branches of the army—of any army—that were richer in fatalities.

They scattered a few months later: when the ambulance and camion services were taken over by the American Expeditionary Force, not many of them re-enlisted. Instead they entered the Lafayette Escadrille, the French or Canadian field artillery, the tanks, the British balloon service, the Foreign Legion, the Royal Air Force; a very few volunteered for the American infantry, doing a simple thing for paradoxical reasons. I had friends in distant sectors: one of them flew for the Belgians, another in Serbia, and several moved on to the Italian front, where John Dos Passos drove an ambulance. Ernest Hemingway was also an ambulance driver on that front, until the July night when an Austrian mortar bomb exploded in the observation post beyond the front lines where he was visiting at the time, like a spectator invited to gossip with the actors behind the scenes. E. E. Cummings was given no choice of service. Having mildly revolted against the discipline of the Norton-Harjes Ambulance Corps, and having become the friend of a boy from Columbia University who wrote letters to Emma Goldman, he was shipped off to a French military prison, where he had the adventures later described in *The Enormous Room*. . . . But even in prison threatened with scurvy, or lying wounded in hospitals, or flying combat planes above the trenches, these young Americans retained their curious attitude of non-participation, of being friendly visitors who, though they might be killed at any moment, still had no share in what was taking place.

Somewhere behind them was another country, a real country of barns, cornfields, hemlock woods and brooks tumbling across birch logs into pools where the big trout lay. Somewhere, at an incredible distance, was the country of their childhood, where they had once been part of the landscape and the life, part of a spectacle at which nobody looked on.

This spectatorial attitude, this monumental indifference toward the cause for which young Americans were risking their lives, is reflected in more than one of the books written by former ambulance drivers. Five of the principal characters in Dos Passos's *Nineteen-Nineteen*—the Grenadine Guards, as he calls them—Dick Savage (a Harvard aesthete), Fred Summers, Ed Schuyler, Steve Warner (another Harvard man, but not of the same college set), and Ripley (a Columbia freshman) first enlist in the

Norton-Harjes Ambulance Corps, and then, when the American army takes it over, go south to the Italian front. In February of the last wartime year, Steve Warner reads that the Empress Taitu of Abyssinia is dead, and the Grenadine Guards hold a wake for her. . . .

"Fellers," Fred Summers kept saying, "this ain't a war, it's a goddam madhouse . . . it's a goddam Cook's tour." It remained, for many of us, a goddam crazy Cook's tour of Western Europe, but for those who served longer it became something else as well.

Ernest Hemingway's hero, in *A Farewell to Arms,* is an American acting as lieutenant of an Italian ambulance section. He likes the Italians, at least until Caporetto; he is contemptuous of the Austrians, fears and admires the Germans; of political conviction he has hardly a trace. When a friend tells him, "What has been done this summer cannot have been done in vain," he makes no answer. . . .

The passage dealing with the Italian retreat from river to river, from the mountains beyond the Isonzo along rain-washed narrow roads to the plains of Tagliamento, is one of the few great war stories in American literature: only *The Red Badge of Courage* and a few short pieces by Ambrose Bierce can be compared with it. Hemingway describes not an army but a whole people in motion: guns nuzzling the heads of patient farm horses, munition trucks with their radiator caps an inch from the tailboard of wagons loaded with chairs, tables, sewing machines, farm implements; then behind them ambulances, mountain artillery, cattle and army trucks, all pointed south; and groups of scared peasants and interminable files of gray infantrymen moving in the rain past the miles of stalled vehicles. Lieutenant Frederick [*sic*] Henry is part of the retreat, commanding three motor ambulances and half a dozen men, losing his vehicles in muddy lanes, losing his men, too, by death and desertion, shooting an Italian sergeant who tries to run away—but in spirit he remains a non-participant. He had been studying architecture in Rome, had become a gentleman volunteer in order to see the war, had served two years, been wounded and decorated: now he is sick of the whole thing, eager only to get away.

As he moves southward, the southbound Germans go past him, marching on parallel roads, their helmets visible above the walls. Frightened Italians open fire on him. The rain falls endlessly, and the whole experience, Europe, Italy, the war, becomes a nightmare, with himself as helpless as a man among nightmare shapes. It is only in snatches of dream that he finds anything real—love being real, and the memories of his boyhood. "The hay smelled good and lying in a barn in the hay took away all the years in between. We had lain in hay and talked and shot sparrows with an air rifle when they perched in the triangle cut high up in the wall of the barn. The barn was gone now and one year they had cut the hemlock woods and there were only stumps, dried tree-tops, branches and fireweed where the woods had been. You could not go back"; the country of his boyhood was gone and he was attached to no other.

And that, I believe, was the final effect on us of the war; that was the honest emotion behind a pretentious phrase like "the lost generation." School and college had uprooted us in spirit; now we were physically uprooted, hundreds of us, millions, plucked from our own soil as if by a clamshell bucket and dumped, scattered among strange people. All our roots were dead now, even the Anglo-Saxon tradition of our literary ancestors, even the habits of slow thrift that characterized our social class. We were fed, lodged, clothed by strangers, commanded by strangers, infected with the poison of irresponsibility—the poison of travel, too, for we had learned that problems could be left behind us merely by moving elsewhere—and the poison of danger, excitement, that made our old life seem intolerable. Then, as suddenly as it began for us, the war ended.

When we first heard of the Armistice we felt a sense of relief too deep to express, and we all got drunk. We had come through, we were still alive, and nobody at all would be killed tomorrow. The composite fatherland for which we had fought and in which some of us still believed—France, Italy, the Allies, our English homeland, democracy, the self-determination of small nations— had triumphed. We danced in the streets, embraced old women and pretty girls, swore blood brotherhood with soldiers in little bars, drank with our elbows locked in theirs, reeled through the streets with bottles of champagne, fell asleep somewhere. On the next day, after we got over our hangovers, we didn't know what to do, so we got drunk. But slowly, as the days went by, the intoxication passed, and the tears of joy; it appeared that our composite fatherland was dissolving into quarreling statesmen and oil and steel magnates. Our own nation had passed the Prohibition Amendment as if to publish a bill of separation between itself and ourselves; it wasn't our country any longer. Nevertheless we returned to it: there was nowhere else to go. We returned to New York, appropriately—to the homeland of the uprooted, where everyone you met came from another town and tried to forget it; where nobody seemed to have parents, or a past more distant than last night's swell party, or a future beyond the swell party this evening and the disillusioned book he would write tomorrow.

Three years after *Exile's Return,* another member of the Lost Generation, John Peale Bishop, also described how war affected expatriate writing, Hemingway's in particular. In "The Missing All," published in the *Virginia Quarterly Review,* Bishop (a Princeton friend of Fitzgerald's) argued that Hemingway and Fitzgerald's most lasting contribution to literature was their rebellion against Puritanism. As products of the Midwest, they revolted against the "New England idea" that religion and morality were sufficient buffers against the evil and deceit of modern life. Only by living overseas, where Europe was resigned to Western civilization's decline, could they find an environment conducive to the truth of their experience.

From "The Missing All" by John Peale Bishop, in *Virginia Quarterly Review,* 13 (Winter 1937): 111–114.

"All modern literature comes out of one book by Mark Twain called 'Huckleberry Finn,'" Hemingway allows himself to say in a conversation in "Green Hills of Africa." And to insist upon it, he adds: "All American writing comes from that. There was nothing before. There has been nothing as good since."

And Fitzgerald, toward the end of "The Great Gatsby," has his narrator meditate on the tragedy which has just occurred and remark that all the principals have come out of the Middle West. The body of Gatsby, after the bullet, floats on the bathing mattress around the artificial pool on his Long Island estate. But all that had made the life of Gatsby had come out of the Midwest. This return toward the East was one of the factors that made the time. The Midwesterner had become the American. He was ready to deny the authenticity of any compatriot not of his kind. Sinclair Lewis's Babbitt had superseded an older conception which Henry James had dared call "The American."

Fitzgerald and Hemingway belong to what was in its day the Younger Generation. It was certainly not the first to be called so, but it was the first to gain capitals from the press. And, as Malcolm Cowley has pointed out, it was really the first literary generation in America. There had been groups before, but they were not united by a communion of youth, a sense of experiences shared and enemies encountered simply because they happened to have been born within certain years. They were those who were of an age to be combatant when America declared war on the Central Powers.

Not all of them fought; but most of them had of their own choice supported a uniform of some sort. When they returned from arms, it was in revolt. What they protested against was called Puritanism, which is a fairer name than it deserves; for the enemy was the New England idea, not in its original purity, but in that corrupt state to which it had arrived through the hundred and more years in which the West was settled.

The pioneer had not gone into the wilderness empty-handed. For beyond those two instruments of the Puritan condemnation of nature, the rifle and the axe, he carried the New England idea. In the shadow of the forest, something of his intellectual toughness was shed. When at last the pioneer strode out on the prairies, his skin was toughened by the sun and the rain; he was hardened to the bone; his distrust of nature had not lessened. That hatred of death which is behind the Puritan hatred of life was still with him, but through varying vicissitudes was lost. The meaning of Puritanism is a contempt for mortality; in the Midwest it was forgotten.

The New England idea had never provided the new country with a particularly satisfactory morality. Along the seaboard, it was counterbalanced by other forces, inherited decencies, values transmitted and transmuted, some brought by sailing vessels, all altered by these shores. There was, in brief, a culture, rather cold, but flowering nevertheless in a lovely and inclement air. But across the Appalachians, New England had begun to go bad. It needed the strictness of the village, it demanded the sense of the community. Else it was disembodied. Beyond the mountains, in the limitless expanse of the West, it was not all wrong. But it certainly was not so good.

Mark Twain has shown its shortcomings. To him, it was all meanness and hypocrisy, so that his serious work is one long protest against a morality that neither aided goodness nor sustained honesty. Huckleberry Finn, who is his creator's exponent of natural morality, becomes in Missouri a notoriously bad boy. All is reversed, so that Huck himself is almost convinced that he is lost.

So long ago did the Midwesterner decide that New England morality was inadequate. But with what could he oppose it, unless with conceptions which had been shaped for him, as for all Americans, in Concord and by Walden Pond? The Midwesterner was self-reliant, he had a profound trust in the natural goodness, the sanctity almost, of unrestricted man. If we look closely, we shall see his beliefs return, altered but recognizable, not only in the "Green Hills of Africa" but in all of Hemingway. We shall find them as well in Fitzgerald.

They came from all over, those who made up the Younger Generation, but it is scarcely an accident that those I consider here as its spokesmen had their origin in the Middle West. There were others, no doubt, who equalled them in talent. But the time was favorable to Hemingway and Fitzgerald. They had, as Hemingway was to say later of the garbage men of Havana, the viewpoint. And more than any others who wrote in prose, they succeeded in communicating their emotional attitudes to their contemporaries. They were never consciously regional, as a somewhat older lot of Middle Western writers were: Masters, Sandburg, and the Anderson of those years when Mr. Mencken was proclaiming that Chicago was the literary capital of America. They had no need to be. They could, as Middle Westerners, assume that they were the country. And in many ways they were right. "Wait and see," Masters had written, not all ironically, in 1918, "Spoon River shall be Americee." And now Middletown was spreading from coast to coast its monstrous and monotonous regimentation of mediocrity. Besides, the Younger Generation were conscious of belonging nowhere. How could they have a place in space, whose roots, whether deliberately or through the uncontrolled accident of war, had been destroyed in time?

They converged on Chicago, and one or two, I believe, stayed there. They came to New York, and once so far, found it as simple to cross the Atlantic as to survive in that costly city. From Land's End to Golden Horn they scattered; carried, as it were a knapsack, their childhood through the Alps: saw girls with print dresses over their starving nakedness throw themselves from bridges of Vienna; saw the hungry eyes of boys, ready for depravity, in the underworld of Berlin; saw the collapse of empires. Some sought the more than sunny warmth of the Mediterranean; some reached Persia; a few, even in those years, penetrated Russia. The world was in throes, but, like the Magi in Eliot's poem, when they had come to the end of their journey, they did not know whether it was a birth or a death they had come for. But most Paris attracted them. In the international intellectual ferment there, they were variously aware of their century, increasingly conscious that they were creatures of its catastrophes. There it seemed possible to know what was happening; not that the event was likely to take place there—Paris was too old; but because it was old and sensitive with a very long memory, it seemed possible that the import of the event would be known there sooner than elsewhere. The collapse of the New England idea was only one more loss in the spiritual débâcle of the times. Meanwhile, one could eat on the sidewalks of Paris, drink at every corner, make love in the streets, under the trees.

Beginning in the 1940s, academic critics began to analyze Hemingway's attitude toward expatriation, attempting to determine the similarities and differences between the Lost Generation and nineteenth-century American writers who lived in Europe—Henry James in particular. In his 1960 essay "Hemingway and Europe," John W. Aldridge argues that James looked to Europe for a sense of tradition and social structure, while Hemingway was more interested in the raw material of his own personal experience. As a result, his plots are "extra-environmental," that is, less reliant on the surrounding culture of France, Italy, or Spain than on the particular morality and psychology of his characters.

From "Hemingway and Europe," by John W. Aldridge, in *Shenandoah*, 11 (1960): 11–14, 18–21.

The problem of the American writer's relation to Europe presented itself with particular urgency to the members of James' generation. In confirmation of this, we need think not only of Henry and William but of, among others, their good friend Henry Adams and his concern with the problem. That generation had the advantage of a unique perspective—an historical moment when the division of cultural allegiances between America and Europe had still not been resolved, and it still seemed possible to move in a direct line from the present into the fathering past simply by crossing the Atlantic. The Jameses happened to be uniquely equipped in both intelligence and experience to make the most of the subject, to show it forth in its full significance, to see it finally as part of the equivocal condition, the extremely complex fate, of being an American. But in differing ways and, for the most part, with less richness of result, the problem presented itself to such diverse minds as Washington Irving, Fenimore Cooper, Melville, Fuller, Howells, Stephen Crane, and Edith Wharton—or at least, in the case of Melville and Crane, the general problem of foreign travel as a whole did. Emerson had strongly negative opinions about the benefits of travel for the American writer, and Hawthorne, uncomfortable and alone in England, wrote of home with powerful nostalgia in his journals.

The problem reasserts itself with equal force in the generation which we now take to have initiated the American literary movement—the generation of Sinclair Lewis, Sherwood Anderson, Gertrude Stein, T. S. Eliot, Ezra Pound, and of Hemingway, Fitzgerald, Dos Passos, Thomas Wolfe, Katherine Anne Porter, Archibald MacLeish, and Henry Miller. Again in these writers one sees the problem being phrased with much more vehemence but in the same sets of dialectical opposites that existed for James—American puritanism vs. European sophistication, American innocence vs. European wisdom, American commercialism vs. European humanism, American social vacuity vs. European social complexity. But in the case of these younger writers, there were additional elements that tipped the scale in favor of Europe—such elements as the stimulus of the European artistic renaissance of the first decades of the century; the opportunity to sit at the feet of modernist European as well as exiled British and American masters; and of course the counter-movement in America toward increasing anti-intellectualism and moral puritanism. None of these factors had been half so compelling for James. Essentially, James was a Europeanized or Anglicized American, but his art derived its unique tensions less from European influences than from the experience of Americanism abroad. But the art of the younger generation came under much more direct European influence. In Hemingway one sees Flaubert, Turgenev, and Conrad as well as Mark Twain. Fitzgerald was influenced as much by Conrad as he was by James, Wharton, and Cather. There are strong echoes of Joyce in much of Thomas Wolfe. The French Symbolist poets show clearly in the early work of Eliot, and through Eliot, in the early work of MacLeish. Gertrude Stein learned a great deal from the French Impressionist painters, and she passed on some of their influence in the instruction she gave Hemingway. These writers confirm the truth of Eliot's remark that it is Americans who have the best chance of becoming real Europeans, of merging their native identities with that of the whole continent of Europe.

But to speak of one of the writers of that now older generation, to speak of Hemingway in his relation to Europe, is to speak in paradoxes; for like all good writers Hemingway defies precise classification, and like all good American writers, he is a curious mixture of American and European qualities. He has, for example, written almost nothing about America directly, although he has written almost always about Americans. Certain of the stories in his first collection *In Our Time* have American settings, mostly in the woods of Michigan where he often vacationed as a boy, and *To Have and Have Not* concerns Key West, Florida, which is about as far out of America as one can get and still be in it. But *The Sun Also Rises* is set in France and Spain, *A Farewell to Arms* in Italy and Switzerland, *For Whom the Bell Tolls* in Spain, *Across the River and into the Trees* in Italy, and *The Old Man and the Sea* in Cuba. Hemingway himself has found it as impossible to live in America as James did, having worked for several years as both a journalist and writer in Paris, settled for a time in Key West, and until the recent change of regime, in Cuba. . . .

In certain respects Hemingway found in Europe what James found: relief from spiritual poverty and social thinness of American life, and the perspective necessary to write both about America from the distance of Europe and about Europe from the distance of the American. But although Hemingway's principal theme is the American in Europe, it is not his major subject, as it was James'. James found in Europe a richly complex culture and society in which the ironic contrast between American innocence and Old World sophistication could be dramatized on a variety of significant levels. He enjoyed all the benefits of his historical moment, and he took advantage of them with the help of a critical and creative intelligence vastly more complicated than Hemingway's. Hemingway found in Europe not so much a society as a certain set of materials peculiarly suited to his creative personality and peculiarly necessary to the operation of his creative talent. In fact, one finds in his books very little portraiture of Europe itself or of Europeans. Europe appears to serve him almost solely as a psychological background for the dramatic situations of his mostly American characters. And once his American characters are "placed" in Europe, it does not seem to matter very much that they *are* in Europe, for they have little to do with Europe, and Hemingway himself is not really interested artistically in Europe. His dramatic situations—or let us say his single recurrent dramatic *situation*—appears to be ultimately extra-environmental, to be composed of a certain set mechanism of challenge, response, failure or success. The situation exists, finally, not in Europe or anywhere else but in the world of his art. The European environment is a still-life painting as it pretty much is in *The Sun Also Rises,* particularly in the descriptions of Spanish landscape, or it is a reflector of moods as it is in *A Farewell to Arms,* or it is a carnival setting which contrasts ironically with the main action—as it does in the Pamplona sections of *The Sun Also Rises.*

In much the same way, Hemingway's books are essentially not about people but about their situation, his stock situation, the situation of test in circumstances in crisis—so that they are in a sense parables of human action rather than portraits of human beings. On the basis of this, one might hazard the distinction that

---

THE RISE OF HEMINGWAY SCHOLARSHIP

By the early 1950s Hemingway was not only the most famous twentieth-century American writer—he was also becoming the subject of several scholarly analyses, some of which he appreciated, others of which he found irksome. The earliest, most influential Hemingway scholar was Princeton professor Carlos Baker, whose *Hemingway: The Writer as Artist* (1952) was the first major study of the author's works. (Baker also went on to write the first authoritative Hemingway biography in 1969 and edit the first collection of letters in 1981.) Although wary of academic critics, Hemingway nevertheless appreciated Baker's interpretation of his writing, mainly because Baker focused on its thematic and symbolic import. He was far less tolerant of scholars interested in its autobiographical origins. He tangled with Yale University instructor Charles A. Fenton over *The Apprenticeship of Ernest Hemingway* (1954), which examined the genesis of the writer's style in his Oak Park youth and subsequent career as a reporter for *The Kansas City Star* and *The Toronto Star.* Hemingway was particularly annoyed when Fenton tried to interview his brothers and sisters, insisting that critics should respect a writer's privacy. But the scholar who most infuriated him was Philip Young, whose psychoanalytic study *Hemingway* (1952) suggested that Hemingway's 1918 wounding in Italy was the psychological key to his writing—an interpretation that the author found reductive. Initially, Hemingway refused Fenton and Young permission to quote from his novels and stories. He quickly relented, however, perhaps realizing that literary critics were going to analyze his work whether he liked it or not.

James was a real novelist because his situation was centered in his people and their relationships to one another and to the social world, while Hemingway is innately a short-story writer because his concern is with situations (or a single situation) and with the relations of people not to one another but to the abstract forces of destiny or fatality. Hemingway has no society in the Jamesean sense, but he does have a situational world composed of metaphorical constructions of his ideas, and this world is, as I have said, extra-environmental, for it draws not upon the observable social scene but upon psychically-engendered elements of crisis and response to crisis.

Yet it is obvious that the world of Hemingway's novels depends to a very important secondary degree upon emotional as well as physical circumstances peculiar to Europe. One notices, for example, how very often his ironic effects are achieved through the use of the point-of-view of the American stranger abroad, and how often his ironic and dramatic effects are achieved through the use of Americans seen in terms of the moral or professional code of Europeans such as bullfighters, soldiers, British white hunters, Italian bartenders, and headwaiters. Even more importantly, the condition of foreignness abroad, of Americans seen out of context and without the support of their native habits, is absolutely central to the dramatic situation with which Hemingway appears to be obsessed. And when the condition of foreignness is coupled with the condition of European crisis, whether it is European war, European emotional fatigue, or European ceremonials and sports, we have the Hemingway dramatic situation in its most characteristic form.

The purest examples of this are to be found, in my opinion, in the first two novels—*The Sun Also Rises* and *A Farewell to Arms*. The people of *The Sun Also Rises* are perfect embodiments of the worst effects of the condition of foreignness. They are portrayed as being unmoored, disenchanted, isolated from every kind of relationship with social and moral order except that which they create for themselves in the form of an "in-group" etiquette. It is not surprising that this etiquette of theirs is no more than a civilian adaptation of the code of survival of men at war, or that it is an American exile adaptation of the code of European men of sport. It insists upon absolute concentration on process and method—the task immediately at hand, whether it be the task of taking another drink or of simply living one's life—

and rigid avoidance of thought and emotion. Robert Cohn of course both thinks and feels, and so constitutes the destructive agent. It is he who breaks the rules, and it is he who at the end is broken by a far stronger set of rules than those he has broken. For the code of the bullfighter Romero is brought up against the code-violator as well as against the American exile code, and it is Romero's code which is finally triumphant, and his values that are shown, like the earth itself, to abide forever. The condition of European crisis is juxtaposed with the condition American foreignness, and the test ends in failure for our side.In *A Farewell to Arms* the situation is basically the same. Frederic Henry is in fact a man at war, but still a foreigner in Europe, and he lives initially by the code of the fighting man, even though as a foreigner he knows that the war is not his war and that he is not really a fighting man. He is, nonetheless, a great respecter of the rules, and is fully aware of the dangers of emotion and thought. But the condition of crisis puts a severe strain on the rules; it is, in fact, one of the major ironies of the novel that it is the war itself which breaks the rules by wounding Frederic and violating his neutrality. And when this occurs, he succumbs to emotion in spite of himself, begins genuinely to love Catherine Barkley, and to find in his love for her a substitute for the security which adherence to the rules had formerly given him. But the condition of crisis still obtains, is, in fact, worsened by the love affair which, by being conducted without regard for the taboos against emotion, is open to the destructive force of fatality. This force exacts its punishment through the death of Catherine in childbirth and the resulting isolation of Frederic in the condition of foreignness. . . .

Writing in the *Sewanee Review* in 1965, Christof Wegelin expands on Aldridge's thesis, applying the contrast between Hemingway and James to a wider variety of Hemingway texts. As Wegelin notes, Hemingway's novels and stories are striking for abandoning the "novel of manners" form associated with James. That is, while James's drama almost always arises from a clash between the habits and customs of different cultures, Hemingway's characters exist in a world where values have deteriorated, thus depriving them of firm standards to guide their conduct.

From "Hemingway and the Decline of International Fiction," by Christof Wegelin, in *Sewanee Review*, 73 (1965): 285, 295–298.

One of the consequences of our colonial origins has been the creation of the literary genre known as "International Fiction." This is the fiction in which Americans are brought in contact with Europeans, usually in Europe, and it is one of the forms which our attempts at self-definition and self-discovery have quite naturally taken. Its development has been tied closely to our changing relations with Europe: its rise in the nineteenth century was expressive of what Daniel Boorstin has called "our tendency to discover ourselves as a kind of non-Europe," that is, the tendency to define ourselves in terms of our deviation from old-world molds; and its decline in the present century reflects the melting of the cis-Atlantic and trans-Atlantic worlds into one world, the consequent mitigation of transatlantic contrasts, and the putative end of the usefulness for national self-definition. All this explains why America produced this functional literary genre, but its lustre derives from the achievement of a few practitioners, preeminent among them Henry James. James's work benefited from the happy conjunction of his cosmopolitanized sensibility with a moment in the social history of his country when the tide of American travellers in Europe rose to unheard-of proportions and, as James later said, Europe was "constantly in requisition as the more salient American stage," a "great lighted and decorated scene" for showing forth the American character. James therefore serves as a norm by which the development of international fiction can be measured and assessed, and what follows is quite simply an attempt to characterize and in part explain Hemingway's European fiction with reference to the Jamesian norm and thereby to place him in this development. . . .

When all is said and done . . . the transformation of international fiction in Hemingway must be characterized by two criteria, one formal, one thematic, though the two impinge on each other. The conflict between the manners of different nations has disappeared as a dramatic principle. Even in the short "Banal Story," the contrast between the tawdry jargon describing what Americans take for "the full life" and the dignity and passion surrounding Maera's death in Spain (one of the simple things) takes shape entirely in the mind of the reluctant expatriate; the piece is mere meditation—it has no plot. Elsewhere in Hemingway the international contrast of manners has disappeared even as a theme, and with it has disappeared the archetypal plot of international marriage which absolutely monopolized the earlier stories of transatlantic contact. The total extinction of the international marriage motif is in fact as striking as its sudden appearance was some fifty years earlier. In one of the prefaces written after the turn of the century, James recalled the historical situation which had practically launched his career: "The international relation had begun to present itself 'socially' . . . as a relation of intermarrying; but nothing was meanwhile so striking as that these manifestations took always the same turn. The European of 'position' married the young American woman, or the young American woman married the European of position—one scarce knew how best to express the regularity of it. . . . The bridal migrations were eastward and without exception—as rigidly as if settled by statute." As he was writing, the conditions recorded in the preface were already passing into history, and after what used to be called The Great War (the very name reminding us that the present of one generation becomes the past of the next), the international scene which engaged the new writers (as the older scene had engaged James and his contemporaries) was transformed. The terms of James's preface do not fit Hemingway's situations. Though the migrations are still eastward, in Hemingway it is mostly the men who migrate. There are no bridal migrations; in fact, there are no brides, in James's sense of the word, nor—for that matter—young men of position. And though Lieutenant Henry and Jake Barnes are American and Catherine Barkley and Lady Brett are British, what gives them their characteristic stamp, what ultimately shapes their lives, are war traumas, not national manners.

Nor is their conduct directed by any standards but those of the classless polyglot avant-garde in which we see them move, unattended by guardians of any kind. The extraordinary freedom with which James *occasionally* endowed his bourgeois heroines by killing off their parents and guardians (one thinks of Isabel Archer or Milly Theale) is now the natural condition of an existence outside the bourgeois order. The love relationship of course remains central; this Hemingway has in common with James. What has changed is the conditions which frame and doom it. The contrast between the two writers and the societies they record can be made ludicrously clear by juxtaposing, for instance, "An International Episode" with *The Sun Also Rises;* in both stories love between Americans and English fails, in James's world of rigid social norms because of a conflict of manners, in Hemingway's because of one of those "simple things." The case of Maria and Robert Jordan differs only slightly. Though there is

TRUE AT FIRST LIGHT: HEMINGWAY'S EXPATRIATE SAGA CONTINUES

Among the many events commemorating the Hemingway centennial in July 1999, none was as important or as controversial as the publication of *True at First Light: A Fictional Memoir*, culled from a sprawling manuscript inspired by Hemingway's 1953–1954 safari to Africa with his fourth and last wife, Mary. As does its nonfiction predecessor *Green Hills of Africa* (to which it inevitably invites comparison), the novel depicts Africa as the last destination in the modern world where the expatriate can put fundamental values such as truth and self-reliance to the test. It also stands (as does *Green Hills*) as an extended meditation on the morality of work and craftsmanship governing both writing and big-game hunting. Yet, in keeping with the general trend of Hemingway's post-1945 work—much of which he had trouble finishing—*True at First Light* also betrays the self-consciousness that the Hemingway legend and persona inflicted on its author. Indeed, the most fascinating aspect of the book is the implicit struggle between two Hemingways: the unflappably stoic hunter whose masculine prowess commands the respect of Kenyan locals, and the aging, sentimental writer who grows infatuated with a native girl dubbed Debba while his aggressive wife Miss Mary stalks her own lion on the plains. While its literary merits are questionable, the autobiographical allure of *True at First Light* more than compensates for its faults. Like *A Moveable Feast*, *Islands in the Stream*, and *The Garden of Eden*, it reveals a writer raging against the dying of his light, trying to convince both himself and his audience that his powers of perception were not diminishing—an effort that Hemingway only abandoned seven years later with a blast from a shotgun.

nothing cosmopolitan about her, though she is the child of her country and momentarily Jordan can "wonder how they will like Maria in Missoula, Montana," none of this counts in the end. Like the lives of Barnes and Lady Brett, their lives are warped by the wrathful time; their marriage, too, fails not for being international but because of another of those simple things.

Another theme of the nineteenth century, the concern with the nature of democratic exile, fell before the transformation of the international scene. Though Robert Jordan couches his political beliefs in the language of the Declaration of Independence, his thinking—and Hemingway's—contains no trace of the traditional American concern with the nature of nobility, with Emerson's "Nature's Gentlemen" or Melville's "kingly commons"—that is, with the contrast between nobility of birth and nobility of talent which permeates the international stories of the earlier time. Nor is Hemingway herein exceptional in his time. There may be traces of this contrast in other writers, but only traces. Dos Passos may be taken as symptomatic. Though his point of view has always been primarily social and political, the question of nobility occurs even in his work at most as a rare passing allusion. He focussed on the phenomena of the new day. And if the multiple colors of his politics merge in what seems at times a blank despair before the threat posed for the individual by the soulless institutional machines of our time—the army, finance capitalism, the Communist party, etc., Hemingway shared the sense of the individual's exposure. But for him the threat lay elsewhere—in a natural order of which the destructiveness of man is a mere part. As he put it in a much-quoted passage in *Death in the Afternoon*, "the unescapable reality, the one thing any man may be sure of, the only security" is death. It was what he considered their "intelligent interest in death" and its manifestation in the bullfight which first attracted him to the Spaniards. The bullfighter—that is, the good bullfighter—may be regarded as his Natty Bumppo, his model of Nature's nobleman. But this is straining the point, for history had abolished the type along with other hallowed abstractions, and a burst of Austrian shrapnel simplified the question of conduct almost beyond recognition. . . .

More recently, critics have begun looking at the historical and biographical implications of expatriation in Hemingway's writing, examining how characters reveal their emotions and attitudes through their relationship to the particular place they inhabit. J. Gerald Kennedy writes about the different meanings that Paris possesses for various Hemingway characters, for example. In this excerpt from his 1996 essay "Hemingway, Hadley, and Paris: The Persistence of Desire," he examines how Hemingway's guilt over his failed first marriage to Hadley Richardson permeates his post 1920s writing, especially "The Snows of Kilimanjaro" and two posthumously published works, *Islands in the Stream* and *The Garden of Eden*.

From "Hemingway, Hadley, and Paris: The Persistence of Desire," by J. Gerald Kennedy, in *The Cambridge Companion to Hemingway*, edited by Scott Donaldson (New York: Cambridge University Press, 1996), pp. 210–213.

By 1936, however, Hemingway had gained the emotional and temporal distance necessary to begin the consuming imaginative project of his later career: the fictional reconstruction or reclamation of his early years in Paris. Using his 1933–34 safari in Africa to construct the immediate setting of "The Snows of Kilimanjaro," he portrayed (in another suggestive move) the situation of a dying writer named Harry who has "destroyed his talent" and who toward the end of his life experiences flashbacks to all of the places and events he has saved to write about and now never will. Reminiscent of the method of Joyce or Faulkner in its use of an italicized flow of images—representing the stream of consciousness—the story offers a virtual resumé of Hemingway's travels from 1922 onward. Within this framework, which fore-grounds the African scene and the writer's bitter exchanges with his wife Helen, Hemingway accords special importance to Harry's memories of Paris.

Remembrance evokes two distinct phases in the writer's life, associated with different wives and different parts of the city. With Helen, the "rich bitch"[2] whom Harry has married cynically in his middle years, he is obliged to ask: "Where did we stay in Paris?" (43). Significantly, he cannot recall the Parisian places he has known with her, the plush quarters at the Hôtel Crillon and at the Pavillion Henri-Quatre (in the suburb of St. Germain-en-Laye), which connote precisely the luxury and excess that Harry intermittently blames for the destruction of his talent. When Helen reminds him that he once "loved it there" at those elegant hotels, the writer replies sardonically, "Love is a dunghill, . . . and I'm the cock that gets on it to crow"(43). His self-contempt, which exceeds even his scorn for Helen, arises from his sense of failure and dissolution. The parts of Paris he has shared with Helen seem in retrospect as meaningless as the marriage that festers on the African plain.

He entertains much richer and more sustaining memories of the Paris that he knew earlier with his first wife, the one he quarreled with but also loved. In an extended flashback the writer admits betraying his first wife while on a journalistic assignment in Constantinople (which Hemingway visited in 1922), and he likewise admits his obsessive longing for another woman, "the one who left him" (48), a shadowy figure who recalls Agnes von Kurowsky, the Red Cross nurse whom Hemingway loved in Italy in 1918. But his feelings for the unnamed first wife nevertheless seem durable and genuine; after returning to Paris after the spectacle of the Greek-Turkish war, Harry feels "glad to be home" safely "back at the apartment with his wife that now he loved again" (49). In a subsequent flashback, he recollects more explicitly the working-class quarter where he has lived with her, remembering "the smell of dirty sweat and poverty and drunkenness at the Café des Amateurs and the whores at the Bal Musette they lived above" (51). "There was never another part of Paris that he loved like that," Hemingway writes, asserting the devotion of the dying writer (and perhaps that of the living author) to the old neighborhood and—implicitly—to the earlier marriage associated with it.

This evocation of the Quarter around the Place Contrescarpe marks an interesting move, for the ostensible focus of Harry's affection—the neighbors, the shopowners, the "sprawling trees," the ancient "white plastered houses," the narrow streets of the quartier, the "two rooms in the apartments where they lived"—conspicuously avoids direct mention of the first wife, who hovers like a ghost about the place where Harry has "written the start of all he was to do" (51). Without naming names, that is, Hemingway invests the scene of prior happiness, the tiny apartment over the bal musette, with nostalgic desire, allowing place to function as a metonym of irreplaceable human presence. Mindful of the pitfalls inherent in the autobiographical fallacy (reading the text naively as a record of the author's life), we must note the obvious about this passage: It portrays in its concrete particulars the very quartier where Hemingway launched his own career in 1922–23, and (ten years after the breakup of his first marriage) it also evokes, albeit indirectly, the memory of the woman inextricably associated with those early years. Hemingway composed the story, perhaps not coincidentally, as his marriage to Pauline foundered upon bitterness, boredom, and mistrust. Suggestively, the memory of the old neighborhood fills the dying writer with a desire for all that has been lost, all that cannot be recovered in his broken life. He observes with remorse that he has "never written about Paris. Not the Paris that he cared about" (52). Yet in "The Snows of Kilimanjaro," Hemingway had indeed begun to write about the Paris that *he* loved, initiating—in however tentative a fashion—the project of restoring Hadley to her place in the narrative. . . .

As events transpired, though, conflict—both matrimonial and military—postponed Hemingway's work on the Paris book. During the Spanish civil war, his visits to the city with his new love, Martha Gellhorn, gave him further occasion to reflect on the persistence of desire and its ineluctable association, in his life, with Paris. During the early 1940s, however, the great problem of liberating France from Nazi occupation overshadowed the private, literary task of reconstructing the Paris years that mattered to Hemingway. A sign of his continuing longing for that lost world emerges in a 1942 letter to Hadley, where he remarks that in life "the good luck is to have had all the wonderful things and times we had. Imagine if we had been born at a time [like the present] when we could never have had Paris when we were young."[3] In 1944, Hemingway participated as a journalist-guerilla fighter in the liberation of "the city [he] love[d] best in all the world," and shortly after the end of the war he embarked on two longer narratives that betrayed his continuing need to excavate the long-repressed story of Paris in the early years.

Several months before Hemingway's fourth marriage to Mary Welsh, he conceived the idea of a three-part sea story that drew on his experiences of the early 1940s, fishing and hunting German submarines in the Gulf of Mexico. In the "Bimini" section that opens the posthumously published *Islands in the Stream* (1970), Hemingway projects details from his own past into the story of painter Thomas Hudson, who cruises the Gulf with his three sons and who remembers Paris in the 1920s, when he was married to the mother of his eldest son, Tom. When his boys ask him to talk about Paris as it was back then, Hudson obliges by reminiscing about acquaintances like Harry Crosby, James Joyce, Ezra Pound, and Ford Madox Ford. As a painter he has also known Picasso, Braque, Miro, Masson, and Pascin. He recalls the flat "over the sawmill," where he lived with baby Tom and his mother, and the nearby Closerie des Lilas and the Jardin de Luxembourg. When he is not fishing, though, Hudson mostly broods on his own loneliness and on the consciousness that through "one disastrous error of judgment" after another, he had broken up his marriage to Tom's mother. "I only really loved one woman and then lost her," he admits to himself. News of young Tom's death in the war colors the action in the "Cuba" section, where Hemingway, in an act of transparent wish-fulfillment, portrays Hudson's brief, intense reunion with the woman whom he has loved and lost. In the third section, "At Sea," the painter reflects on the ephemerality of happiness, on "the time of innocence" when Hudson and his first wife would go to the Closerie together: "They would put Tom to bed and sit there together in the evenings at the old café, completely happy to be with each other." . . . This crucial remembrance of things past occurs just before Hudson receives a presumably fatal wound from a sniper hidden in a mangrove thicket. The painter's preoccupation with the Paris of his youth suggests Hemingway's implicit urge to memorialize his *own* past, but the fictionalizing of the *Islands* manuscript also suggests a countervailing need to disguise the autobiographical element.

The Garden of Eden, another narrative begun in 1946 and destined never to be completed, evokes the early years of Paris mainly through a subplot dropped from the abbreviated edition of the novel that appeared in 1986. While focusing mainly on the androgynous experiments of David Bourne, a young American novelist, and his sexually ambivalent wife, Catherine, this surprising novel about expatriate liaisons and gender reversals originally contained a parallel account of the sexual "changings" undertaken by painter Nick Sheldon and his wife Barbara, who live on a cobblestone street in a small, unheated studio in the fifth *arrondissement* near the Place Contrescarpe. Though they sometimes dine at the Brasserie Lipp, the Sheldons have little money and content themselves with giving each other small gifts, like the brioche Nick brings his wife for breakfast. Not coincidentally Barbara bears a striking physical resemblance to Hadley: "Her face was fresh scrubbed and very delicately freckled and her red-gold hair was shining brushed and came down to the square collar of her sweater."[4] In this subplot Hemingway seems poised to convert deeply personal material from his life with Hadley into sensational fiction. But he refrained: Except for a few wholly imagined episodes set in the south of France—one portraying Barbara's infidelity and Nick's almost simultaneous death in a bicycle accident—Hemingway dropped the Sheldons and focused most of the bulky manuscript on the Bournes and their bisexual friend Marita. *The Garden of Eden* draws its main imaginative force not from the author's nostalgia for the early days in Paris but—insofar as autobiographical sources may be discerned—from the more complicated triangular relations that developed in Schruns and on the Riviera after Pauline entered the lives of Ernest and Hadley in 1925–26. . . .

Donald Pizer has also examined the influence that memories of Hadley and Paris in the early 1920s exerted over Hemingway later in life. In this excerpt from *American Expatriate Writing and the Paris Moment* (1996), Pizer explores how the twin imperatives of artistic and marital dedication are for Hemingway subject to a combination of discipline and chance in *A Moveable Feast.*

From *American Expatriate Writing and the Paris Moment* by Donald Pizer (Baton Rouge: Louisiana State University Press, 1996), pp. 16–19.

Hemingway links two major themes to this central trope of the capacity of Paris to nurture the artist. The first, present throughout *A Moveable Feast,* is that Paris is a place to work, not to play. Hemingway is shocked when Fitzgerald, unable to work, "laid the failure to Paris, the town best organized for a writer to write in." What Hemingway means by *organized* is that he has shaped his own life into a circuit of nourishment and productivity. Most daytime hours are carefully hoarded—especially after January 1924, when the Hemingways return to Paris with their child—for the slow process of writing and rewriting, and anything distracting him from or interfering with this activity must be resisted. Hemingway describes in some detail, in "The End of an Avocation," the seductive appeal of race handicapping, which he resists finally, "because it took too much time, I was getting too involved" (62). And he describes his resentment on several occasions when his workplace sanctuary, the Closerie des Lilas, is invaded by outsiders or threatened with change by the installation of an "American bar."

Hemingway of course devoted much effort throughout his career to cultivating a sometimes self-serving image of the commitment and pain necessary in pursuit of the writer's craft. But whatever doubts there might be about the actual amount of time Hemingway devoted to his literary labors during his early Paris years, the *idea* of work functions successfully as a literary construct in *A Moveable Feast.* The sketches, in their various ways, present an account of a young writer drawing strength and inspiration from his surroundings while resisting their sapping blandishments, and thereby achieving the skill necessary to produce *In Our Time* and *The Sun Also Rises.* Hemingway's work ethic in *A Moveable Feast* functions much like the trope of artistic potency in that both reveal how an American writer can at once draw upon the distinctive beneficial attributes of a foreign culture and yet retain his distinctive American values. The avid consumer of Turgenev novels borrowed from Shakespeare & Co. and of Cézannes viewed at the Musée du Luxembourg was also anxious to return home to his wife and child and was contemptuous toward the bohemian wastrels and sexual "misfits" of Montparnasse.

The second major theme that Hemingway links to the trope of Paris's capacity to satisfy the artist's hunger is that of luck. Hemingway describes himself in *A Moveable Feast* as someone who practices many of the conventional artifices for placating fate. He carries a rabbit's foot and will knock on wood to ward off misfortune. But he also connects the idea of luck to the hunger motif. Several times during the work he and Hadley congratulate themselves on their good luck in being young and happy and living and working in Paris. In addition, they are often lucky at the track, though Hemingway is quick to note that skill and inside information also help in picking winners.

All these themes come together in the sketch "A False Spring." Hemingway and Hadley have won at the races, and after some seafood at an expensive restaurant they walk through the heart of Paris reminiscing about the good fortune they have experienced since arriving in Europe. They pause on a bridge over the Seine. "We looked and there it all was: our river and our city and the island of our city. 'We're too lucky,' she said" (55). They are hungry again and examine a menu outside a restaurant. . . .

Hemingway is asking us, in this sketch, to view his and Hadley's happiness in the context of time as time is expressed within the motifs of hunger and luck. All life seems simple and literal to Hemingway initially, because he is living in the present. He has won at the races and is therefore lucky, and he has had his hunger assuaged by a good meal. Hadley's comments that "memory is hunger" and that she meant "lucky in other ways" disturb and confuse him because he is still "too stupid" to understand her recognition and acceptance of mutability—that the freshness and excitement of youth, of living in the "moonlight," will pass, leaving the hunger of memories (that is, a desire for the good life of the past) and a realization that to be happy, given that all things change, is to be lucky. Paris, as a "very old city," is the proper setting for this interplay between the innocence of youth (Hemingway's role) and the wisdom of experience (Hadley's role). Eventually, of course, Hemingway will enter the world of experiential knowledge and will act out fully, in the writing of *A Moveable Feast,* his hunger for the lucky days of the past.

The interrelated motifs of sustenance (including the work theme) and luck reach a tragic climax in the conclusion of *A Moveable Feast,* set in Schruns, with Hemingway's earlier characterization of himself as an innocent playing a large role in the climax. Schruns is in one sense a surrogate for Paris, since it is an excellent place to work on the criteria Hemingway has established in connection with Paris. There is much good food and drink, pleasant companionship, and Hadley. In its isolation as a mountain town in winter it is also a kind of private Eden, seemingly timeless and inviolate in its routine of writing, skiing, eating, reading, and lovemaking. It constitutes, in brief, a "happy and innocent" place and moment (207). But "during our last year in the mountains new people came deep into our lives and nothing was ever the same again" (207). These interlopers—not named by Hemingway—are the "pilot fish" John Dos Passos and two others he guides, Sara and Gerald Murphy. The Murphys are a more ingratiating variation on the fashionable literati surrounding Pound whom Hemingway had eluded in Paris. But now, reassured by Dos Passos, he allows himself to be praised and taken up by them and thus finds himself, in his "inexperience" (208), drawn into the orbit of the idle rich whose sycophantic clinging and whose jealous interruption of the pattern of hunger and creativity break the productive circuit of the writer in luck. And he succumbs, only to discover that the rich, "when they have passed and taken the nourishment they needed, leave everything deader than the roots of any grass Attila's horses' hooves have ever scoured" (208).

This ravaging of the writer's landscape of creative fertility is completed by another rich "infiltrator" (209), the charming young woman Pauline Pfeiffer—also not named—who in the role of companion to the often neglected Hadley makes herself desirable to Hemingway. "The husband now has two attractive girls around when he has finished work. One is new and strange and if he has bad luck he gets to love them both" (210). In one sense, of course, Hemingway's use of *luck* in this instance can be viewed as an effort to dodge his personal responsibility for becoming involved with Pauline. But the term also relates, in the context of its earlier usage, to the theme of the inevitability of change in human affairs and especially to the transitory character of happiness. "Luck" is to possess happiness, "bad luck" is to see the happy moment pass.

Hemingway consummates his relationship with Pauline later that winter in Paris, on his way back from New York to Schruns, but once he has returned to Schruns he and Hadley are temporarily reunited. "I worked well and we made great trips, and I thought we were invulnerable again, and it wasn't until we were out of the mountains in late spring, and back in Paris that the other thing started again" (211). With this fall from innocence, "Paris was never the same again" (211). The Paris that Hemingway creates before his fall is thus a kind of writer's Eden in which the city's capacity to nourish his creative potency is richly productive. But his moment of luck is susceptible to time and thus change, with the idle rich and the seductive woman the agents of a fall from the innocence of a pure work ethic and a pure sexuality. Paris can never be the same, Hemingway concludes, because he himself has changed. He has become less the American innocent he was and more the bohemian expatriate he had resisted becoming. And this, to his mind, is a fall from grace. . . .

As these various essays suggest, life in Paris affected Hemingway in different ways. His work likewise reflects diverse responses to the challenge of life abroad. Additional secondary sources about expatriation are offered in the "For Further Study" section of the bibliography of this guide.

NOTES

1. Shari Benstock, *Women of the Left Bank: Paris 1900–1940* (Austin: University of Texas Press, 1986), p. 35.

2. Ernest Hemingway, "The Snows of Kilimanjaro," in his *The Complete Short Stories of Ernest Hemingway* (New York: Scribners, 1987), p. 45. Subsequent references to Hemingway's stories are cited in the text.

3. Ernest Hemingway to Hadley Mowrer, 23 July 1942, in *Ernest Hemingway: Selected Letters, 1917–1961,* edited by Carlos Baker (New York: Scribners, 1981), p. 537.

4. Ernest Hemingway, *The Garden of Eden*, Unpublished manuscripts, Item 422a, Folder 37, The Ernest Hemingway Collection, John F. Kennedy Library, Boston.

5. Ernest Hemingway, *A Moveable Feast* (New York: Scribners, 1964), p. 192. Subsequent references to this work are cited within the text.

EXPATRIATE MODERNISM AND OTHER ART FORMS

Thus far, expatriate modernism has been described only as a literary movement—a reasonable approach, since Hemingway's *métier* was the written word and since he most influenced the novel and the short story. Yet, one should not assume that Paris in the 1920s was a haven exclusively populated by writers. The expatriate community included painters, musicians, photographers, and dancers who also found the city liberating. Just as Hemingway, Gertrude Stein, Ezra Pound, and others aimed to reinvent literature, these artists pledged allegiance to the new and developed original techniques that transformed their respective fields. Hemingway's affiliation with these other arts was tangential at best. He expressed little affinity for modernist music or ballet, premieres of which sometimes proved so scandalous that they provoked riots. He was, however, a devotee of painting, often describing his goal as achieving on paper what artists such as Paul Cézanne (1839–1906) had achieved on canvas.

Hemingway was by no means unique in drawing literary ideas from other art forms. Modernist innovation in one medium typically inspired experimentation in others, leading to a sense of a fruitful cross between literature and the visual and performance arts. And while expatriate modernists did not subscribe to one strict set of goals—indeed, they often debated each other's methods—the different arts did share parallels. In general, modernists rejected "civilized" ideals of artistic taste, embracing instead "primitive" modes of expression that they believed were more instinctive and therefore more authentic. They were also concerned with the effect of technology on human life, the reason their work evokes the shapes and sounds of machines. Finally, they wanted to breathe new life into overly familiar emotions through the use of radical colors, perspectives, and dance moves. These techniques allowed them to communicate through abstraction; rather than depict their subject matter in a literal or realistic fashion, modernists reinvented it through visionary modes of expression.

The first modernist wave in Paris was led by painters somewhat ambiguously categorized as postimpressionists. By the late 1890s the reserved colors and dreamy rural vistas associated with artists such as Claude Monet and August Renoir had lost the shock value that in the 1870s and 1880s led critics to dub them impressionists. Their work was too sleepy and calm, even too escapist, to convey the industrialism and technology that marked the ebb of the nineteenth century. Cézanne had passed through an impressionistic period, but he came to rebel against its soft color scheme and shapelessness, preferring bolder reds and greens and starker, more defined edges. In impressionist landscapes, objects often blur together into a fuzzy whole. In famous Cézanne canvases such as *Bathers* (1898–1905) or *Mont Ste-Victorie* (1904–1906), however, the individual element possesses its own form and presence, creating a checkerboard effect as each stands out in contrast to the others. "Treat nature according to the sphere, the cone and the cylinder," Cézanne said in a phrase that became a mantra for Paris-based painters. The two most celebrated followers of this advice, French-born Henri Matisse and Spanish expatriate Pablo Picasso, developed

Picasso's 1906 portrait of Gertrude Stein: the flattened, mask-like features reflect the painter's fascination with the primitivism of African tribal art.

Cézanne's interest in shape by breaking down the implied angles of perspective into two dimensions instead of three. Instead of molding shapes to convey the contour and depth that the eye normally perceives, they flattened their subject's physical dimensions, presenting it in a radically unfamiliar way.

Matisse gained his initial notoriety with one painting exhibited at the 1905 Autumn Salon in Paris. *La Femme au chapeau* (Woman with Hat) outraged sensibilities for its unconventional use of color. In accenting this portrait of his wife, the painter employed strokes of orange, blue, and lilac. Along her nose and upper lip, where one would expect gray to suggest the shadow of the angle of the light, he drew a long strip of green. Equally bizarre for the time, the brush strokes were broad and unrefined, making little effort to blend the various parts of the composition together. In *The Autobiography of Alice B. Toklas,* Gertrude Stein, who with her brother Leo purchased the portrait shortly after the exhibition, recalls the derision Matisse inspired: "People were roaring with laughter at the painting and scratching at it. . . . It bothered her [Stein] and angered her because she did not understand why because to her it was so alright."[1] Unlike Stein, many saw Matisse's technique as barbaric. His primitivism repudiated the idea that the value of art lies in the skill and exactitude of its presentation. Accordingly, the painter and other artists of the Autumn Salon were dubbed *les fauves* or "wild beasts."

Picasso was not part of this group, having arrived in Paris only the previous year. He was then in what became known as his "Rose Period," in which he painted human figures (many of them *saltimbanques* or circus workers) in soft grays and pastels. When Leo Stein purchased *Jeune Fille aux Fleurs* (Girl with a Basket of Flowers) and brought it home to 27, rue de Fleurus, his sister proclaimed it "appalling," comparing the girl's extremities to monkey paws. The Steins nevertheless became early patrons of the artist, placing his canvases alongside Cézanne's and Matisse's in what became one of the most valuable collections of modern art. The Steins' friendship with Picasso led to his 1906 portrait of Gertrude Stein, a pivotal moment in both artists' careers. By her account, Stein posed some eighty to ninety times at Picasso's studio on the rue Ravignan in a North Paris neighborhood known as the *bateu-lavoir* (laundry boat). "During these long poses and these long walks [to and from Picasso's studio] Gertrude Stein meditated and made sentences," she writes in *The Autobiography.* "She was then in the middle of her negro story Melanctha Herbert, the second story of *Three Lives.*"[2] "Melanctha" is Stein's most influential work, cited by modernists as diverse as Hemingway, James Weldon Johnson, and Richard Wright for its dreamlike use of repetition. Stein's claim that she conceived the story during her sittings with Picasso has led critics to search for parallels with the portrait. In actuality, the two are quite different. Nevertheless, in Stein's mind, the sittings were epochal because art and literature were being reinvented right in the same room: "In the long struggle with the portrait of Gertrude Stein, Picasso passed from the Harlequin, the charming early italian period to the intensive struggle which was to end in Cubism. Gertrude Stein had written the story of Melanctha . . . which was the first definite step away from the nineteenth century and into the twentieth century in literature."[3]

What makes Picasso's portrait of Stein important is the representation of her face, parts of which are flat and disproportionate, with a dominating nose and irregularly shaped eyes usually described as "mask-like." Picasso struggled with the features for months, at one point painting the face blank. When the canvas was finally hung at the Steins' studio, few thought the image resembled Gertrude. "Everybody says that she does not look like it," Stein describes Picasso telling Alice B. Toklas. "That does not make any difference, she will."[4] Sure enough, as Stein's reputation grew, the portrait seemed a canny prediction of the imperious presence she would exert in the American expatriate colony. For Picasso the painting marked a decisive turn toward abstraction. Within a year he exaggerated the facial distortions even further, drawing inspiration from African tribal art to create *Les Demoiselles d'Avignon* (The Women of Avignon). In this scene of prostitutes on display at a brothel, he fashioned bodies out of overlapping squares and ovals, conveying a sense of both disconnection and dehumanization. This emphasis on form as shape was only a step away from the wholesale use of geometric patterns that became known as Cubism.

In its various stages, the Cubism of Picasso and his close ally Georges Braque not only broke down figures and landscapes into planes and angles; they often also arranged these interlocking elements to suggest that the eye was viewing an object from multiple perspectives. Later, cubists incorporated actual objects into their work, gluing squares of newspaper and packages onto their canvases. (This stage of the movement is usually referred to as "synthetic Cubism," as opposed to the earlier "analytic Cubism.") The resulting collage effect became one of the most inspirational devices in all modernist art. The notion that one could juxtapose materials of different textures—whether shapes, words, or musical phrases—gave artists a tool for conveying the increasingly patchwork feel of modern life.

By the time Hemingway arrived in Paris, the techniques associated with postimpressionism, and Cubism in particular, were no longer as shocking or controversial as they had been in the previous two decades. Nevertheless, upon visiting Stein's studio in 1922 Hemingway was impressed by her art collection, especially her Cézanne canvases, and began contemplating ways to achieve comparable effects in prose. He later claimed that "Big Two-Hearted River" was an effort to render both the scope of the landscape and its details in Cézanne fashion. In the original ending of that story (known as "On Writing"), Nick Adams specifically identifies the postimpressionist as his role model: "He, Nick, wanted to write about the country so it would be there like Cézanne had done it in painting."[5] Critics have argued for the influence of other painters on his writing. The arrangement of stories in *In Our Time* evokes Picasso's cubist collages, for by alternating concise vignettes with longer narratives, Hemingway achieves the same sense of startling contrast. He was also an admirer of Spanish painter Joan Miró, whose cubist masterpiece *The Farm* he purchased in 1925. One of his few forays into art criticism is an appreciation of that work, written for *Cahiers d'Art* in 1934. Another significant modernist painting Hemingway owned was *The Guitar Player* by Juan Gris, which Hemingway and his second wife, Pauline, purchased in 1931. As a sign of the affinity he believed art and literature shared, Hemingway in later works created protagonists who were modernist painters. Sections of *The Garden of Eden* cut from the 1986 published version include an expatriate artist named Nick Sheldon, and *Islands in the Stream* (posthumously published in 1970) centers on a painter named Thomas Hudson, who in Paris in the 1920s associated with Picasso, Braque, Miró, and others. In one scene, Hemingway compares Hudson's career to that of a writer friend, Roger Davis, who is struggling to regain his squandered talent: "It is luckier to be a painter . . . because you have more things to work with. We have the advantage of working with our hands and the métier we have mastered is an actual thing."[6]

In the 1920s Hemingway was also a casual acquaintance of Man Ray, the best-known American disciple of Cubism, who applied its techniques to photography as well as to the painter's canvas. Ray was a commercial artist in New York in 1913 when he attended the Armory Show, the first exhibition of modernist art in America. The exhibition was a highly controversial event. Such Stein-owned paintings as Matisse's *Blue Nude* (1907) were ridiculed by critics and newspaper columnists, and, at one point, when the show moved to Chicago, art students even burned Matisse in effigy. (Picasso escaped attack only because his most controversial works, including *Les Demoiselles,* were not included in the exhibition.)[7] Ray experimented with the cubist style in works such as *AD MCMXIV* (1914), inspired by the outbreak of World War I, and *The Rope Dancer* (1916). In the avant-garde circles of New York, he became acquainted with Marcel Duchamp, whose *Nude Descending a Staircase* (1912) was the most divisive work in the Armory Show; one detractor described it as an "explosion in a shingle factory." Duchamp and Ray, along with another French expatriate, Francis Picabia, began to craft an anti-artistic style that later became known as Dadaism, which employed absurdity to convey the disorder and anarchy of modern life. The chief spokesman of Dadaism, Tristan Tzara, claimed to have founded the literary arm of this movement in Zurich in 1916, but Duchamp, Picabia, and Ray were expressing its philosophy of self-conscious lunacy in the visual arts during the same period. Challenging audience preconceptions of what was meant by the term "serious art," they created works that struck many as hoaxes and stunts. (For one exhibition, Duchamp, under the alias "R. Mutt," submitted a porcelain urinal as a sculpture, replete with a title, *Fountain* [1917].) Not all modernists appreciated this nihilistic, nothing-means-anything aesthetic. Believing that art should reinstitute order rather than proliferate chaos, Hemingway was contemptuous of Dadaism. One of his first published writings, "A Divine Gesture" (1922), is a parody of the devotion to nonsense in the movement.[8] Two years later, when Ford Madox Ford printed Tzara's intentionally meaningless prose in *transatlantic review*, Hemingway slipped insults against the poet into the editorial column of the magazine behind Ford's back. As late as the mid 1930s Dadaism continued to arouse Hemingway's ire. "The Snows of Kilimanjaro" describes Tristan Tzara by name as a drunken fop forever lounging at the Café du Dôme.

George Antheil and his Ballet Mécanique, caricatured by the *New York Sun* on the eve of the Carnegie Hall premiere of the work in April 1927.

Hemingway never attacked Ray, who photographed him on several occasions in the 1920s. Hemingway was apparently oblivious to Ray's art, however, the absurdist strategies of which involved incorporating common mechanical objects into his canvases to call attention to the many banal, everyday devices in human life. Ray's 1916 *Self-Portrait* consists of two electronic bells and a buzzer arranged on a black-and-aluminum background to suggest a pair of eyes and a mouth. Spectators who fancied themselves smart enough to get the point—the human face imagined in machine form—soon found their assumptions undermined, for the buzzer was disconnected, leaving observers poking at the object in the expectation that something might happen. In another clever moment Ray hung a framed canvas unevenly. A passerby attempting to right the object did not know that a second nail not only kept it from being straightened but also set the frame rocking like a pendulum. By tricking viewers into displaying their desire for even, orderly aesthetics (elemental aspects), *Portrait Hanging* literally demonstrated that modern art could not be set straight.

Ray moved to Paris in July 1921, immersing himself in the vibrant but often fractious world of Dadaism that included such colorful literary figures as Tzara, André Breton, and Phillipe Soupault. When Ray discovered that he could not make a living from painting, he turned to photography, which eventually overshadowed his other work, much to his frustration. Initially, he earned small commissions for reproducing canvases and sculptures for art-gallery catalogues. Within a short time he also garnered a reputation as a portraitist, becoming the preferred photographer for Sylvia Beach's bookshop, Shakespeare and Company, where his prints of James Joyce, Hemingway, and other leading writers were prominently displayed. (Until the early 1930s, when a dispute over money drove them apart, Gertrude Stein anointed Ray her official photographer.) French aristocrats sought his services as well, and soon he was earning five hundred dollars—the equivalent of expenses for five months in expatriate Paris—for a fashion spread in *Vogue*. But Ray did not just regard the camera as a paycheck. More than any artist in the post–World War I years, he exploited the capacity of photography for optical trickery, developing darkroom techniques that elevated the medium into an art form. One early innovation was the "rayograph." Placing an object directly upon photographic paper and exposing it to light, he created silhouettes whose shadows and shapes recalled the cubists' fascination with geometric forms.

By the mid 1920s a faction of the Dadaist movement in Paris abandoned Tzara's absurdity to form a less confrontational school known as Surrealism. Interested in the psychology of perception, Surrealists took as their subject the dreams and hallucinations of the irrational mind. The purpose was to suggest that perception, just as a camera lens, was not an objective interpreter of reality but its creator. Many of Ray's trademark photographic techniques—such as double exposure, soft focus, and the use of backlighting—lent themselves to Surrealist ideals. One of his most famous images is *Le violin d'Ingres* (The Violin of Ingres, 1924), dedicated to the mid-nineteenth-century painter Jean-August-Dominique Ingres. In the picture, Ray's Parisian mistress, a model popularly known as Kiki of Montparnasse, sits with her nude back to the camera, her face in profile. Just above her hips is the image of the two *f*s carved in the body of violins. (Hemingway was fond of Kiki; he wrote an introduction to her 1928 memoirs of life in Montparnasse.) Just as Ray's earlier *Self-Portrait* had, the picture conveys one of his favorite themes, the transformation of the human body into an instrument—in this case, a musical instrument. A decade later, Ray immortalized another lover in an important Surrealist painting. *A l'heure de l'Observatoire—Les amourex* (Observatory Time—The Lovers, but known in English as *The Lips* [1932–1934]) juxtaposes a vista of the Luxembourg Gardens and the Paris Observatory with a huge pair of red lips floating above. Inspired by the artist's romantic travails with his protégé Lee Miller, the canvas captured the Surrealist belief that desire dominates the human landscape, dwarfing nature and science with its overwhelming presence.

As with many expatriates, the advent of World War II forced Ray to abandon his beloved Paris and return to America. Although never as famous as his fellow Surrealist Salvador Dalí, who was more adept at self-promotion, Ray continued his optical experiments in painting, photography, and sculpture late into life. During a 1957 exhibition in Paris, Ray's *Object to Be Destroyed* (1932)—a metronome with a picture of an eye paper-clipped to its ticking arm—was indeed destroyed by art students protesting Dadaism and Surrealism. Rather than prosecute, Ray commended the students' gesture. To point out the futility of their actions, he then arranged for the mass production of the object. A few years later, five thousand reproductions of his 1921 sculpture *Cadeu* (The Gift), a flatiron with tacks glued to its surface, were also created and sold for several hundred dollars apiece. Both efforts demonstrated Ray's belief—one shared by his fellow artists—that modern art must break from old notions of beauty and originality, drawing its inspiration from the material objects defining human life in the twentieth century.

Modernist trends in music and dance parallel innovations in the visual arts. The embrace of primitivism, the rejection of cultivated standards of taste, and the emphasis on originality and novelty are also common. Music and dance often excited a level of audience outrage that Dadaists and Surrealists could only dream of achieving. The watershed moment in the development of modern music was Igor Stravinsky's *The Rite of Spring,* a ballet commissioned for Sergey Pavlovich Diaghilev's Ballets Russes (Russian Ballet), which premiered at the Théâtre des Champs-Elysées in Paris in May 1913. The work was a dual assault on the senses, with the choreography by legendary dancer Vaslov Nijinsky matching the innovations of the score. In *The Autobiography of Alice B. Toklas,* Stein describes attending the second performance of the ballet, which proved as uproarious as its opening night:

> No sooner did the music begin and the dancing than they [the audience] began to hiss. The defenders began to applaud. We could hear nothing, as a matter of fact I never did hear any of the music of the *Sacre du Printemps* because it was the only time I ever saw it and one literally could not, throughout the whole performance, hear the sound of music. The dancing was very fine and that we

could see although our attention was constantly distracted by a man in the box next to us flourishing his cane, and finally in a violent altercation with an enthusiast in the box next to him, his cane came down and smashed the opera hat the other had just put on in defiance. It was all incredibly fierce.[9]

"Fierce" is a good word to describe Stravinsky's music. Rather than complementing its brief snatches of melody (drawn from ancient Slavic folk songs), the score of *The Rite of Spring* was built out of harsh, atonal chords the dissonance of which sounded loose and unstructured. Equally important, Stravinsky employed asymmetrical, syncopated rhythms that gave the music a jagged, jutting sense of progression. These intentionally awkward rhythms accompanied the story line of the ballet, which describes an ancient fertility ritual in which a young girl is sacrificed to the gods by dancing herself to death. The primitivism of the music was a detour for Stravinsky, who subsequently returned to more-conventional forms and structures. For aspiring modernist composers, however, the piece served as the ideal against which they measured their own experimental efforts. But Stravinsky was only one influence. Paris was also home to Claude Debussy and Erik Satie, as well as the renowned teacher Nadia Boulanger, who instructed promising students in the rigors of composition. For classically trained American expatriates, the City of Light was the capital of modern music, the only place where the future of the medium could be determined.

Ultimately, the most important expatriate composer was Aaron Copland. In the 1920s and 1930s, however, two of Copland's peers, George Antheil and Virgil Thomson, garnered more attention, in part because they were closely aligned with expatriate writers who promoted their reputations. Antheil was a concert pianist from Trenton, New Jersey, who promoted himself as the "bad boy of music." (To dissuade audiences from rioting at his concerts, he placed a pistol on his piano.) Antheil's performances tricked audience expectations by beginning with selections from Bach, Mozart, and Chopin—all chosen to endear classical devotees to him. Then, toward the end of his program, he abruptly shifted to "ultra-modern" pieces—sometimes Stravinsky's work, sometimes his own—that sounded all the more brash and untamed compared with their more melodious predecessors. His 1945 autobiography describes how his Paris debut twenty-two years earlier had affected attendees: "Man Ray was punching somebody in the nose in the front row. Marcel Duchamp was arguing loudly with somebody else in the second row. In a box nearby Erik Satie was shouting, 'What precision! What precision!' and applauding. The spotlight was turned on the audience by some wag upstairs. It struck James Joyce full in the face, hurting his sensitive eyes. A big burly poet got up in one of the boxes and yelled, 'You are all pigs!'

In the gallery the police came in and arrested the Surrealists, who, liking the music, were punching everybody who objected."[10] Such chaotic scenes were the quickest route to celebrity in expatriate Paris. Antheil became the *"sauvage"* (savage) of modernism, his power and intensity as a performer and composer embodying the promise of primitivism that *The Rite of Spring* heralded.

Beginning in 1923 Antheil lived in a small apartment above Sylvia Beach's Shakespeare and Company bookshop. Working on a piano provided by Beach's companion, Adrienne Monnier, he began his best-known composition, *Ballet Mécanique,* which exaggerated Stravinsky-like rhythms and transformed the piano into a rhythm instrument. When the piece was performed, supporters and detractors recognized that for Antheil the keyboard was a drum, though they disagreed on the significance of that innovation. Supporters considered *Ballet Mécanique* as close as a modernist had come to fashioning music out of the industrial soundscape of the modern age. Pound wrote an entire treatise on Antheil's work, declaring that "with the performance of the *Ballet Mécanique* one can conceive the possibility of organizing the sounds of a factory, let us say of boilerplate, or any other clangorous noisiness, the actual sounds of the labor, the various tones of the grindings. . . . We have here the chance, a mode, a music that no mere loudness can obliterate, but that serves us, as the primitive chanteys for rowing, for hauling cables."[11] The composition achieved a primary goal of modernism—dramatizing the effect of the machine age on human life.

As with many expatriate artists who gained early fame, Antheil's "savage" reputation proved detrimental to his career. Although *Ballet Mécanique* was praised in Paris, it had a hostile reception at its 1927 Carnegie Hall premiere in New York. American critics by this point had tired of the posturing and publicity surrounding expatriate rebels' work. Perhaps the most remarked-upon element of the performance was the use of an actual airplane propeller to augment the barrage of pianos performing the score. As Antheil later complained, he had allowed gimmickry to overwhelm the music: "Because the entire concert was now expanding into a highly *visible* proposition, our industrious publicists suddenly decided to smuggle a *real* propeller on the stage. . . . It was confidently expected that the noise would make them [the audience] quite afraid of being blown out of their seats."[12] The following morning the composer awoke to dismissive reviews such as "Don't make a mountain out of an Antheil" and "Forty million Frenchmen CAN be wrong!" His career was damaged for years. (A revival of the ballet was scheduled, however, for late 1999 at the University of Massachusetts, Lowell, and a spring 2000 performance at Carnegie Hall, which marks the New York encore of the piece, seven decades after its premiere.) Although he wrote ballets and Hollywood movie scores, Antheil's legendary Paris years prejudiced his mature work. One notable exception was his 1953 adaptation of the Hemingway short story "The Capital of the World," performed at the Metropolitan Opera House by the American Ballet Theater. After badgering Hemingway in the 1920s to collaborate on a ballet, Antheil finally realized his dream of translating modernist literature into music.

While Antheil was extravagant and flamboyant, Virgil Thomson was measured and cautious. He first visited Paris not as a tourist but as a tenor in the Harvard Glee Club. A yearlong fellowship allowed him to remain there in 1921–1922 to study composition with Boulanger, who served for musicians the same expatriate godmother role that Stein played for writers. Thomson was forced to leave Paris for three years, but after his 1925 return he remained one of the more committed expatriates of the city. His most famous work during this time was a collaboration with Stein, whom he met in 1926. Their friendship was a rocky one, for both were strong-willed. Yet, they also shared many of the same characteristics, including a playfulness that was atypical of more somber modernists. (Thomson enjoyed composing parodies; his *Variations on Sunday-School Tunes* poked fun at various genres such as hymns that he felt diminished the reputation of the organ.) Within a few months of their initial meeting, Thomson arranged a piano and vocal score for one of Stein's poems, "Susie Asado," an action that flattered the matron of Montparnasse, despite her inability to read music. Thomson recognized that Stein's use of language as sound rather than content lent itself to musical settings more easily than the styles of other modernists. (Antheil, for example, abandoned an effort to score *Ulysses*, frustrated by its verbal complexity.) By the late 1920s Thomson had composed accompaniment for several Stein compositions, including "Preciosilla," "The Portrait of F. B.," and *Capitals Capitals*—a four-part conversation between major cities of southern France. What proved to be their most celebrated collaboration was a full-length piece titled *Four Saints in Three Acts* (1928), which in the mid 1930s became the longest-running opera on Broadway.

The long gestation period between the conception of *Four Saints in Three Acts* and its 1934 debut is one of the legendary stories of expatriate modernism. Stein and Thomson commenced work in early 1927, choosing as their subject the lives of two sixteenth-century Catholic saints—Thérèsa (or Teresa as she became in the score), a Carmelite mystic from the Spanish city of Âvila, and Ignatius Loyola, her contemporary in Barcelona. As with most of Stein's writing, the libretto of *Four Saints in*

Three Acts is antinarrative, refusing to tell a story or set a scene according to the dramatic dictates of the Italian opera tradition that Thomson chose as their medium. There are minimal hints of scenes—including a funeral, a wedding procession, and a glimpse of heaven—but these are barely evoked. (When the opera was finally staged, its most vivid scenes, including St. Ignatius's dream of the Last Supper, were introduced into the script by the director.) As Stein toured America in early 1935, she described the opera, oddly enough, as a piece of landscape writing. Her goal, she insisted, was "to tell what happened without telling stories" and "to tell what each [saint] is without telling stories." Because "a landscape does not move," she believed that capturing the essence of her main characters meant viewing them as a painter would a vista. "The story is only of importance if you like to tell or like to hear a story," she claimed. For her, the goal was to convey the "relation" between aspects of her characters' personalities, just as a visual artist seeks to depict the relation between "the trees to the hills the hills to the fields the trees to each other any piece of it to any sky and then any detail to any other detail."[13]

In his 1966 autobiography Thomson offered a more accessible interpretation. The opera, he suggested, was an allegory of the artist's life in Paris, of people living near one another often collaborating on artistic projects,

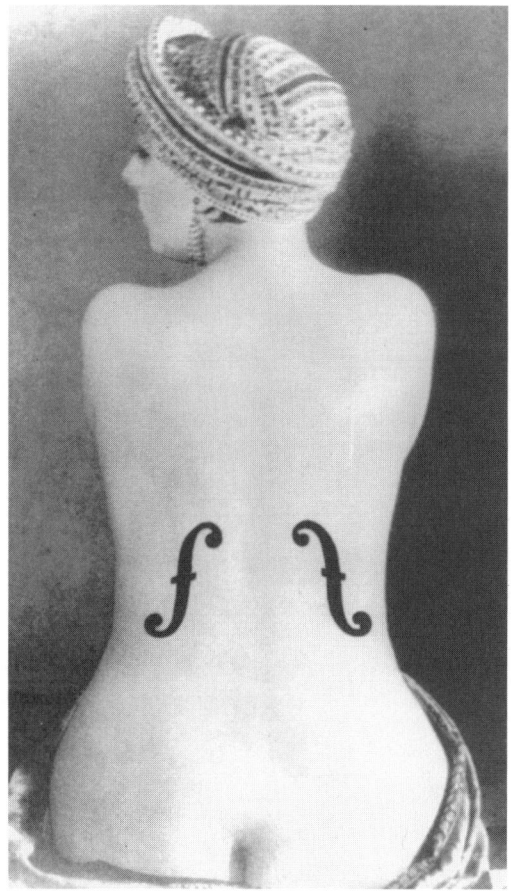

Man Ray's *Le Violin d'Ingres*, a seminal Surrealist work, featuring his lover Kiki, one of the celebrated Montparnassian personalities.

all of them devoting their lives to the disinterested effort of being better artists and making good art. "We couldn't write about art that way, but we could write about saints with the understanding between ourselves that it was artists we were writing about, and were treating the saints as if they were artists and viewing artists as if they were possibly saints."[14]

It is a testimony to Thomson's vision of the opera as a story of artistic collaboration that his score is credited with bringing the inherent music of Stein's phrasing to life. The accompaniment draws upon a variety of musical forms—including the waltz, the tango, and cowboy campfire ballads. In effect, Thomson created an aural montage that was the sonic counterpart of a Picasso collage.

Although Thomson completed his score to Stein's libretto by 1928, six frustrating years passed before it finally reached the stage. In the intervening time Stein and Thomson's friendship cooled. (In her customary manner, she sent him a card that curtly read "Miss Stein declines further acquaintance with Mr. Thomson.") Fortunately, he refused to abandon their collaboration, arranging for a group playfully known as the Friends and Enemies of Modern Music, headed by one of his former college friends, to underwrite a performance in Hartford, Connecticut. Thomson secured the contributions of an experimental choreographer and set designer to ensure the presentation was as avant-garde as the libretto and score. The most arresting device of the performance was also his idea. In the lead roles and chorus, Thomson hired all African-American performers. As many reviewers subsequently commented, the cast gave the score a quality that was at once spiritual and surreal—spiritual because the black gospel tradition that the singers evoked deepened the religious context of the opera, surreal because the sight of African Americans portraying Catholic saints singing "pigeons on the grass alas alas" struck many as bizarre.

The work was such an unqualified critical and commercial success that performances on Broadway and in Chicago were quickly arranged. Coming only months after the success of *The Autobiography of Alice B. Toklas,* the positive publicity of the opera contributed to the growing acceptance of Stein's artistry among critics and heightened demand for her return to America. During her profitable 1934–1935 stateside lecture tour—her first visit home in three decades—she attended the Chicago premiere of the play and was pleased with Thomson's production. He later scored two additional Stein librettos, *Yes Is For A Very Young Man* and *The Mother of Us All,* both pieces written in the last years before Stein's 1946 death. In the same era Thomson won the Pulitzer Prize for his score for the movie *Louisiana Story* (1948), the only piece of music written for a movie to receive that honor.

Classical music was not the only form thriving in expatriate Paris. Jazz was also prevalent during the 1920s, with several African-American musicians catering to the demand for new sounds. As early as 1900, ragtime became a Parisian rage when John Philip Sousa and his orchestra performed at the Exposition Universelle. With a repertoire prominently featuring Scott Joplin compositions, Sousa and his players introduced Europeans to energetic rhythms that seemed instinctive rather than studied. A few years later, after the United States entered

World War I, African-American soldiers serving in segregated military regiments staged public jazz performances that enlivened the mood of the battle-weary capital. With nicknames such as "Harlem's Hellfighters" and "Seventy Black Devils," these regiments exaggerated the racial stereotypes of Europe and fed the fascination with primitivism that had inspired Picasso. By the mid 1920s, jazz nightclubs opened in Montmartre in North Paris. The most important was Le Grand Duc at 52, rue Pigalle. There Florence Jones sang until the mid 1920s. Her successor was an orange-haired entertainer known as Bricktop (Ada Smith), who made the nightclub a hub for expatriate celebrities such as F. Scott and Zelda Fitzgerald. Poet Langston Hughes briefly worked as a dishwasher at Le Grand Duc. In his memoir he recounts the effect of jazz in the *ville lumière* (City of Lights):

> When all the other clubs were closed, the best of the musicians and entertainers from various other smart places would often drop into the Grand Duc, and there'd be a jam session until seven or eight in the morning. . . . The cream of the Negro musicians then in France, like Cricket Smith on the trumpet, Louis Jones on the violin, Palmer Jones on the piano, Frank Withers on the clarinet, and Buddy Gilmore at the drums, would weave out music that would almost make your heart stand still at dawn in a Paris night club in the rue Pigalle. . . . Blues in the rue Pigalle. Black and laughing, heartbreaking blues in the Paris dawn, pounding like a pulse-beat, moving like the Mississippi![15]

With the exception of ragtime and jazz, the experimental boundaries of modernist music were established by non-American composers, whether French-born (Debussy, Maurice Joseph Ravel) or expatriates from other European countries (Stravinsky was Russian). However innovative, Antheil's *Ballet Mécanique* and Thomson's *Four Saints in Three Acts* build upon the breakthroughs of

HEMINGWAY AND MURPHY

The painter with whom Hemingway was closest in the 1920s was Gerald Murphy. This wealthy expatriate, the prototype for Dick Diver in F. Scott Fitzgerald's *Tender Is the Night,* was not, by his own admission, a major artist. He was, however, highly conversant in theories of modernist painting. Linda Patterson Miller explores the artistic affinities between Murphy's *Watch* (1925) and Hemingway's "Hills Like White Elephants":

"Hemingway's 'Hills' and Murphy's Watch demonstrate the importance to modernist art of both visible and invisible spaces. . . . The role of invisible space is more readily identifiable in painting than in writing, and it was Hemingway's literary adaption of this artistic principle that made him the father of modern American prose. The artist can paint by relying entirely upon negative space, and particularly the latter. As such, he shades in everything that is not there—the space which surrounds objects. When he has filled in all the spaces, the objects stand out in visible contrast, now defined as counterreaction as negative white spaces. The invisible has now created the invisible. The writer must inevitably work in the opposite direction, using the visible to illuminate the invisible. As Hemingway recognized, it was precisely what he chose to make visible that determined the dimensions of those negative spaces. When Murphy was filling his canvases 'with forms which were to have no faintest resemblance to any real object,' he was essentially working from the principle of negative space—using the invisible to see what would then become visible. The objects which gradually emerged always came as a surprise, and they were seen fresh and for themselves."

Linda Patterson Miller, "'Nourished at the Same Source: Ernest Hemingway and Gerald Murphy," *Mosaic,* 21 (1988): 86.

the preceding European generation. The same is true of classical dance. From 1909 to 1929 the leading ballet company of Paris, Ballets Russes, was headed by a Russian expatriate, Diaghilev. As much as for its score, *The Rite of Spring* prompted outrage for its choreography, which dispensed with the formal positions that are the foundation of ballet in favor of self-consciously primitive steps and gestures. Descriptions of the original staging of *The Rite of Spring* include such unflattering phrases as "knock-kneed," "stoop shouldered," and "frog hopping"—and these descriptions are from *admirers* of the presentation. For many years reconstructing the choreography that Nijinsky conceived was deemed impossible, for when the ballet closed after only six performances, the production notes were lost, leaving only a few sketches by an opening-night eyewitness as a record. (Nijinsky's sister was able to reconstruct the steps, however, allowing the Joffrey Ballet to stage a re-creation in 1990.) Although *The Rite of Spring* was not considered a success until years later, Diaghilev nevertheless capitalized upon its avant-garde notoriety, inviting an array of modernist painters—including Picasso, Braque, and Gris—to design sets and costumes. The results were what today would be called "multi-media" spectacles in which dance, music, and painting combined to create the impression of a unified direction of experimentation among artists. While Hemingway never participated in these collaborative efforts, many of his fellow writers did. John Dos Passos, for example, helped paint sets for the 1923 Diaghilev/Stravinsky production of *Les Noces*. Dos Passos became a Diaghilev enthusiast through his friends Gerald and Sara Murphy, the wealthy expatriate couple who inspired the portraits of Dick and Nicole Diver in Fitzgerald's *Tender Is the Night* (1934) and who socialized with Hemingway in the late 1920s and 1930s. Gerald Murphy described the appeal of the Ballets Russes to expatriates in Paris to his biographer: "In addition to being the focal center of the whole modern movement in the arts, the Diaghilev ballet was a kind of movement in itself. Anybody who was interested in the company became a member automatically. You knew everybody, you knew the dancers, and everybody asked your opinion on things."[16]

While the controversy generated by the Ballets Russes until Diaghilev's death in 1929 proved that the world of classical dance was never quite amenable to modernism, the same was not true of its contemporary counterpart. As early as 1892, an American expatriate named Loie Fuller (1862–1928) gained fame in Paris for the striking optical illusions she created on stage through costuming and lighting effects. Veiled in layers of skirts or draperies, she imitated various natural phenomena— including the birth of a butterfly and fire—by twirling her long, flowing outfits in constant fits of motion. Fuller was one of the first dancers to exploit the possibilities of electrical lighting by incorporating colored gels and slide projections into her act. Her greatest innovation may be the use of underlighting. For her *Fire Dance* (1895), she performed on a pane of frosted glass that splintered the illumination rising from beneath it into eerie, flamelike shafts. Originally Fuller performed for the Folies Bergére, a nightclub, but by the turn of the century she was overseeing her own theater at the Paris International Exhibition, a highbrow showcase for the arts. There she founded an all-female dance troupe that employed a multicultural array of dance forms, including the pantomime.

Fuller is one of the least-remembered Americans who relocated to Paris, in part because her fame was overshadowed by Isadora Duncan (1878–1927), whose theatricality, both in public and private life, made her the expatriate grand dame for nearly thirty years. Duncan arrived in Paris just after the turn of the century, her first appearances sponsored by Fuller. Although she despised the modernist fascination with primitivism, her style seemed to complement it, for she rejected the formality associated with classical ballet in favor of a personal, fluid style emphasizing self-expression over technique. Duncan danced barefoot, did away with the elaborate backdrops and props associated with ballet, and even eschewed the obligatory tutu in favor of flowing, free-form tunics, all of which enhanced her reputation as a free spirit. Just as modernist poets did, she revered Greek culture and insisted that her repertoire embodied an Hellenic ideal.

By the end of her life Duncan's celebrity overshadowed her artistic reputation. That she was an unwed mother of two children by different fathers was a closely guarded secret—until the children drowned in the Seine River in Neuilly, France, in 1913. That tragedy became melodramatic fodder for the international press, which subsequently seized upon rumors of her financial problems, love affairs, and alcoholism. In 1921 she opened a dance school in newly communist Russia and was promptly denounced as a "Red" and a "Bolshevik hussy." A few years later, when she attempted a comeback at almost fifty, she was mercilessly ridiculed for her age and weight. Robert McAlmon's autobiography *Being Geniuses Together* recalls one Paris performance: "Although she must have known that her dancing days were over, she tried to do one leap, and it was grotesque and sad, and she was aware of it. But long before this I had seen a constantly despairing and rather shamed look in her eyes."[17] Her macabre death in 1927 sealed her legend. When her flowing scarf caught in the wheel of her moving car, she was choked to death. Many expatriate memoirs describe her funeral, which drew a crowd of five thousand. She was buried in one of the most famous cemeteries in Paris, Père Lachaise, where Stein and Toklas came to rest in later decades.

Two years before Duncan's death, another American dancer in Paris created a sensation. Like Fuller and Duncan, Josephine Baker had little formal dance training, having worked mainly as a chorus girl in vaudeville and on Broadway. She was brought to Paris in 1925 as a member of La Revue Nègre, an American-style variety show featuring African-American musicians and dancers. Nightclub owner Andre Dáven was on the verge of insolvency when an acquaintance, the cubist painter Fernand Léger, offered a surefire prescription for attracting Parisian audiences: "Give them Negroes." Baker, plucked from obscurity to become the troupe's featured performer, was an instant hit when Dáven's revue opened. Dubbed the "Black Venus," she became notorious for her suggestive routines, in which she was draped in little more than a girdle of feathers. Baker and her fellow performers built their act around the dance steps then popular in urban America. They performed the Charleston, as well as the Mess Around, the Itch, and the Tack Annie. If a particular act did not exude enough "primitive" eros, Dáven cut it—thus, a tap dance segment was removed, as were slow-moving spirituals. The emphasis on eroticism and the stereotypical linking of black skin with sexuality made Baker a symbol of the libidinal temptations that Paris represented for expatriates. When Fitzgerald needed an image to convey the allure of dissipation for his short story "Babylon Revisited" (1931), he described his protagonist as attending a Baker performance to watch her "go through her chocolate arabesques.[18] Years later, Hemingway claimed to A. E. Hotchner that he had danced a night away with Baker, "the most sensational woman anybody ever saw," at Le Jockey, a Montparnasse nightclub. "Very hot night but she was wearing a coat of black fur," Hemingway supposedly recalled. "She never took off her fur coat. Wasn't until the joint closed she told me she had nothing on underneath."[19] Both stories suggest how Baker came to symbolize the eros expatriates associated with African primitivism.

Baker's act created such a stir in the mid 1920s that the Folies Bergère offered her $5,400 per month for a solo act, making her by far the highest paid African-American entertainer in expatriate Paris. To satisfy audiences, her act became even bawdier. Gone were the feathers, replaced by a more suggestive skirt of bananas. When interviewed, Baker played up her primitive image by telling reporters she learned her dance steps by watching kangaroos at the St. Louis Zoo. According to biographer Phyllis Rose, such pronouncements obscured her dedication to dancing as a craft and tradition, which she had studied since her early teen years: "She invoked the zoo and animals no doubt to please an audience that loved her as a child of nature. . . . But underneath the seeming total spontaneity were known steps and dances . . . and years of daily practice. When she seemed the most unstrung, there had been the most careful preparation."[20] While her provocative image won her many fans, it also prevented her from earning serious critical regard. At least one critic was not above invoking a racial slur to dismiss Baker's primitivism, calling her act a "lamentable example of the transatlantic exhibitionism which makes us revert to the ape in less time than it took to descend from it."[21]

Baker's example demonstrates clearly that the modernist fascination with primitivism was built in part upon racial stereotypes. Nevertheless, painting, music, and dance, much like literature, embraced it in rebellion against the reserve of most nineteenth-century art. If the various art forms practiced by expatriate modernists can be said to share one overriding aim, it was the creation of new forms of expression that demonstrated just how irrelevant the ideals of the previous century were in the modern age.

NOTES

1. Gertrude Stein, *The Autobiography of Alice B. Toklas* (New York: Harcourt, Brace, 1933), p. 35.

2. Ibid., p. 49.

3. Ibid., p. 54.

4. Ibid., p. 12.

5. Ernest Hemingway, "On Writing," in *The Nick Adams Stories*, edited by Philip Young (New York: Scribners, 1972), p. 239.

6. Hemingway, *Islands in the Stream* (New York: Scribners, 1970), p. 103.

7. In his history of the Armory Show, Milton W. Brown quotes a *Chicago Tribune* writer who singled out both *Blue Nude* and Gertrude Stein for ridicule: "I called the canvas *Cow with Cud* / And hung it on the line, / Altho' to me 'twas vague as mud, / 'Twas clear to Gertrude Stein." See *The Story of the Armory Show* (New York: Abbeville Press, 1988), p. 163.

8. See Dennis Ryan, "'A Divine Gesture': Hemingway's Complex Parody of the Modern," *The Hemingway Review*, 16 (Fall 1996): 1–17.

9. Stein, *The Autobiography of Alice B. Toklas*, p. 137.

10. George Antheil, *Bad Boy of Music* (Garden City, N.J.: Doubleday, Doran, 1945), pp. 7–8.

11. Ezra Pound, *Antheil and the Treatise on Harmony* (New York: DeCapo Press, 1968), pp. 146–147.

12. Antheil, *Bad Boy of Music*, pp. 192–193.

13. Stein, *Lectures in America* (New York: Random House, 1935), pp. 21, 25.

14. Virgil Thomson, *Virgil Thomson* (New York: Knopf, 1966), p. 161.

15. Langston Hughes, *The Big Sea* (New York: Hill & Wang, 1963), pp. 161–162.

16. Quoted in Calvin Tompkins, *Living Well Is the Best Revenge* (New York: Viking, 1972), pp. 8–9.

17. Robert McAlmon, *Being Geniuses Together, 1920–1930* (San Francisco: North Point Press, 1984), p. 304.

18. F. Scott Fitzgerald, "Babylon Revisited," in his *The Short Stories of F. Scott Fitzgerald,* edited by Matthew J. Bruccoli (New York: Scribners, 1989), p. 619.

19. Quoted in A. E. Hotchner, *Papa Hemingway: A Personal Memoir* (New York: Random House, 1966), p. 23.

20. Phyllis Rose, *Jazz Cleopatra: Josephine Baker in Her Time* (New York: Doubleday, 1989), pp. 46–47.

21. Quoted in Rose, *Jazz Cleopatra: Josephine Baker in Her Time*, p. 32.

ADDITIONAL DEPICTIONS OF
EXPATRIATE LIFE

emingway was hardly the first American writer to explore the theme of expatriation. Nor was he the only modernist in Paris to transform his experiences abroad into fiction; in the 1920s and early 1930s novels and stories about expatriate life were an established trend. As the constant waves of Americans arriving in the city slowed to a trickle during the Great Depression, many Montparnasse regulars wrote memoirs about their glory days, further enhancing the legend of the expatriate literary scene. While *The Sun Also Rises* and *A Moveable Feast* remain among the best remembered of such books, other fictions and autobiographies provide additional accounts of the years between the two world wars. Although not as well known as Hemingway's work, they are nevertheless useful for helping readers understand the range of modernist writing achieved in this important period of literary history.

The Autobiography of Alice B. Toklas, by Gertrude Stein (New York: Harcourt, Brace, 1933). A surprise best-seller upon its publication, Stein's *Autobiography* finally won the enigmatic author the critical and commercial success she had coveted since expatriating to Paris in 1903. Written as if told by her companion Alice B. Toklas, the memoir on the surface reads like a social register as wave after wave of modernist luminaries journey to 27, rue de Fleurus to pay homage to the "Matron of Montparnasse." The portrait of Hemingway remains controversial for its pungent insults ("That is Hemingway, he looks like a modern and he smells of the museums") and its claim that Stein and Sherwood Anderson "formed" the young writer. Stein also declares Hemingway's virile persona a facade: "What a book . . . would be the real story of Hemingway, not those he writes but the confessions of the real Ernest Hemingway. . . . One he should tell himself but alas he never will. After all, as he himself once murmured, there is the career, the career" (236–237). Other modernists discussed include Henri Matisse, Pablo Picasso, Ezra Pound (dis-

Gertrude Stein, expatriate godmother of the Lost Generation, pictured with Alice B. Toklas in the 1920s at 27, rue de Fleurus.

patched with another pity comment: "He was a village explainer, excellent if you were a village but if you were not, not" [200]), T. S. Eliot, F. Scott Fitzgerald, Virgil Thomson, and many more. Beyond its cast of characters, the book is interesting for its insights into Stein's creative process, explained here in more accessible form than in other writings such as *How to Write* (1931) or *Lectures in America* (1935).

Scholars further find *The Autobiography* fascinating for the playful way it undermines the rules and expectations governing memoir writing. By telling her story through Alice, Stein violates the founding premise of the genre, which presumes the "I" in the text is the author. The book also possesses an unusual structure. Rather than unfolding in chronological order, it opens with two chapters describing why Toklas moved to Paris in 1907, one on the four years Stein lived in the city before the women met (1903–1907), and a fourth on Stein's background and the reasons she immigrated to France. Only then do the chapter titles suggest a linear progression through the decades. Yet, within her paragraphs Stein continues to hop back and forth in time, exhibiting little concern for calendar continuity. Close inspection reveals that the form of the book is circular, with Alice's arrival in the expatriate capital as its epicenter. This unusual arrangement conveys the symbolic importance of Toklas's entry into Stein's life while suggesting a radical new way of dating one's personal history. Instead of measuring the formation of personality from birth to death, *The Autobiography* argues that one determines a sense of identity through a pivotal moment or event that becomes the narrative center point of one's life.

The popularity of *The Autobiography* led to a highly successful 1934–1935 lecture tour of America, Stein's first trip home in three decades. Her stateside adventures with Alice are recounted in the sequel to the memoir, *Everybody's Autobiography* (1937).

The Autobiography of William Carlos Williams, by William Carlos Williams (New York: New Directions, 1951). Williams's memoir recounts his friendship with Ezra Pound, his dislike of T. S. Eliot's *The Waste Land* (1922), and his reasons for maintaining his New Jersey medical practice while composing his classic modernist poems. Hemingway is a slight presence in the book, remembered mainly as a tennis foe whose serve could not be broken. Williams also describes Gertrude Stein. When Williams visited the rue de Fleurus, the imperious Stein asked him what she should do with her many unpublished manuscripts. "If they were mine," he candidly answered, "I should probably select what I thought were the best and throw the rest in the fire." To which Stein replied: "No doubt. But then writing is not, of course, your *métier.*" As Williams adds, "That closed the subject and we left soon after" (254).

"Babylon Revisited," by F. Scott Fitzgerald, in *The Short Stories of F. Scott Fitzgerald,* edited by Matthew J. Bruccoli (New York: Scribners, 1989). First published in *Scribner's Magazine* in 1931, Fitzgerald's most-anthologized short story documents the author's mixed feelings toward expatriate Paris. Having recovered from a breakdown brought on by alcoholism and his wife's death, Charlie

RIGHT BANK VS. LEFT BANK

When critics compare Hemingway's depiction of Paris to that of other expatriates—and Fitzgerald in particular—they often cite his familiarity with the Left Bank, the "artistic" half of the city that lies south of the Seine River. Yet, Jean Méral cautions readers against identifying Hemingway only with the Left Bank; as he points out, in later years of his life the author was a habitué of Right Bank watering holes and accommodations, including the Ritz Hotel:

"The oft-invoked distinction between Hemingway's Paris and Fitzgerald's Paris is not simply a question of Left Bank versus Right Bank. While it may be true that Fitzgerald's Paris was largely restricted to the Right Bank, Hemingway's city, on the other hand, is much more widespread, rich and fused with his most intimate experiences. It is not limited to Montparnasse and the Latin Quarter. As Hemingway gained fame and fortune, he moved from one bank to the other, and his knowledge of the capital was considerable. Stadiums, velodromes, boxing rings, racecourses—all of these, scattered throughout the city—were destinations of the author's constant to-and-fro between Left Bank and Right Bank. In one pointed anecdote related by the narrator of *A Moveable Feast,* which takes its place alongside the other perfidies—doubly posthumous—launched against Fitzgerald, he quotes Georges, a former bellboy at the Ritz who has become a barman, as saying that he has not the slightest recollection of this M. Fitzgerald whose name is on everyone's lips. Thus Hemingway establishes his supremacy over a territory ordinarily attributed to his friend and rival."

From Jean Méral, *Paris in American Literature,* translated by Lourette Long (Chapel Hill: University of North Carolina Press, 1989), pp. 145-146.

Wales returns to the city to reclaim his daughter, Honoria, from his sister-in-law, Marion Peters, and her husband, Lincoln. On the one hand, Charlie recognizes the destructiveness of his 1920s lifestyle, which was financed by profits from the booming American stock market. Yet, in the bleaker, postcrash 1930s, he also seems nostalgic for the carefree fun and frivolity of the 1920s. "It was nice while it lasted," he decides early in the story. Expatriates "were a sort of royalty, almost infallible, with a sort of magic around us" (619). Charlie's plan to reclaim his daughter is ruined when two drunken friends from the past barge into Marion and Lincoln's apartment demanding that Charlie go carousing with them. Doubting that Charlie has truly settled down, Marion refuses to release Honoria to him. The story ends with Charlie returning to the Ritz Bar, where he recognizes how expatriation and easy money have destroyed his life. "I heard you lost a lot in the crash," the bartender says. "I did," Charlie answers, "but I lost everything I wanted in the boom" (633).

Bad Boy of Music, by George Antheil (Garden City, N.J.: Doubleday, Doran, 1945). This autobiography by the composer of *Ballet Mécanique* includes a flattering mention of Hemingway—unexpectedly, perhaps, considering the two expatriates bickered throughout the mid 1920s. Antheil met Hemingway while living in an apartment above Sylvia Beach's Shakespeare and Company bookshop. Antheil takes credit "in a small way" for "the first widely distributed publication" of Hemingway's first printed work. At the time, Antheil supplemented his income by serving as a talent scout for the German magazine *Der Querschnitt.* Through a friend named George O'Neil (the George of "Cross-Country Snow"), Antheil met Hemingway, who showed him some unpublished stories. Antheil recommended them to his editor, Hans von Wedderkop, who not only printed them but actually paid Hemingway for his contributions (147–148). (*A Moveable Feast* includes a chapter in which Hemingway, plagued by poverty and hunger, receives a check from Wedderkop.) Interestingly, Antheil does not mention Hemingway's public insult of Antheil's music in the *transatlantic review* in 1924. Nor does Antheil describe how he tartly responded with a note that read "Dumb people must have something to talk about and appear smart. Hemingway is among the dumbest."[1] Antheil was virtually alone in not drudging up old grudges to vilify Hemingway.

Being Geniuses Together 1920–1930, by Robert McAlmon and Kay Boyle (Garden City, N.Y.: Doubleday, 1968; republished, San Francisco: North Point Press, 1984). First published in London in 1938 as by McAlmon alone, this memoir by the expatriate publisher of Hemingway's *Three Stories and Ten Poems* (1923) was widely unavailable until 1968, when Boyle added her own reflections on expatriate Paris to an expanded edition. McAlmon first met Hemingway in Rapallo, Italy, in 1923 and traveled with him that spring to Spain for Hemingway's first bullfight. McAlmon criticizes Hemingway's hard-boiled persona by recalling how, during their trip, the two happened upon a dog's decaying corpse that sickened McAlmon. For Hemingway, the reaction meant McAlmon was a romantic unable to stomach "the sight of grim reality." Returning the insult, McAlmon denounces Hemingway as a closet sentimentalist whose "false-naive type of writing" suggests "an older person who insists upon trying to think and write like a child": "There is altogether too much attitudinized insistence upon the starry-eyed innocence and idealism and sentimentality of not only the child but the 'sensitive' roughneck" (158–159). McAlmon expresses affection for Joyce but condemns Stein, whose thousand-page *The Making of Americans* he published in 1925.

The Best Times, by John Dos Passos (New York: New American Library, 1966). Appearing only two years after *A Moveable Feast,* this memoir is intriguing for its lack of bitterness over Hemingway's "pilot fish" slur, which blamed Dos Passos for ruining Ernest and Hadley's marriage by introducing them to rich, frivolous expatriates.

Instead of retaliating, Dos Passos offers a balanced portrait of his literary peer, admiring the writer's "extraordinary dedication to whatever his interest was for the moment" (155) while acknowledging Hemingway's tendency in the 1930s toward egomania. Dos Passos skirts the issue of their long-running feud, noting only that "the troubles that arise between a man and his friends are often purely and simply the result of growing up" (218).

The Confessions of a Harvard Man, by Harold Stearns (Sutton West, Ontario & Santa Barbara, Cal.: Paget Press, 1984). Originally published in 1935 as *The Street I Know,* this 1984 reprint offers one of the most in-depth explanations for why Americans in the 1920s chose to live in Paris. Having edited *Civilization in the United States* (1922), a collection of essays bemoaning the anti-intellectualism of the United States, Stearns was a well-known critic of America. He does not romanticize Paris life in *Confessions,* however. He discusses his own poverty (he supported himself as a handicapper for the Parisian racetracks) and his excessive drinking. The brief comments on Hemingway are positive, although Hemingway satirized Stearns in *The Sun Also Rises.* (Stearns appears as the sodden expatriate Harvey Stone.) As Stearns notes, Hemingway was always willing to lend him money, despite Hemingway's own poverty.

The Diary of Anaïs Nin, 1931–34, by Anaïs Nin, edited by Gunther Stulhmann (New York: Swallow Press, 1966). Long before its publication in 1966, Nin's diary was legendary among expatriates for its account of the author's friendships with Henry Miller, French actor Antonin Artaud, and René Allendy and Otto Rank—two pioneers of psychoanalysis. As the daughter of a Spanish father and a Danish-Creole American mother, Nin grew up with a sense of cultural and ethnic displacement. Born in France but raised in Spain and America, she returned to Paris in the 1920s as the wife of an American banker. *The Diary* is an account of her struggle to determine her identity through creative expression, a struggle that involves breaking her dependency on various charismatic men who have passed through her life, including Miller and her absentee father, who reenters her life after twenty years. The book ends with Nin realizing her identity through independence: "Psychoanalysis did save me because it allowed the birth of the real me, a most dangerous and painful one for a woman, filled with dangers" (359).

Nin published several additional volumes of her diary. This 1966 version is heavily edited; Nin cut the more-graphic passages detailing her

Montparnassians in front of the Dingo, the Paris cafe which Hemingway and Fitzgerald first met in 1925. Among those pictured are James "Jimmy the Barman" Charters (center); Duff Twysden, the model for Brett Ashley in Hemingway's *The Sun Also Rises* (front left); and Kiki (front right).

---

affair with Miller. Since her death, many of these passages have been published in *Henry and June: The Unexpurgated Diary of Anaïs Nin* (1986) and *Incest: From a Journal of Love—The Unexpurgated Diary of Anaïs Nin, 1932–1934* (1992).

The Enormous Room, by E. E. Cummings (New York: Boni & Liveright, 1922; reprinted 1970). This novel was based on Cummings's three-month internment in La Ferté Macé, a French prison camp, on trumped-up charges of fostering pro-German sentiment. Having enlisted in the French ambulance corps in 1917, Cummings had befriended another enlistee, William Slater Brown, on his journey to Europe. During their time in the corps, the duo exasperated their commander with their anti-authoritarianism and friendships with French soldiers. The commander eventually confiscated several of Brown's letters and found them detrimental to the Allies because they discussed a series of mutinies among French forces that almost resulted in German victory. When Cummings refused to condemn his friend, he too was sentenced to be detained for the duration of the war. Sent home to America after three months (Brown was held for an additional two), Cummings began *The Enormous Room* at the request of his father, who planned to use the account as evidence in a suit he intended to file against the French government for its treatment of his son. That *The Enormous Room* would have fared well in a courtroom setting, however, seems doubtful, for its tone is defiant as it skewers the insistence of the military hierarchy on complete subservience to order.

Great Companions: Critical Memoirs of Some Famous Friends, by Max Eastman (New York: Farrar, Straus & Cudahy, 1959). In Hemingway studies, Eastman is best known as the author of a negative review of *Death in the Afternoon* (1932) that culminated in an altercation between the writers in New York in 1937. But Eastman was also active in Montparnasse circles in the early 1920s, and his memoir offers several glimpses of the young "unspoiled" Ernest. In one episode, Eastman encounters a somber Hemingway in front of the Café du Dôme. Hungover, Hemingway asks Eastman whether he feels guilty for lusting after "the girls in those [Paris] nightclubs." Eastman says that he enjoys his lustful feelings and accuses Hemingway of feigning guilt and not "talking real": "To my regret, Ernest jumped up suddenly and, waving me back into my own world with a laugh, continued more briskly his walk up the street. I have no interpretation of that incident—only the vivid memory and a regard that with my brusque remark . . . I blocked a tendency of our friendship to become more confiding than it had been" (50).

The Heart to Artemis: A Writer's Memoirs, by Bryher (Winifred Ellerman) (New York: Harcourt, Brace & World, 1962). British-born Bryher, daughter of shipping magnate Sir John Ellerman, married Robert McAlmon in the early 1920s, although "neither of us felt the slightest attraction towards each other but remained perfectly friendly" (201). Their marriage was one of convenience, designed to hide her lesbianism from her parents and to secure him the funds necessary to start his expatriate press. "It was a marvelous apprenticeship and I am thankful to have shared in a historic moment that seems so much richer today than when I was in the middle of it," she writes of the 1920s. "Although I realized the exhilaration around me, I was a Puritan in Montparnasse and Paris could not give me the same sense of enchantment that it offered my companions" (205). *Artemis* recites fond memories of Hemingway, including a fencing invitation that Bryher declined because one look "at his broad shoulders and [I] knew his reach would be much longer than my own." She also defends Hemingway against accusations of machismo: "Then or now, Hemingway has never seemed to me a 'tough' writer. . . . Hemingway is rather the last of the great Victorians who still believed in loyalty and honor. . . . He never forgot the command of our generation to put down truth as we saw it" (213–214).

It Was the Nightingale, by Ford Madox Ford (Philadelphia: Lippincott, 1933). Published the same year as Stein's *Autobiography of Alice B. Toklas,* Ford's memoir is surprisingly positive in its depiction of Hemingway, despite Hemingway's making no bones about his dislike of this British editor and novelist. (In *The Sun Also Rises* Hemingway parodied Ford as a pompous expatriate named Braddocks.) Ford describes how his young assistant editor at the *transatlantic review* "shadow boxed at . . . the files of unsold reviews, and at my nose, shot tree-leopards that twined through the rails of the editorial gallery and told magnificent tales of the boundless prairies of his birth" (333). He offers some decidedly original legends about the writer's background. ("Mr. Hemingway had, I think, been a cowboy before he became a tauromachic [bullfighting] expert" [335].) Ford also remembers Hemingway's father, Clarence, who committed suicide in late 1928, as "an extraordinarily gentle, swarthy, bearded man who should have been an Elizabethan poet-adventurer" (338).

Kiki's Memoirs, by Kiki (Alice Prin), translated by Samuel Putnam (Paris: Titus, 1928; reprinted, Hopewell, New Jersey: Ecco Press, 1996). One of the most colorful figures in Montparnasse, Kiki was Man Ray's model/lover in the 1920s and an irrepressible presence in expatriate cafés and bars; no memoir of the crazy years in Paris is complete without mention of her. Her autobiography, first published in 1928, is most notable for its inclusion of several Ray photographs; Kiki's own prose, translated by Samuel Putnam, is exuberant but hardly revelatory: "I was so very gay that any poverty didn't make even so much as a dent; and such words as 'kill-joy,' 'gloom,' 'the blues' were just so much Hebrew as far as I was concerned" (129). Hemingway wrote the introduction to the book, calling Kiki "a monument to herself and to the era of Montparnasse."

FICTIONALIZING HEMINGWAY

In addition to massive amounts of scholarship and literary criticism, Hemingway has also inspired several novels that either feature him as a fictional character or that borrow from his life and legend:

Hemingway's Suitcase, by MacDonald Harris (1990). Based on the famous December 1921 incident in which Hadley Hemingway lost a suitcase of her husband's writings at a Paris subway station, this novel explores the intrigue that arises when these early works mysteriously resurface years later.

Hemingway Hoax, by Joe Haldeman (1991). A Hemingway aficionado tries to dodge a time-traveler out to stop him from forging Hemingway works.

Murder in the Latin Quarter, by Tony Hays (1993). Hemingway, James Joyce, Ezra Pound, and Sylvia Beach all make prominent appearances in this mystery novel to catch a murderer in the expatriate community.

I Killed Hemingway, by William McCranor Henderson (1993). A farcical commentary on the Hemingway legend and the American fascination with celebrity in general, the story revolves around a ghostwriter who is hired to write the memoirs of an old salt nicknamed "Pappy."

Hemingway's Chair, by Michael Palin (1998). An unassuming British postmaster lives vicariously through the Hemingway myth by collecting memorabilia. But when an American scholar begins outbidding him for coveted possessions, his personality undergoes a Papaesque transformation.

The Crook Factory, by Dan Simmons (1999). This wartime thriller dramatizes Hemingway's exploits tracking German submarines on his fishing boat, the *Pilar,* during World War II.

Ladies Almanack, by Djuna Barnes (Paris: Privately printed, 1928). *Ladies Almanack* is a satirical celebration of Natalie Barney's lesbian salon at 20, rue Jacob, a gathering place for many female expatriate authors. Because of its salacious subject matter, the book was credited to "A Lady of Fashion" instead of to Barnes, though most expatriates knew the author's identity. Although the book is structured like an almanac, with each chapter built around a different month of the year, it is also a narrative, tracing the efforts of Evangeline Musset (Barney) to accumulate "converts" to her Sapphic circle, known as the Temple of Love.

The Left Bank, by Jean Rhys (Paris: Privately printed, 1927). Best known for her novel *Wide Sargasso Sea* (1966), Rhys's collection of stories about expatriates in Paris is notable both for its satirical portraits of Montparnasse inhabitants (such as artists, art collectors, and drunkards) and for its evocation of Left Bank vistas. In several stories, Rhys highlights the indifference of frolicking Americans to harsher Parisian realities. In "In a Café," for example, a Frenchman sings a song about *les grues de Paris,* "the sellers of illusion of Paris, the frail and sometimes pretty ladies"—in other words, the accommodating local girls with whom expatriate men would dally. After performing his woeful tale of a *grue* rejected by a man who chose to marry a proper woman, the singer sells his sheet music to a young American lady who seems to think herself removed from the conditions of the French women. The story, however, implies that she, too, will suffer the same fate as the *grues* amid the liberalities of Paris. The theme of sexual exploitation runs throughout *The Left Bank;* in another story, set in the Luxembourg Gardens, a young man pursues an attractive girl, hoping a carnal conquest will cure his depression. In yet another story, an aspiring fashion artist gets drunk in a Montparnasse bar in an effort to overcome her failed dreams of being discovered in Paris. All of Rhys's stories depict a sense of defeated expectation and a fear of hunger and poverty, making *The Left Bank* one of the more pessimistic glimpses of expatriate life to emerge in the 1920s.

A Long Way from Home, by Claude McKay (New York: L. Furman, 1937; reprinted, New York: Harcourt, Brace & World, 1970). This autobiography by a leading member of the Harlem Renaissance movement is important for its description of the African-American expatriate experience. As McKay writes, he went abroad not, like white expatriates, in the name of art, sex, or a more economical existence, but because of "color-consciousness": "It was something with which my white fellow-expatriates could sympathize but which they could not altogether understand. For they were not black like me. Not being black and unable to see deep into the profundity of blackness, some even thought that I might have preferred to be white like them. They couldn't imagine that I had no desire merely to exchange my black problem for their white problem. For all their knowledge and sophistication, they couldn't understand the instinctive and animal and purely physical pride of a black person resolute in being himself and yet living a simple civilized life like themselves" (245). McKay praises James Joyce's *Ulysses* (1922), questions the influence of Stein's "Melanctha" (1909) among fellow Harlem writers, and recalls debating a Hemingway detractor over the merits of *In Our Time* at the Café du Dôme.

Lunar Baedeker, by Mina Loy (Paris: Contact Press, 1923); revised as *The Lost Lunar Baedeker,* edited by Roger Conover (Highlands, N.C.: Jargon Society, 1982). A regular contributor to the Parisian little magazines, Loy published this poetry collection with Robert McAlmon's Contact Press in 1923 in the same series of books as Hemingway's *Three Stories and Ten Poems.* Highly praised, *Lunar Baedeker* briefly made Loy one of the most celebrated female expatriate poets. Her work is rich in metaphor and dense in imagery, reasons undoubtedly why modernists such as Eliot and Pound were impressed with the collection. A passage from "English Rose" is typical of her work: "Early English everlasting / quadrate Rose / paradox-Imperial / trimmed with some travestied flesh / tinted with bloodless duties dewed / with Lipton's teas and grimed with crack-packed / herd-housing / petalling. . ." (133).

Sherwood Anderson's Memoirs, by Sherwood Anderson (New York: Harcourt, Brace, 1942). Published less than a year after the author's death, this autobiography includes an account of the 1926 *The Torrents of Spring* controversy. Although *Torrents* marked a decline in Anderson's reputation, he speaks of Hemingway without bitterness. Instead, he describes *Torrents* as evincing his former friend's insecurity; fearful that he might owe a debt to Anderson, Hemingway felt the need to declare his literary independence. As proof, Anderson describes how Hemingway showed up at his Paris hotel room toward the end of 1926, offering to mend fences over a beer. Once served, Hemingway consumed his in a gulp and hurried away, leaving a confused Anderson behind. After that, according to Anderson, he wanted nothing more to do with Hemingway. Anderson insists that *Torrents* did not really bother him, partly because he did not think it good, but partly because he was accustomed to satire. Although William Faulkner had parodied Anderson in the same period, he and Faulkner remained friends because the latter could express his doubts about Anderson's work without stabbing him in the back.

"Miss Toklas' American Cake," by Allen Tate, in his *Memories and Opinions* (Chicago: Swallow Press, 1975). This 1971 essay recounts a famous 1929 dinner party at 27, rue de Fleurus at which Gertrude Stein reportedly declared that Fitzgerald's "flame" or talent burnt brighter than Hemingway's. Tate's recollections of expatriate Paris are opinionated and funny. Upon meeting Hemingway, he was challenged to account for a negative review of *The Sun Also Rises* he had written for *The Nation* several years earlier. But most interesting is his account of the imperious Stein, whose dinner party consisted of a "short course in American literature, beginning with Washington Irving, whose works Miss Stein did not distinguish very clearly from those of James Fenimore Cooper." According to Tate, Stein insisted that "the true genius of America was for abstraction . . . there was . . . the sad case of Henry James, whose novels had abstract design but were ruined by his getting bogged down in the American experience of Europe. . . . The climax, the entelechy towards which all American literature was striving, I need not describe, for the reader has already perceived it" (65). In other words, Stein's lecture ended with a discourse on her own work, which she believed to be the pinnacle of American literature.

My Thirty Years War: The Autobiography: Beginnings and Battles to 1930, by Margaret Anderson (New York: Covici-Friede, 1930; reprinted, New York: Horizon, 1970). As the founding editor of the *Little Review* in 1914, Anderson was an early advocate of modernism, publishing chapters of Joyce's *Ulysses* even after being prosecuted upon obscenity charges in the early 1920s. She was also one of the first Hemingway supporters, printing several poems and the *in our time* vignettes in 1923. In her 1930 autobiography, she recalls visiting Paris in 1924, where Hemingway read to her his "Mr. and Mrs. Elliot," a "gem of a story" that she immediately published. As Stein, McAlmon, and others did, Anderson distinguishes his public and private persona: He "is so soft-hearted that it must be as much as he can bear to beat a punching-bag; and he is so afraid of falling often in love that he doesn't go about as blithely as he used to. He knows that falling in love, for him, is the absorbing emotional experience which leaves him no time for eating, sleeping, working, living" (258–259).

Nightwood, by Djuna Barnes (London: Faber & Faber, 1936 / New York: Harcourt, Brace, 1942). Barnes's 1936 novel offers one of the more hallucinatory visions of modernist Paris. The story revolves around a miscellaneous group of exiles cast out of mainstream society by virtue of their ethnicity, sexual preference, and gender identity. At the heart of the narrative is Robin Vote, an American who wanders perpetually from country to country, relationship to relationship, looking for a home but unable to reconcile herself to it. Much of the narrative centers upon the frustrations of Nora Flood, who loves Robin but whose possessiveness drives her into the arms of Jenny Petherbridge, who is

Josephine Baker symbolized the modernist fascination with African primitivism in the mid 1920s.

also unsuccessful in controlling her. The other main characters include Felix Volkbein, a Jewish orphan who believes himself an aristocrat and is searching for a woman to sire his male heir, and Dr. Matthew O'Connor, a cross-dressing physician who intrudes into the narrative to protest the impossibility of love in the modern age. Barnes based *Nightwood* partly on her affair with American sculptor Thelma Wood (1901–1970), with whom she lived for most of the 1920s. The novel is notable for its dense, challenging style, which mixes slang from the 1920s with Shakespearean soliloquies.

Nineteen-Nineteen, by John Dos Passos (New York: Harcourt, Brace, 1932); reprinted in *U.S.A.: The 42nd Parallel, Nineteen-Nineteen, The Big Money* (Boston: Houghton Mifflin, 1960). The second part of Dos Passos's *U.S.A.* trilogy, *Nineteen-Nineteen* explores the corruptions afflicting the Lost Generation in the year following the 1918 armistice that ended World War I. Because the author's goal is to show how global political and business entities determine the individual's fate, the novel juxtaposes major news events of the time against its plot, which revolves around a half-dozen major characters. Foremost among these is Richard Ellsworth Savage, a Harvard-educated poet who is dismissed from the Red Cross ambulance service when he grows disillusioned with the war. He plans to go to Spain, where he will dedicate himself to poetry, but instead he returns to the United States. There he eventually accepts a commission in the American army and returns to Europe to serve as a courier for the 1919 Paris Peace Conference. He is introduced to J. Ward Moorehouse, a capitalist whose behind-the-scenes influence on the conference suggests big business's power over politics. By entering Moorehouse's circle, Dick sacrifices his literary and cultural ideals and becomes a mere cog in the machine, growing hard and indifferent to suffering in his public and private lives. As he works in Paris, he falls in love with Anne Elizabeth Trent, but he abandons her out of self-interest when she reveals she is pregnant.

As a running contrast to Dick's corruption, Dos Passos also follows the story of an unnamed "I," often called the "Camera Eye" narrator by critics because this character's perspective is presented as an everyman's parallel to Dick's skewed view of the world. Many of the Camera Eye's experiences parallel Dick's: the "I," too, serves in the ambulance corps, but instead of becoming an officer, he remains a lowly enlisted man and must suffer constant exposure to the absurd regulations of military bureaucracy. Once discharged, he also settles in Paris, but he settles in an artistic area of the city where the vibrancy and excitement of life prove stimulating. In one impressionistic record of his enthusiasm, he explains how modernist painting, music, and writing will lead to a new world. Paris is a "Nouvelle Athène," and modernism is a "revolution round the spinning Eiffel Tower . . . that burns up our last year's diagrams the dates fly off the calendar we'll make everything new today is the Year 1 Today is the sunny morning of the first day of spring We gulp our coffee splash water on us jump into our clothes run downstairs step out wideawake into first morning of the first day of the first year" (344–345). Perhaps borrowing a motif from Hemingway, Dos Passos locates the world of the Camera Eye in the working-class environs of the Place de Contrescarpe (where Hemingway and Hadley resided in 1921–1922). He associates with radicals, observing a failed May Day revolution in the streets of Paris and attending a picnic hosted by anarchists, which strikes him as an absurd contradiction. Unlike Dick, however, he does not betray his ideals. Even at the end of the novel, as he is reduced to menial labor until he can secure identification papers that prove he was discharged from the army, he recommits himself to establishing an aesthetic life that rejects American materialism and hypocrisy.

The stories of Richard Savage and the Camera Eye make up only a portion of the encyclopedic look at the postwar epoch in the novel. Other sections follow working-class characters in America who become involved in leftist politics. Given its scope of settings and techniques, Dos Passos's novel remains one of the most experimental products of expatriate modernism.

Paris France, by Gertrude Stein (London: Batsford, 1940). Less an autobiography than a meditation on French life and character, this book represents Stein's attempt to account for why "Paris was the place that suited those of us that were to create twentieth century art and literature" (12). The city was both old and new, Stein notes, at once attuned to the changes modernity brought while remaining respectful of tradition. America was too infatuated with progress, while England denied the changing times. Only France, with its relaxed attitude and mellow pace, could accept the transformations of the twentieth century without worrying about them. "When the twentieth century was going to start," Stein writes, "the Frenchmen were very content to be in it but not part of it" (107). France's sense of its secure connection to tradition and history thus provided a stable perspective from which artists could view the tumult of the times: "It begins to be reasonable that the twentieth century whose mechanics, whose crimes, whose standardization began in America, needed the background of Paris, the place where tradition was so

SAVE ME THE WALTZ, TENDER IS THE NIGHT, AND THE GARDEN OF EDEN

Although Hemingway declared *Tender Is the Night* a failure when it was published in 1934, the novel was clearly on his mind in the late 1940s and 1950s as he struggled through versions of *The Garden of Eden*. Like Fitzgerald's novel, Hemingway's story of domestic dissolution explores the troubling effects of expatriation, adultery, and madness. Accordingly, critics have been tempted to read Hemingway's posthumously published novel as a response to Fitzgerald's story of jealousy and dependency. As Nancy R. Comley notes, Hemingway's Catherine Bourne possesses many of the qualities that Hemingway attributed to Zelda Fitzgerald—in particular her emotional instability. Comley, however, suggests yet another source for *The Garden of Eden*—Zelda's own *Save Me the Waltz* (1932):

"Hemingway appropriated the Fitzgeralds' story of the talented writer with the crazy wife, but he would adapt it to a character like himself as writer. Zelda, as his model for madness, spoke not only in his memory, and through Fitzgerald's texts, but also through her own. To Maxwell Perkins ... Hemingway wrote, 'Zelda I found to be completely and absolutely unreadable';... having considered Zelda 'crazy' from his first meeting with her, Hemingway suggests that she, as well as her novel, are texts he either cannot or does not wish to read.... Zelda herself and Zelda's text were too closely wedded for Hemingway to read comfortably. Yet the two conjoined provided the discourse of madness that Hemingway would draw on in creating the Catherines of *The Garden of Eden*."

From Nancy R. Comley, "Madwomen on the Riviera: The Fitzgeralds, Hemingway, and the Matter of Modernism," in *French Connections: Hemingway and Fitzgerald Abroad*, edited by J. Gerald Kennedy and Jackson R. Bryer (New York: St. Martin's Press, 1994), p. 287.

firm that they could look modern without being different, and where their acceptance of reality is so great that they could let any one have the emotion of unreality" (18). The affection of *Paris France* for tradition proved bittersweet when, shortly before its publication, the city fell to Adolf Hitler's forces.

Paris Was Our Mistress: Memoirs of a Lost and Found Generation, by Samuel Putnam (New York: Viking, 1947). This autobiography describes how Hemingway changed over the course of his Paris years. Having met the writer in Chicago in the early 1920s, Putnam insists that Hemingway became more affected as he became part of the Montparnasse literary scene. In one episode at a café, Hemingway pretentiously discourses on the writer's duty to truth. "Apothegms dropped from his lips," Putnam writes, "as from those of a brilliant sophomore doing his best not to appear too brilliant" (128).

The Passionate Years, by Caresse Crosby (New York: Dial, 1953). The widow of Harry Crosby, whose 1929 suicide is analyzed in Malcolm Cowley's *Exile's Return*, recounts the founding of the couple's small press, Black Sun: "We knew that someday we must see our poems in print—it did not occur to us to submit them to a publishing house—the simplest way to get a poem into a book was to print the book!" (146). *Years* also offers an extended portrait of poet Hart Crane, whose *The Bridge* (1930), a poetic repudiation of Eliot's *The Waste Land*, appeared under the Crosby imprint.

Quartet, by Jean Rhys (New York: Simon & Schuster, 1929) and **Good Morning,**

Midnight, by Jean Rhys (London: Constable, 1939); reprinted together in Jean Rhys, *The Complete Novels* (New York: Norton, 1985). The publication of Rhys's *The Left Bank* owed a debt to Ford Madox Ford, who published selections in the *transatlantic review* and advised the young author. With that assistance, however, came a bizarre demand: Ford coerced Rhys into a ménage à trois with his mistress Stella Bowen. That painful relationship is treated in *Quartet,* Rhys's 1929 semi-autobiographical novel, in which Marya Zelli becomes entangled romantically with H. J. Heidler, an art dealer, when her husband, Stephen, is imprisoned on theft charges in Paris.

A year after *Quartet,* Rhys published *Good Morning, Midnight,* a much better novel that also explores the isolation and desperation of economically insecure women expatriates. The heroine in this novel is Sasha Jansen, a middle-aged woman who, while revisiting Paris, is haunted by memories of past loves. As with all Rhys heroines, Sasha is plagued by economic uncertainty. While she lives off a small inheritance, she has bitter memories of working in grungy dress shops for employers who forever cheated her of her pay. Toward the end of the novel she tries to escape her loneliness by taking up with a gigolo named René, but her inhibitions and guardedness prevent her from opening up to the young man. During one encounter, she tries to pay René not to make love to her but to leave her. When she discovers that he has departed without taking the money, she realizes he has a heart and calls for him to come back. In a bizarre twist, the man who enters her room is not René but a fellow hotel guest who takes advantage of her confusion. This strange seduction scene is typical of Rhys's writing, in which people are incapable of establishing lasting relationships. In her work, Paris is a site of profound spiritual and emotional emptiness.

Shakespeare and Company, by Sylvia Beach (New York: Harcourt, Brace, 1953). The owner of Paris's legendary expatriate bookstore (and the publisher of Joyce's *Ulysses*) describes Hemingway as her "best customer." Beach recalls Hemingway showing her his war wounds on their initial meeting, tutoring her and her companion Adrienne Monnier in boxing and bicycling, and reading her his early fiction: "We were impressed by his originality . . . his storyteller's gift and sense of the dramatic, his power to create—well, I could go on, but as Adrienne summed him up: 'Hemingway has the true writer's temperament'" (81). The book ends with Hemingway's reappearance on the rue de l'Odéon in 1944 during the liberation of Paris from the Nazis: "He wanted to know if there was anything he could do for us. We asked him if he could do something about the Nazi snipers on the roof tops in our street. . . . He got his company out of the jeeps and took them up to the roof. We heard firing for the last time. . . . Hemingway and his men came down again and rode off in their jeeps—'to liberate,' according to Hemingway, 'the cellar at the Ritz'" (220).

Tender Is the Night, by F. Scott Fitzgerald (New York: Scribners, 1934). Fitzgerald's long-delayed novel traces the dissolution of Dr. Dick Diver, a talented psychiatrist. As the novel opens on the Riviera in 1925, there is little hint of the instability that will destroy him. Instead, a young silent-movie actress, Rosemary Hoyt, views the expatriate lifestyle as glamorous and exciting as she is introduced to Dick and his wife, Nicole, who embody the aristocratic ideal of sophistication and taste. In her youthful naiveté, Rosemary imagines them as magnetic personalities whose charm attracts the attention of other expatriates. Undercurrents of trouble in the Divers' seemingly idyllic existence begin to surface, though, as the couple's coterie journeys to Paris. Rosemary and Dick contemplate an affair; the Divers' friend Abe North succumbs to alcoholism; and Nicole eventually suffers an emotional breakdown when an acquaintance of North is murdered in Rosemary's hotel room.

A flashback scene accounts for Nicole's emotional problems. Originally Dick's patient at a psychiatric clinic in Switzerland, she was a victim of incest who was drawn to her doctor as she searched for a paternal substitute to protect her in the way her own father had failed to. But her dependence on Dick appeals to his central weakness, his vain belief in his own poise and strength of character. The flashback reveals that the Divers' marriage is built upon the same shaky premise as his flirtation with Rosemary—both young girls fall in love with an image of Dick that proves faulty. When the action shifts back to 1925, it becomes clear that Dick's discovery of his own weakness and fallibility is the main point of the novel. Following his dissipation through a return to the Riviera in 1929, the novel documents Dick's corruption through drinking, fistfights, and an increasing reliance on Nicole's inherited wealth. Complementing his descent is Nicole's rising independence. By the time she begins an affair with Tommy Barban and prepares herself to leave her marriage, she has outgrown her need for Dick's protective oversight. The novel ends with Dick returning to America, broken, and disappearing into the obscure, unremarkable life of a general practitioner in upstate New York: "He was not young any more with a lot of nice thoughts and dreams to have about himself" (334).

That Summer in Paris: Memories of Tangled Friendships with Hemingway, Fitzgerald, and Some Others, by Morley Callaghan (New York: Coward-McCann, 1963). Canadian novelist Callaghan first met Hemingway during the latter's short 1923 tenure in Toronto as a reporter for the *Star.* Callaghan describes how Hemingway encouraged his writing, even publishing his stories in the *transatlantic review.* Most of the memoir, however, is concerned with the repercussions of a famous incident in 1929 when Hemingway and Callaghan were sparring partners in Paris. During one boxing session at the American Club, Callaghan landed a punch that knocked Hemingway on his back. The incident never would have happened had not Fitzgerald, who was serving as the timekeeper for the match, forgotten to call the round at the right moment. Furious, Hemingway insisted that Fitzgerald intentionally let the sparring go on and insulted him in front of Callaghan. Some time later, a notice appeared in the *New York Herald Tribune* describing how Callaghan had knocked Hemingway out at the Dôme café. The publicity led to strained relations among the three writers; according to Callaghan, the incident taught him the "grim lesson" that "you can't be sustained by the praise and admiration of a few friends. You lose them along the way anyway, and since you should always be changing and becoming something else, the friends, if they stay alive, may not stay with you" (253–254).

The Way It Was, by Harold Loeb (New York: Criterion, 1959). Loeb, the model for Robert Cohn in *The Sun Also Rises,* published this memoir in 1959, recounting his experience in Paris as the editor of the short-lived little magazine *Broom* and the July 1925 excursion to Pamplona that inspired Hemingway's novel. The memoir is notable for the affectionate portrait of Duff Twysden (or Twitchell, as Loeb calls her), upon whom Brett Ashley was based. Loeb recounts the couple's tryst in St.-Jean-de-Luz, noting Hemingway's jealousy and his own crush on Duff. *The Way It Was* ends without Loeb's mentioning Hemingway's unflattering portrait of him in *The Sun Also Rises.*

This Must Be The Place: Memoirs of Montparnasse, by Jimmie, the Barman, by James Charters, edited by Morrill Cody (London: Joseph, 1934). Known as "Jimmy the Barman," Charters was the expatriates' favorite bartender. That he could publish an autobiography in 1934 testifies to the appetite for stories about the Lost Generation at the time. As with *Kiki's Memoirs,* Hemingway wrote the introduction to the book, which is notable for its bitter response to Stein's recently published *Autobiography of Alice B. Toklas.*

Tropic of Cancer, by Henry Miller (Paris: Guardian Obelisk, 1934; reprinted, New York: Grove, 1961). Upon its publication *Tropic of Cancer* gained instant notoriety for its graphic depiction of the author's sexual adventures in the City of Light. Deemed pornographic, the novel was available in America only as contraband until the early 1960s. While many readers come away from *Tropic of Cancer* shocked and offended by its cavalier depiction of women, it is nevertheless an important expatriate text, notable for the link between creativity and eros that it celebrates. "There is only one thing which interests me vitally now," Miller writes, "and that is the recording of all that which is omitted in books" (11). Accordingly, *Tropic of Cancer* takes readers on a whirlwind tour of brothels, bidets, back alleys, bedbugs, genitalia, poverty, and hunger. Miller's essential point is that in a world ridden with disease and decay, the only expressions of vitality possible are primal impulses. "It may be that we are doomed, that there is no hope for us, *any of us,* but if that is so then let us send up a last agonizing, bloodcurdling howl, a screech of defiance, a war whoop! Away with lamentation! Away with elegies and dirges! . . . Let us living ones dance about the rim of the crater, a last inspiring dance. But what a dance!" (257). Like Walt Whitman (to whom he often compared himself), Miller located the source of knowledge in feeling—linking sensuality to intuition and insight. Consequently, *Tropic of Cancer* rants against the debilitating effects of repression as it revels in its own bawdy impulses.

A Voyage to Pagany, by William Carlos Williams (New York: New Directions, 1970). This 1928 semi-autobiographical novel is based on the author's 1924 journey abroad. "Pagany" is his name for Europe, so dubbed because its pre-Christian cultural heritage makes a more hospitable home for culture and art than puritanical America. Like Williams, the chief protagonist is a middle-aged general practitioner, Dr. "Dev" Evans, who takes a sabbatical from his profession to tour the great continental sites. Along the way, he indulges in an affair on the Riviera with another expatriate and later, in Vienna, briefly studies pediatrics at Leipzig University. Without much plot, *Voyage* often reads like a travel book, with Williams meditating on French, Italian, and Austrian landmarks. In the end, Evans decides to return to America, believing (unlike other expatriates depicted in the book) that America possesses the resources possible for great art but lacks artists to sing its praises. During a picnic near the Seine with his sister Bess, he realizes that where one lives should not determine how one writes, for "art is a country by itself" (251).

NOTE

1. Quoted in Michael S. Reynolds, *Hemingway: The Paris Years* (New York: Blackwell, 1989), p. 227.

RESOURCES FOR
MODERNISM STUDY

STUDY QUESTIONS

1. Select two Hemingway works set in Paris (*The Sun Also Rises* and *A Moveable Feast*). Examine the influence of place upon the major characters. Focus specifically upon the different sites that they frequent. How do the revelers at the Café du Dôme and the Sélect differ from the young Hemingway at the Closerie des Lilas? How do their surroundings reflect the characters' values?

2. Read three or more Hemingway war works set in Italy (for example, *A Farewell to Arms,* "Now I Lay Me," and "In Another Country"). What is the Hemingway hero's attitude toward war? How do the characters' near-death experiences and/or wounding affect them?

3. Examine two Hemingway works set in Spain (the Pamplona section of *The Sun Also Rises,* "A Clean, Well-lighted Place," and *For Whom the Bell Tolls* are good examples). What is Hemingway's attitude toward this country? In what ways does his depiction of the settings contribute to the characters' drama?

4. Select several of Hemingway's marriage tales (for example, "Out of Season," "Cat in the Rain," *The Garden of Eden, A Moveable Feast*). How does living abroad affect these couples' relationships? What problems seem to be compounded by their expatriation?

5. Examine three or more of Hemingway's sports stories (for example, "My Old Man," "Fifty Grand," "The Undefeated," and the bullfighting scenes in *The Sun Also Rises*). What values do these athletic endeavors embody? What challenges must characters confront to maintain their professional ethics? Are they still heroes even if they fail to uphold their ethics?

6. Read *Death in the Afternoon* and *Green Hills of Africa*. Characterize Hemingway's self-presentation. What similarities does he find between bullfighting and game hunting on the one hand and writing on the other? How does he portray critics of his work?

7. Read Fitzgerald's *Tender Is the Night* and Hemingway's *The Garden of Eden*. Do Dick Diver and David Bourne compare in any way? Why does expatriation wreck Dick, while David is able to survive and overcome his conflicts?

8. Read *In Our Time*. What modernist techniques does Hemingway employ? How does the arrangement of the stories and interchapters reinforce the themes and difficulties in the various stories?

9. Examine Hemingway's use of dialogue in two stories ("Hills Like White Elephants" and "The Sea Change" are examples). What literary devices (repetition, for example) does the author use to convey the characters' problems? How do the characters talk around their conflicts rather than addressing them directly? How does their expatriation contribute to their problems?

10. Contrast a Hemingway war story (the *In Our Time* vignettes or "Now I Lay Me," for example) to John Dos Passos's "The Body of an American," from *Nineteen-Nineteen*. How do the authors' different approaches to depicting the effects of war shape their works? Do Hemingway's techniques in any way parallel Dos Passos's?

11. Select a Hemingway biography, focusing in particular on the depiction of Hemingway's early years in Paris (1921–1924). How differently does each biographer depict the young Hemingway's expatriation? What problems did Ernest and Hadley face? How did Hemingway relate to other expatriates such as Gertrude Stein, Ford Madox Ford, and F. Scott Fitzgerald?

12. Choose a Hemingway story ("Big Two-Hearted River" or "Soldier's Home," for example) and, with the help of Hemingway biographies, discuss the autobiographical aspects of that work. What events in the text actually occurred? What parts did Hemingway invent?

13. Read *A Farewell to Arms, For Whom the Bell Tolls,* and two or more Nick Adams stories. What values does each Hemingway hero possess?

14. Compare/contrast Brett Ashley in *The Sun Also Rises,* Catherine Barkley in *A Farewell to Arms,* and Maria in *For Whom the Bell Tolls.* What do these different Hemingway heroines say about Hemingway's attitude toward women? Is he more sympathetic to some? Why? Which characters seem flat or unrealistic?

15. Read *Green Hills of Africa, True at First Light,* and "The Snows of Kilimanjaro." What do these texts say about Hemingway's attitude toward Africa? What values does the continent embody for him?

16. Compare an early Hemingway story (for example, "Soldier's Home" or "Mr. and Mrs. Elliot") to Gertrude Stein's "Miss Furr and Miss Skeene" (from *Geography and Plays,* 1923). What techniques did Hemingway learn from Stein? In what ways did he use these techniques differently? After you draft your initial response, read Wyndham Lewis's essay "The Dumb Ox" (reprinted in *Hemingway: The Critical Heritage,* edited by Jeffrey Meyers) and compare/contrast your findings to his.

17. Examine the stream-of-consciousness passages in "The Snows of Kilimanjaro." After consulting Hemingway biographies and *A Moveable Feast,* explore the ways in which Hemingway fictionalized his early Paris years with Hadley. What do these passages reveal about his feelings toward his first marriage?

18. Examine the representations of women in "The Short Happy Life of Francis Macomber" and "The Snows of Kilimanjaro." Consult Bernice Kert's *The Hemingway Women* (1983) for more information.

19. Explore the thematic importance of eating in Hemingway's fiction. Select texts in which food is an important motif (for example, *The Sun Also Rises, A Farewell to Arms,* and *A Moveable Feast*). What does the way in which Hemingway's heroes eat reveal about their values?

20. Explore the thematic importance of drinking in Hemingway's fiction. Select texts in which drinking is an important motif (for example, *The Sun Also Rises,* "Hills Like White Elephants," and "The Sea Change"). What does the way in which Hemingway's heroes drink reveal about their values?

21. Examine the portrait of Ezra Pound in *A Moveable Feast.* Using Hemingway biographies, explore why Pound was one of the few expatriate friends with whom Hemingway maintained good relations. Why did these writers continue to respect each other when Stein and other former friends turned against Hemingway?

22. Read chapter 1, section 5 of Malcolm Cowley's *Exile's Return* (titled "Ambulance Service"). Then read Hemingway's *A Farewell to Arms,* the Richard Savage chapters of John Dos Passos's *Nineteen-Nineteen,* and E. E. Cummings's *The Enormous Room.* Do these works support Cowley's "spectatorial attitude" thesis? If so, how? If not, why not?

23. Compare Hemingway's *A Moveable Feast* to another memoir of Paris, whether Stein's *The Autobiography of Alice B. Toklas* or Robert McAlmon's *Being Geniuses Together.* How differently does Paris

inspire each author's creativity? What Parisian sites does each associate with his or her art?

24. Classify the different types of expatriates that appear in Hemingway's works. Revise the categories offered in chapter 4. In other words, instead of labeling Brett Ashley a decadent, is there another way of describing her behavior?

25. Explore Hemingway's thematic obsession with death. How do Hemingway characters confront their fear of death in the *In Our Time* vignettes? Is their response similar to or different from Frederic Henry's in *A Farewell to Arms* or Robert Jordan's in *For Whom the Bell Tolls?*

PARIS EXPATRIATES IN THE 1920S AND 1930S

The following list offers introductory biographical material on the most influential expatriates in the heyday of the Lost Generation, with particular emphasis on those most relevant to Hemingway's development.

MARGARET C. ANDERSON (1886–1973). Anderson was the founder of the *Little Review* (1914–1929), which published excerpts from James Joyce's *Ulysses* (1922) as well as the early Hemingway vignettes of *In Our Time* (1925).

SHERWOOD ANDERSON (1876–1941). Author of *Winesburg Ohio* (1919), *The Triumph of the Egg* (1921), and *Death in the Woods* (1933)—all influential short-story collections—Anderson met Hemingway in 1921 in Chicago, encouraging him to move to Paris. Later Hemingway parodied Anderson's novel *Dark Laughter* (1925) in *The Torrents of Spring* (1926).

GEORGE ANTHEIL (1900–1959). Flamboyant composer and pianist, Antheil wrote *Ballet Mécanique* (1925) in Paris while living above Sylvia Beach's Shakespeare and Company bookstore. Later in life he turned Hemingway's short story "The Capital of the World" (1936) into a ballet.

DJUNA BARNES (1892–1982). Barnes was a journalist, poet, short-story writer, and novelist who relocated to Paris in the early 1920s, where she fell in love with Thelma Wood, a relationship that inspired *Nightwood* (1936), her best-known novel. She was also author of *Ryder* (1928), *Ladies Almanack* (1928), and several volumes of stories. Many critics speculate that Hemingway borrowed Barnes's last name for the hero of *The Sun Also Rises* (1926).

NATALIE CLIFFORD BARNEY (1877–1972). Heiress to a railroad-car-works fortune, Barney established a salon at 20, rue Jacob frequented by lesbian writers. An aficionado of Greek culture, she fashioned herself into a modern-day Sappho.

SYLVIA BEACH (1887–1962). Owner and operator of Shakespeare and Company, the preeminent expatriate bookstore, Beach also published the first edition of Joyce's *Ulysses*.

WILLIAM BIRD (1888–1963). Journalist and founder of Three Mountains Press, Bird was publisher of Hemingway's *in our time* (1924).

JOHN PEALE BISHOP (1892–1944). A Princeton contemporary of F. Scott Fitzgerald and Edmund Wilson, Bishop wrote poetry and fiction but is best remembered as an essayist whose work includes at least two important accounts of the Lost Generation—"Homage to Hemingway" (1936) and "The Missing All" (1937).

KAY BOYLE (1902–1992). Boyle arrived in Paris at nineteen, served an apprenticeship under Robert McAlmon and Eugene Jolas, helped edit the little magazine *This Quarter,* and went on to become a prolific novelist. In the late 1960s she contributed her autobiographical reflections on the 1920s to an expanded version of McAlmon's memoir *Being Geniuses Together* (1968).

BRYHER (WINIFRED ELLERMAN) (1894–1962). Daughter of a shipping magnate, Bryher married Robert McAlmon to conceal her lesbianism from her parents. She wrote *Two Selves* (1923) in addition to several other volumes of poetry, prose, and memoirs.

JAMES CHARTERS (1897–?). Also known as "Jimmy the Barman," Charters, an Irishman, was the bartender of choice among expatriates. His *This Must Be the Place* (1934) recounts the American colony's colorful exploits throughout the 1920s.

MALCOLM COWLEY (1898–1989). Cowley was a writer and critic; his *Exile's Return* (1934) and *A Second Flowering* (1973) are two of the most important analyses of the Lost Generation.

HART CRANE (1899–1932). An innovative poet, Crane's major work, *The Bridge* (1930), sings the praises of American popular culture, technology, and advertising, as well as its manmade and natural landmarks. Two years after publishing *The Bridge*, Crane committed suicide by jumping from an ocean liner.

HARRY CROSBY (1898–1929). Nephew of oil-magnate J. P. Morgan, Crosby established the Black Sun Press in Paris, where he published both his own work and D. H. Lawrence's. He died as a result of a bizarre murder-suicide pact with his mistress. Cowley's *Exile's Return* analyzes Crosby's excesses.

CARESSE CROSBY (1892–1970). Wife of Harry Crosby, Caresse Crosby carried on their independent publishing venture after his death. Her *Passionate Years* (1953) is a highly readable memoir.

E. E. CUMMINGS (1894–1962). One of the most influential of American poets, Cummings gained early fame for *The Enormous Room* (1922), an experimental account of his imprisonment during the waning days of the Great War.

HILDA DOOLITTLE (H.D.) (1886–1961). A poet originally considered a protégé of Pound for her Imagist verse, H.D. also wrote fiction—including *Palimpsest* (1925), a trio of long short stories, and *Hermione* (written in 1927 but not published until 1981), a semi-autobiographical novel.

JOHN DOS PASSOS (1896–1970). A prolific author, Dos Passos is best known for his *U.S.A.* trilogy (1938), which includes *The 42nd Parallel* (1930), *Nineteen-Nineteen* (1932), and *The Big Money* (1936), all of which include his trademark techniques (the newsreel, camera eye, and interpolated biography). Dos Passos befriended Hemingway in the mid 1920s but later broke with him over the Spanish Civil War. Dos Passos's memoir, *The Best Times* (1966), recounts his acquaintance with Hemingway, Fitzgerald, and Cummings. His *Manhatten Transfer* (1925) was among the earliest American modernist novels.

T. S. ELIOT (1888–1965). Although never a resident of Paris, Eliot was nevertheless a central influence among expatriates. He was revered by the American colony for *The Waste Land* (1922), a dense, cryptic survey of the emptiness of modern life.

F. SCOTT FITZGERALD (1896–1940). Author of *The Great Gatsby* (1925), *Tender Is the Night* (1934), and several classic short stories, including "Babylon Revisited," Fitzgerald wrote extensively about expatriation in the late 1920s and early 1930s.

ZELDA FITZGERALD (1900–1948). Wife of Scott Fitzgerald, Zelda was a talented if undisciplined painter and writer, though mostly remembered as the inspiration for her husband's literary heroines. Her novel, *Save Me the Waltz* (1932), includes a fictionalized account of the Fitzgeralds' experiences on the French Riviera.

JANET FLANNER (1892–1978). A long-time commentator for *The New Yorker* on the expatriate Paris scene, Flanner regularly corresponded with Hemingway.

FORD MADOX FORD (FORD MADOX HUEFFER) (1873–1939). English expatriate, author of *The Good Soldier* (1915), *It Was the Nightingale* (1933), and several volumes of fiction and criticism, Ford founded the *transatlantic review* in 1924, taking on Hemingway as both an assistant editor and contributor. Hemingway depicts him unfavorably in both *The Sun Also Rises* and *A Moveable Feast* (1964).

EUGENE JOLAS (1894–1952). Jolas was a columnist for the *Paris Tribune* and the founder of *transition,* an important little magazine that promoted James Joyce.

JAMES JOYCE (1882–1941). Irish expatriate and author of *Dubliners* (1914), *Ulysses* (1922), and *Finnegans Wake* (1939), Joyce was declared by Hemingway (among others) as the greatest of modernist writers.

KIKI OF MONTPARNASSE (ALICE PRIN) (1901–1953). Flamboyant habitué of Montparnasse bars and cafés, Kiki was Man Ray's lover and model throughout the 1920s.

WYNDHAM LEWIS (1882–1957). Cofounder of Vorticism with Ezra Pound, Lewis was both a painter and writer. He wrote a scathing estimation of Hemingway and Gertrude Stein in "The Dumb Ox" (1933).

HAROLD LOEB (1891–1974). Founder of *Broom,* an important little magazine, Loeb wrote several novels before becoming an economist in the 1930s. Best remembered as the inspiration for Robert Cohn in *The Sun Also Rises,* his memoir *The Way It Was* (1959) recounts his Paris years.

MINA LOY (1882–1966). Loy is the author of *Lunar Baedeker* (1923), a celebrated collection of poems written in the 1920s.

ROBERT MCALMON (1896–1956). Nominal husband of Bryher, McAlmon used money from his wife's wealthy family to found Contact Press, which published Hemingway's *Three Stories and Ten Poems* (1923) and Stein's *The Making of Americans* (1925). McAlmon was also an author, writing *A Hasty Bunch* (stories; 1922), *Post-Adolescence* (published posthumously, 1991), and *Being Geniuses Together* (1938).

CLAUDE MCKAY (1890–1948). A poet and fiction writer, McKay was a leading contributor to the Harlem Renaissance movement; his *Home to Harlem* (1928) remains a much studied work.

HENRY MILLER (1891–1980). Controversial author of *The Tropic of Cancer* (1934), a celebration of Paris's decadent sensuality, Miller also wrote several volumes of fiction, letters, and social commentary. He is often linked with Anaïs Nin.

ADRIENNE MONNIER (1892–1955). Monnier was Sylvia Beach's long-term companion who operated her own French bookstore, La Maison des Amis des Livres, on the rue de l'Odéon, across the street from Beach's Shakespeare and Company.

GERALD MURPHY (1888–1964) AND **SARA MURPHY (1883–1975).** Heir to the Mark Cross luxury leather goods fortune, Gerald Murphy was a painter and literary enthusiast who, with his wife Sara, befriended both the Hemingways and the Fitzgeralds in the mid 1920s. The Murphys were partial models for Dick and Nicole Diver in *Tender Is the Night.* In *A Moveable Feast,* Hemingway, although not mentioning them by name, implies their money corrupted him.

ANAÏS NIN (1903–1977). French-born Nin was the author of several volumes of fiction before publishing the first of a series of diary excerpts in 1966. She was also a friend and early supporter of Henry Miller.

ELLIOT PAUL (1891–1958). Columnist for the *Paris Tribune,* Paul also wrote several novels.

EZRA POUND (1885–1972). Perhaps the single most influential poet of the twentieth century, Pound was the author of "Hugh Selwyn Mauberly" (1920) and the *Cantos* (1917–1968). Most expatriate writers remembered him fondly for helping them publish their writing.

SAMUEL PUTNAM (1892–1950). Translator, biographer, and essayist, Putnam arrived in Paris in 1927. He worked with Kiki on her memoirs and also published Henry Miller's work in his short-lived little magazine *New Review* (1931–1933).

JEAN RHYS (1890–1979). A British expatriate, Rhys's story collection *The Left Bank* (1927) and several novels from the late 1920s to the early 1930s document the economic frustrations and loneliness of independent women living in Paris.

HAROLD STEARNS (1891–1943). A critic and intellectual whose *America and the Young Intellectual* (1921) fomented the expatriate movement, Stearns is noted in expatriate memoirs for his habitual presence at the Sélect Café.

GERTRUDE STEIN (1874–1946). Modernism's most misunderstood figure, Stein was the author of poems, novels, and criticism—almost all written in her hermetic, obscure style. She won a popular audience with *The Autobiography of Alice B. Toklas* (1933) and later published an intriguing account of living through both world wars in France (*Wars I Have Seen*, 1945).

ALLEN TATE (1890–1979). Poet, novelist, and critic, Tate became a leading member of the Agrarians, a group of influential Southern writers. His essay "Miss Toklas's American Cake" (1971) recounts a tension-laden evening at Stein's residence at 27, rue de Fleurus with Hemingway and Fitzgerald.

VIRGIL THOMSON (1896–1989). Composer with Stein of *Four Saints in Three Acts* (1928), Thomson also scored Stein's *The Mother of Us All* (1947), an opera about Susan B. Anthony.

ALICE B. TOKLAS (1877–1967). Gertrude Stein's long-term companion, Toklas became an expatriate publisher when she and Stein founded their Plain Edition in the early 1930s.

CARL VAN VECHTEN (1880–1964). Journalist, novelist, dramatist, and devotee of Stein, Van Vechten helped arrange Stein's 1934–1935 return to America.

WILLIAM CARLOS WILLIAMS (1883–1963). An influential poet who also wrote fiction and criticism, Williams—although he toured Europe in the mid 1920s—preferred New Jersey, which became the subject of his extended poetry cycle *Paterson* (1946–1958). His expatriate novel *A Voyage to Pagany* (1928) is unjustly ignored.

LITERARY TERMS AND MOVEMENTS

Abstraction: In common usage, abstract refers to language in which the meaning is imprecisely expressed. In modernist art, it has a more positive connotation. Through abstraction, a writer suggests the general characteristics of the subject matter by depicting its particulars in a new, provocative way.

Aesthetics: Formally, aesthetics is a branch of philosophy concerned with defining elemental aspects of beauty. Informally, in literary criticism the term is used to designate the qualities of art valued by a specific author or literary movement.

Allusion: An allusion is a reference to a literary work, character, or setting. It is used to suggest unexpressed significance that a reader may or may not perceive, depending upon his or her knowledge of myth, history, and literature. Allusions allowed modernist writers to establish a connection to the past in their poetry and fiction. In a line of his "Hugh Selwyn Mauberly," Ezra Pound uses two allusions to describe his main character's artistic ideals: "His true Penelope was Flaubert." Pound assumes readers know that 1) Penelope was the wife to whom Odysseus in the Greek epic *The Odyssey* was attempting to return home; and 2) that French writer Gustave Flaubert believed that writing was a search for *le bon mot* (the right word). Together, Pound's allusions suggest that, just as Odysseus was devoted to Penelope, Mauberly was devoted to Flaubert's idea of writing as verbal craftsmanship.

Ambiguity: Not unlike abstraction, ambiguous ordinarily means unclear or unspecific. As a literary technique, however, ambiguity often reflects a writer's desire to convey the complexity of the moral or psychological conflict of a work without oversimplification. For example, Jake Barnes's dilemma in *The Sun Also Rises* can be described as ambiguous because Hemingway never explicitly explains Jake's motives for introducing Brett Ashley to Pedro Romero. Does he facilitate their affair because he genuinely wants Brett to be happy, or is he perversely punishing himself for his own inability to love her? While ambiguity can be frustrating for readers, it can also be liberating in allowing them to explore their own responses to events in a story.

Archetype: An archetype is a character, theme, image, or event common to a broad array of cultures and social groups. Adam and Eve's expulsion from the Garden of Eden can be considered archetypal, for instance, since similar stories of humanity's fall from grace and initiation into evil are found in religions other than Christianity. Modernists often employed archetypes in the same way they used allusions—to heighten the mythic aspect of their writings and connect them with ancient traditions.

Compression: Compression is a writing technique that avoids explaining or elaborating upon the significance of a character or event, suggesting it instead through a symbol or image. Hemingway's style in *In Our Time* can be considered compressed because his sentences are generally short, descriptive, and devoid of unnecessary words. See also *Iceberg Principle.*

Cubism: Cubism is a style of modernist painting (ca. 1907–1915) led by Pablo Picasso and Georges Braque in which forms are broken down into geometric shapes. Its earliest phase (called "analytical cubism") juxtaposed these shapes, creating the illusion of viewing an object from many angles simultaneously. In its later, post-1912 stage ("synthetic cubism") artists incorporated pieces of newspaper and fabric into the composition, creating a collage effect. One modernist text that aims to translate Cubists' visual techniques into writing is Gertrude Stein's *Tender Buttons* (1914).

Dada: A French term meaning *hobby horse,* Dada became the name for a modernist art movement that lasted roughly from 1916 until the mid 1920s. Dadaism claimed to counteract the artificiality of modern life with works that were self-consciously absurd and meaningless. Provocative and confrontational, the members of the movement—including Tristan Tzara, Man Ray, and Marcel Duchamp—insisted that art possessed no intrinsic merit. At best, it could only outrage or shock the middle class by ridiculing its materialism.

Decadence: Normally, decadence refers to behavior that violates the mores of a culture by indulging an individual's desire for gratification. Thus, promiscuity is considered decadent because it disregards social standards of monogamy for the self's craving for physical pleasure. In the late nineteenth century, a literary genre known as the decadent movement arose; it condoned deviancy as a way to achieve individual enlightenment. It also encouraged its mem-

bers to explore the effects of drugs and sexual taboos in their writing. By the 1920s, decadent was a common synonym for the expatriate movement, although only a handful of modernists openly believed in stimulating the imagination through artificial means.

Diachronic: Meaning "across" or "through" time, diachronic describes the measurement of a characteristic or quality as it changes over the course of history. Its opposite is synchronic.

Dramatis Personae: This term refers to the cast of characters in a play and, by extension, in other fictional works.

Exile: As opposed to expatriate, exile connotes banishment from one's homeland, usually for political or moral reasons.

Expatriation: Expatriation is the act of voluntarily living outside of one's native country.

Fragmentation: Fragmentation is a literary technique by which modernists broke down a story or plot into a single episode or image. Traditionally, a narrative is supposed to possess unity, meaning it progresses from a beginning to a middle to an ending resolution. Modernists, however, often flashed upon individual moments of significance without supplying background, character development, or a conclusion. The vignettes in Hemingway's *In Our Time* can be considered examples of fragments—they fix upon a moment of violence without explaining what happened before or after it. Ezra Pound in "Hugh Selwyn Mauberly" and T. S. Eliot in *The Waste Land* employ a different sort of fragmentation: they shift scenes, speakers, and settings without cuing readers or explaining their transitions. For modernists, fragmentation was a way of conveying the sense that modern life possessed little continuity with the past.

Fauvism: This term is used to describe the style of primitive painting associated with Henri Matisse and other artists at the 1905 Autumn Salon. These painters were described as "wild" or "beast-like" because of their unconventional use of colors and unblended brush strokes.

Futurism: A school of literary modernism that took shape mainly in Italy under the direction of Filippo Tommaso Marinetti (1876–1944), futurism was a forerunner of Dadaism. Futurism flagrantly violated rules of grammar and word use. Its main goal was to break with the past and embrace the energy or "dynamism" of the future, especially as embodied by modern technology.

Genre: Genre is a French term describing categories of literature. Poetry is a genre, as are the novel and the short story. A genre is often the result of an effort to classify different types of writing, distinguishing them by the characteristics unique to their class. Definitions of genres are always changing, however, as critics challenge and revise previous scholars' descriptions of the traits of various categories.

Harlem Renaissance: This term describes a movement of African-American writers in the 1920s to expand the possibilities of black writing in America. Writers such as Langston Hughes, Claude McKay, Nella Larsen, and Zora Neale Hurston described the varieties of life in African-American urban communities. They often blended folkloric tales and styles with modernist techniques borrowed from James Joyce, T. S. Eliot, and Ezra Pound. The movement was seen as a renaissance or rebirth because its authors were celebrating black communities rather than defending them from racist attacks or protesting prejudices. Although the movement identified Harlem as its central site, several writers—including Hughes, McKay, and Countee Cullen—also visited Paris for brief periods of time in the 1920s.

Iceberg Principle: This phrase is commonly used among critics to describe Hemingway's style of omission. In *Death in the Afternoon,* Hemingway writes: "If a writer of prose knows enough about what he is writing about he may omit things that he knows and the reader, if the writer is writing truly enough, will have a feeling of those things as strongly as though the writer had stated them. The dignity of movement of an iceberg is due to only one-eighth of it being above water." A good example of Hemingway's omission is the absence of the word *abortion* in "Hills Like White Elephants."

Imagism: Ezra Pound announced the birth of this school of modern poetry in 1912. Its principal aim was to avoid excess verbiage that marred contemporary verse. It also conveyed intense emotions through a concentrated description of an object. The quintessential imagist poem is Pound's "In the Station of the Metro," which reads in its entirety: "The apparition of these faces in the crowd, / Petals on a wet, black bough." Pound eventually abandoned Imagism out of annoyance with American poet Amy Lowell, who became the school's chief public spokeswoman. Something of Imagism's intense brevity can be found in Hemingway's terse style, which Pound encouraged.

Initiation Story: Also known as the "coming-of-age" tale, initiation story refers to a type of plot in which an adolescent recognizes the moral complexity of adulthood, either by failing his/her own value system or by observing the hypocrisy of an adult authority.

Juxtaposition: Juxtaposition is a modernist technique of contrast by which two different elements of a painting or poem are set next to each other, thus emphasizing the differences. Eliot's *The Waste Land* offers several examples, such as when the poem opposes fragments of modern discourse to excerpts from classical and Renaissance literature. One episode recounts the empty, insincere farewells of patrons at a working-class bar:

Goonight Bill. Goonight Lou.
Goonight May. Goonight.
Ta ta. Goonight. Goonight.
Good night, ladies, good night, sweet
ladies, good night,
good night.

The last lines, drawn from Ophelia's final speech in William Shakespeare's *Hamlet,* serve as an emotional counterpoint to the modern dialogue, whose meaninglessness is emphasized by the contrast.

Metaphor: A figure of speech by which a single word or a phrase dramatizes the qualities of another object or emotion, metaphors differ from similes in that the similes assert a similarity between two things, marked by "such as" or "like," whereas with metaphors the relationship between the two terms is implied. Thus, "love is a rose" is a metaphor, while "love is like a rose" is a simile.

Métier: One of Gertrude Stein's favorite terms, this French word refers to a genre, form, or activity to which someone's talents are well suited. Thus, writing was Hemingway's métier, while painting was Pablo Picasso's.

Modernism: A broad term that describes movements in the arts from roughly 1900 to the end of World War II. In literature, the adjective *modernist* is typically applied to works of this era that are complex and experimental, that strive to present new ways of describing perception and consciousness, and that are pessimistic about human evolution and progress. There are many subcategories of modernism—including futurism, cubism, and Vorticism—to name but three. The term "high modernism" is also used frequently to distinguish the most technically dense and difficult modernist works, including James Joyce's *Ulysses* and T. S. Eliot's *The Waste Land.*

Postimpressionism: This term in the 1890s and early 1900s described the generation of painters who rebelled against impressionism. Postimpressionists preferred sharper outlines and bolder colors than their predecessors. Of this group, Paul Cézanne was the most influential among modernists.

Primitivism: Primitivism is a rebellious tendency in the arts to break from rules and prescriptions for what Western art should be to explore sensuous (and sensual) emotions. In modernist art, the primitivist attitude can be seen in several techniques and forms of expression. Fauvists' harsh brush strokes are a good example, as are the figures in Pablo Picasso's *Les Demoiselles d'Avignon,* which are flat and unrealistic. Modernists cultivated primitive techniques as a result of their fascination with African culture. Because Europeans and Americans considered African cultures "uncultivated," they viewed their various forms of artistic expression as more spontaneous and authentic than approaches learned through formal training.

Roman à clef: Literally, this French phrase means "novel with a key." The term refers to narratives in which fictional characters are modeled on real-life people whom readers are meant to recognize. *The Sun Also Rises* is a roman à clef because Hemingway based Brett Ashley, Mike Campbell, Bill Gorton, and others in the novel on Parisian friends and acquaintances, including Duff Twysden, Pat Gutherie, and Donald Ogden Stewart respectively.

Stream of consciousness: Originally coined by Gertrude Stein's teacher William James (philosopher brother of novelist Henry James), stream of consciousness is a literary technique that presents a character's perceptions as a rush of sensations rather than as an orderly arrangement of ideas. James Joyce popularized the use of this device in *Ulysses;* other famous examples include Virginia Woolf's *Mrs. Dalloway* (1925) and William Faulkner's *The Sound and the Fury* (1929). Hemingway experimented with stream of consciousness, most effectively in the passages detailing Harry's memories in "The Snows of Kilimanjaro." With the exception of his use of stream of consciousness in this story, the technique is not considered his strength.

Surrealism: Meaning "superrealism," this term describes a literary movement that arose from disagreements among Dadaists in the mid 1920s. Surrealist writers such as André Breton and Louis Aragon and painters such as Man Ray aimed to tap into the creative resources of the unconscious mind with dreamlike visions of unconventional images.

Symbol: A symbol is an object or action that stands for an idea. Thus, in "The Snows of Kilimanjaro," both the snow and the mountain symbolize different aspects of Harry's life and personality as he prepares for

death—though just what those aspects are largely depends upon the reader's interpretation.

Synchronic: Synchronic means "above" or "out of" time; unlike diachronic, it refers to qualities or characteristics without concern for historical context.

Vorticism: Ezra Pound and Wyndham Lewis founded this avant-garde school of modernism in the 1910s. Vorticists rebelled against genteel nineteenth-century poetry and art, insisting that modern works must acknowledge the effects of technology, violence, and dynamic motion in their work. Julian Symons explains that the central image of the movement, the vortex, reflected a desire to establish art as "the still point of maximum energy in the midst of conflicting forces, as there is said to be stillness at the heart of a whirlpool." In other words, art and literature should not only reflect the chaos of cultural change but also should be a catalytic force in shaping its future.

BIBLIOGRAPHY

PRIMARY SOURCES

Anderson, Margaret. *My Thirty Years War: The Autobiography: Beginnings and Battles to 1930.* New York: Covici-Friede, 1930; republished, New York: Horizon Press, 1970.

Anderson, Sherwood. *Memoirs.* New York: Harcourt, Brace, 1942.

Anderson. *France and Sherwood Anderson: Paris Notebook 1921,* edited by Michael Fanning. Baton Rouge: Louisiana State University Press, 1976.

Anderson. *Winesburg, Ohio.* New York: Huebsch, 1919; republished, New York: Oxford University Press, 1997.

Antheil, George. *Bad Boy of Music.* Garden City, N. Y.: Doubleday, Doran, 1945.

Barnes, Djuna. *Ladies Almanack.* Paris: Contact Press, 1928; · republished, New York: New York University Press, 1992.

Barnes. *Nightwood.* London: Faber & Faber, 1936.

Beach, Sylvia. *Shakespeare and Company.* New York: Harcourt, Brace, 1953.

Bricktop (Ada Smith), with James Haskins. *Bricktop.* New York: Atheneum, 1983.

Callaghan, Morley. *That Summer in Paris: Memories of Tangled Friendships with Hemingway, Fitzgerald, and Some Others.* New York: Coward-McCann, 1963.

Charters, James. *This Must Be The Place: Memoirs of Montparnasse.* London:

H. Joseph, 1934; republished, New York: Colliers Books, 1989.

Crosby, Caresse. *The Passionate Years.* New York: Dial, 1953.

Dos Passos, John. *The Best Times: An Informal Memoir.* New York: New American Library, 1966.

Dos Passos. *The Fourteenth Chronicle: Letters and Diaries of John Dos Passos,* edited by Townsend Ludington. Boston: Gambit, 1973.

Dos Passos. "A Lost Generation," in his *John Dos Passos: The Major Nonfiction Prose,* edited by Donald Pizer. Detroit: Wayne State University Press, 1988, pp. 92–93.

Dos Passos. *Nineteen-Nineteen.* New York: Harcourt, Brace, 1932; republished in *U. S. A.: The 42nd Parallel, Nineteen-Nineteen, The Big Money.* Boston: Houghton Mifflin, 1960.

Eastman, Max. *Great Companions: Critical Memoirs of Some Famous Friends.* New York: Farrar, Straus & Cudahy, 1959.

Eliot, T. S. "*Ulysses,* Order, and Myth," in *Selected Prose of T. S. Eliot,* edited by Frank Kermode. New York: Harcourt Brace Jovanovich, 1975, pp. 175–178.

Eliot. *The Waste Land. The Complete Poems and Plays, 1909–1950.* New York: Harcourt Brace Jovanovich, 1971, pp. 37–55.

Ellerman, Winifred "Bryher." *The Heart to Artemis: A Writer's Memoirs.* New

York: Harcourt, Brace & World, 1962.

Fitzgerald, F. Scott. "Babylon Revisited," in *The Short Stories of F. Scott Fitzgerald,* edited by Matthew J. Bruccoli. New York: Scribners, 1989, pp. 616–633.

Fitzgerald. *The Crack-Up,* edited by Edmund Wilson. New York: New Directions, 1945.

Fitzgerald. *The Great Gatsby.* New York: Scribners, 1925; republished, edited by Bruccoli. Cambridge: Cambridge University Press, 1991.

Fitzgerald. *A Life in Letters,* edited by Bruccoli. New York: Touchstone, 1994.

Fitzgerald. *The Notebooks of F. Scott Fitzgerald,* edited by Bruccoli. New York: Harcourt Brace Jovanovich/ Bruccoli Clark, 1978.

Fitzgerald. *Tender Is the Night.* New York: Scribners, 1934.

Fitzgerald. *This Side of Paradise.* New York: Scribners, 1920.

Ford, Ford Madox. *It Was the Nightingale.* Philadelphia: Lippincott, 1933.

Hawthorne, Nathaniel. *The Centenary Edition of the Works of Nathaniel Hawthorne,* edited by William Charvat and others, 16 volumes. Columbus: Ohio University Press, 1962–1985.

Hemingway, Ernest. *Across the River and into the Trees.* New York: Scribners, 1950.

Hemingway. "The Art of the Short Story," in *New Critical Approaches to the Short Stories of Ernest Hemingway,* edited by Jackson J. Benson. Durham, N.C.: Duke University Press, 1991, pp. 1–13.

Hemingway. *By-Line: Ernest Hemingway: Selected Articles and Dispatches of Four Decades,* edited by William Wiser. New York: Scribners, 1967.

Hemingway. *The Complete Short Stories of Ernest Hemingway.* New York: Scribners, 1987.

Hemingway. *Death in the Afternoon.* New York: Scribners, 1932.

Hemingway. *88 Poems,* edited by Nicholas Georgiannis. New York & San Diego: Harcourt Brace Jovanovich/Bruccoli Clark, 1979.

Hemingway. *Ernest Hemingway: Selected Letters, 1917–1961,* edited by Carlos Baker. New York: Scribners, 1981.

Hemingway. *A Farewell to Arms.* New York: Scribners, 1929.

Hemingway. *For Whom the Bell Tolls.* New York: Scribners, 1940.

Hemingway. *The Garden of Eden.* New York: Scribners, 1986.

Hemingway. *Green Hills of Africa.* New York: Scribners, 1935.

Hemingway. Item 179a–1. Unpublished manuscript. The Ernest Hemingway Collection, John F. Kennedy Library, Boston, Massachusetts.

Hemingway. Item 202c. Unpublished manuscript. The Ernest Hemingway Collection, John F. Kennedy Library, Boston, Massachusetts.

Hemingway. *A Moveable Feast.* New York: Scribners, 1964.

Hemingway. *The Only Thing That Counts: The Ernest Hemingway/Maxwell Perkins Correspondence, 1925–1947,* edited by Bruccoli. New York: Scribners, 1996.

Hemingway. "On Writing," in his *The Nick Adams Stories,* edited by Philip Young. New York: Scribners, 1972, pp. 233–242.

Hemingway. *The Sun Also Rises.* New York: Scribners, 1926.

Hemingway. *The Sun Also Rises: A Facsimile Edition,* edited by Bruccoli, 2 volumes. Detroit: Omnigraphics, 1990.

Hemingway. *The Torrents of Spring.* New York: Scribners, 1926.

Hemingway. "The True Story of My Break With Gertrude Stein," *New Yorker,* 3 (12 February 1927): 23–24; republished in *The Critical Response to Ger-*

trude Stein, edited by Kirk Curnutt. Westport, Conn.: Greenwood Press, 2000, pp. 254–255.

Hughes, Langston. *The Big Sea.* New York: Hill & Wang, 1963.

Irving, Washington. *The Complete Writings of Washington Irving,* edited by Richard Dilworth Rust and others, 30 volumes. Boston: Twayne, 1978–1989.

James, Henry. *Hawthorne, in The Art of Criticism: Henry James on the Theory and Practice of Criticism,* edited by William Veeder and Susan M. Griffin. Chicago: University of Chicago Press, 1986, pp. 101–131.

Kiki (Alice Prin). *Kiki's Memoirs,* translated by Samuel Putnam. Paris: Titus, 1928; Hopewell, N.J.: Ecco Press, 1996.

Loeb, Harold. *The Way It Was.* New York: Criterion, 1959.

Loy, Mina. *Lunar Baedeker.* Paris: Contact Press, 1923; republished and enlarged as *The Lost Lunar Baedeker,* edited by Roger Conover. Highlands, N.C.: Jargon Society, 1982.

McAlmon, Robert. *Being Geniuses Together, 1920–1930.* London, 1938; revised and enlarged with supplementary chapters by Kay Boyle. Garden City, N.Y.: Doubleday, 1968; republished, San Francisco: North Point Press, 1984.

McKay, Claude. *A Long Way from Home.* New York: L. Furman, 1937; republished, Harcourt, Brace & World, 1970.

Miller, Henry. *Tropic of Cancer.* Paris: Guardian Obelisk, 1934; republished, New York: Grove, 1961.

Nin, Anaïs. *The Diary of Anaïs Nin, 1931–1934,* edited by Gunther Stulhmann. New York: Swallow Press, 1966.

Owen, Wilfred. "Dulce et Decorum Est," in *The Norton Book of Modern War,* edited by Paul Fussell. New York: Norton, 1991, p. 166.

Pound, Ezra. *Antheil and the Treatise on Harmony.* Paris: Contact Press, 1925; republished, New York: DeCapo Press, 1968.

Pound. *The Selected Poems of Ezra Pound.* New York: New Directions, 1957.

Putnam, Samuel. *Paris Was Our Mistress: Memoirs of a Lost and Found Generation.* New York: Viking, 1947.

Stearns, Harold. *America and the Young Intellectual.* New York: Doran, 1921.

Stearns. "Apologia of an Expatriate." *Scribner's Magazine,* 85 (March 1929): 338–341.

Stein, Gertrude. "An American and Paris," in her *What Are Masterpieces,* edited by Robert Bartlett Haas. New York: Pitman, 1970, pp. 61–70.

Stein. *The Autobiography of Alice B. Toklas.* New York: Harcourt, Brace, 1933.

Stein. "He and They, Hemingway," in her *Portraits and Prayers.* New York: Random House, 1934, p. 193.

Stein. *Lectures in America.* New York: Random House, 1935.

Stein. "Miss Furr and Miss Skeene," in her *Geography and Plays.* New York: Four Seas, 1922, pp. 17–22.

Stein. *Paris France.* London: Batsford, 1940.

Tate, Allen. "Miss Toklas' American Cake," in his *Memories and Opinions.* Chicago: Swallow Press, 1975, pp. 46–66.

Thomson, Virgil. *Virgil Thomson.* New York: Knopf, 1966.

Williams, William Carlos. *The Autobiography of William Carlos Williams.* New York: New Directions, 1951.

Williams. "The Voyage of the Pilgrims," in his *The William Carlos Williams Reader,* edited by M. L. Rosenthal. New York: New Directions, 1966.

Williams. *A Voyage to Pagany.* New York: Macaulay, 1928; republished, New York: New Directions, 1970.

Woolf, Virginia. "Mr. Bennett and Mrs. Brown," in her *The Captain's Death Bed and Other Essays*. New York: Harcourt, Brace, 1950, pp. 94–119.

Yeats, William Butler. "The Second Coming," in his *The Poems of William Butler Yeats,* edited by Richard J. Finneran. New York: Macmillan, 1983, p. 187.

SECONDARY SOURCES:

BOOKS

Baker, Carlos. *Hemingway: The Writer as Artist*. Princeton, N.J.: Princeton University Press, 1952; revised and expanded, 1972.

Benstock, Shari. *Women of the Left Bank: Paris 1900–1940*. Austin: University of Texas Press, 1986.

Bradbury, Malcolm. *The Expatriate Tradition in American Literature*. Durham, U.K.: BAAS Pamphlets in American Studies, 1982.

Brown, Milton W. *The Armory Show.* Greenwich, Conn.: New York Graphic Society, 1963; republished, New York: Abbeville Press, 1988.

Bruccoli, Matthew J. *Fitzgerald and Hemingway: A Dangerous Friendship*. New York: Carroll & Graf, 1994.

Coben, Stanley. *Rebellion Against Victorianism: The Impetus for Cultural Change in 1920s America*. New York: Oxford University Press, 1991.

Cowley, Malcolm. *Exile's Return: A Narrative of Ideas*. New York, 1934; revised and enlarged as *Exile's Return: A Literary Odyssey of the 1920s*. New York: Viking, 1951.

Crowley, John W. *The White Logic: Alcoholism and Gender in American Modernist Fiction*. Amherst: University of Massachusetts Press, 1994.

Earnest, Ernest. *Expatriates and Patriots: American Artists, Scholars, and Writers in Europe*. Durham, N.C.: Duke University Press, 1968.

Flora, Joseph. *Hemingway's Nick Adams*. Baton Rouge: Louisiana State University Press, 1982.

Ford, Hugh, ed. *The Left Bank Revisited: Selections from the Paris Tribune, 1917–1934*. University Park: Pennsylvania State University Press, 1972.

Ford. *Published in Paris: American and British Writers, Printers, and Publishers in Paris, 1920–1939*. New York: Macmillan, 1975.

Fussell, Paul, ed. *The Norton Book of Modern War*. New York: Norton, 1991.

Glad, John, ed. *Literature in Exile*. Durham, N.C.: Duke University Press, 1990.

Griffin, Peter. *Along with Youth: Hemingway, the Early Years*. New York: Oxford University Press, 1985.

Holder, Alan. *Three Voyagers in Search of Europe: A Study of Henry James, Ezra Pound, and T. S. Eliot*. Philadelphia: University of Pennsylvania Press, 1966.

Hotchner, A. E. *Papa Hemingway: A Personal Memoir*. New York: Random House, 1966.

Huddleston, Sisley. *Bohemian Literary and Social Life in Paris: Salons, Cafés, Studios*. London: Harrap, 1928.

Kennedy, J. Gerald. *Imagining Paris: Place, Writing, and American Identity*. New Haven, Conn.: Yale University Press, 1993.

Mellow, James R. *Hemingway: A Life without Consequences*. New York: Houghton Mifflin, 1992.

Méral, Jean. *Paris in American Literature,* translated by Laurette Long. Chapel Hill: University of North Carolina Press, 1989.

Meyers, Jeffrey, ed. *Hemingway: The Critical Heritage*. London: Routledge & Kegan Paul, 1982.

Pizer, Donald. *American Expatriate Writing and the Paris Moment: Modernism and Place*. Baton Rouge: Louisiana State University Press, 1996.

Rahv, Philip, ed. *Discovery of Europe: The Story of American Experience in the Old World.* Boston: Houghton Mifflin, 1947.

Read, Herbert. *Art Now.* New York: Pitman, 1936; revised and enlarged as *Art Now: An Introduction to the Theory of Modern Painting and Sculpture,* 1968.

Reynolds, Michael S. *Hemingway: The American Homecoming.* New York: Blackwell, 1992.

Reynolds. *Hemingway: The Final Years.* New York: Norton, 1999.

Reynolds. *Hemingway: The Paris Years.* New York: Blackwell, 1989.

Reynolds. *The Young Hemingway.* New York: Blackwell, 1986.

Rose, Phyllis. *Jazz Cleopatra: Josephine Baker in Her Time.* New York: Doubleday, 1989.

Symons, Julian. *Makers of the New: The Revolution in Literature, 1912–1939.* New York: Random House, 1987.

Tompkins, Calvin. *Living Well Is the Best Revenge.* New York: Viking, 1962; reprinted, 1972.

Townsend, Kim. *Sherwood Anderson.* Boston: Houghton Mifflin, 1987.

Young, Philip. *Hemingway: A Revaluation.* University Park: Pennsylvania State University Press, 1966.

SECONDARY SOURCES:

ARTICLES AND ESSAYS

Aldridge, John W. "Hemingway and Europe." *Shenandoah,* 11 (1960): 10–24.

Aldridge. "*The Sun Also Rises*: Sixty Years Later," in his *Classics and Contemporaries.* Columbia: University of Missouri Press, 1992, pp. 39–48.

Bagger, Eugene. "Uprooted Americans." *Harper's,* 159 (September 1929): 474–484.

Barrett, Richmond. "Babes in the Bois." *Harper's,* 156 (May 1928): 724–736.

Blythe, Samuel G. "La Grande Fête Amèricaine." *Saturday Evening Post* (22 March 1913): 10–11.

Carter, John F., Jr. "Those Wild Young People." *Atlantic Monthly,* 126 (1920): 301–304.

Child, Maude Parker. "Expatriated Americans." *Saturday Evening Post* (13 June 1925): 22, 86, 90, 94.

Curnutt, Kirk. "'In the Temps de Gertrude': Hemingway, Stein, and the Scene of Instruction at 27, rue de Fleurus," in *French Connections: Hemingway and Fitzgerald Abroad,* edited by J. Gerald Kennedy and Jackson R. Bryer. New York: St. Martin's Press, 1998, pp. 121–140.

Farrell, James T. "Ernest Hemingway, Apostle of a 'Lost Generation.'" *New York Times Book Review* (1 August 1943): 6, 141.

Kennedy, Thomas E. "The New Expatriates: American Writers in Europe Today." *Cimarron Review,* 100 (1992): 9–13.

Levin, Harry. "Literature and Exile," in his *Refractions: Essays in Comparative Literature.* New York: Oxford University Press, 1966, pp. 62–81.

McCarthy, Mary. "A Guide to Exiles, Expatriates, and Internal Emigrés," in *Altogether Elsewhere: Writers on Exile,* edited by Marc Robinson. Boston: Faber & Faber, 1994, pp. 49–58.

Perloff, Marjorie. "Ninety-Percent Rotarian: Gertrude Stein's Hemingway." *American Literature,* 62 (December 1990): 668–683.

Preston, John Hyde. "Gertrude Stein: A Conversation." *Atlantic Monthly,* 156 (August 1935): 187–194.

Ryan, Dennis. "'A Divine Gesture': Hemingway's Complex Parody of the Modern." *Hemingway Review,* 16 (Fall 1996): 1–17.

Schwartz, Delmore. "The Hero as Good Sport," in *Readings on Ernest Hemingway,* edited by Katie de Koster. San Diego: Greenhaven Press, 1997, pp. 61–65.

Smith, Paul. "Hemingway's Apprentice Fiction: 1919–1921," in *New Critical Approaches to the Short Stories of Ernest Hemingway,* edited by Jackson J. Benson. Durham, N.C.: Duke University Press, 1991, pp. 137–148.

"Whom America Has Failed." *Literary Digest* (26 May 1928): 23–24.

Zehr, David Morgan. "Paris and the Expatriate Mystique: Hemingway's *The Sun Also Rises.*" *Arizona Quarterly,* 33 (1977): 156–164.

FOR FURTHER STUDY

Adair, William. "Hemingway's Sense of an Ending: Repetitious and Pathetic." *ANQ,* 12 (Spring 1999): 32–35.

Baker, Carlos. *Hemingway: A Life Story.* New York: Scribners, 1969. The first scholarly biography; remains essential reading.

Beegel, Susan F. "The Critical Reputation of Ernest Hemingway," in *The Cambridge Companion to Ernest Hemingway,* edited by Scott Donaldson. New York: Cambridge University Press, 1996, pp. 269–300. Overview of critical trends in Hemingway criticism from 1950 to 1990.

Beegel, ed. *Hemingway's Neglected Short Fiction: New Perspectives.* Tuscaloosa: University of Alabama Press, 1992. Valuable collection of essays, including many on expatriate stories such as "My Old Man."

Beegel. "'A Room on the Garden Side': Hemingway's Unpublished Liberation of Paris." *Studies in Short Fiction,* 31 (Fall 1994): 627–638. Unpublished Hemingway story set in World War II Paris that reveals his attitude late in life toward the city of his literary apprenticeship.

Benson, Jackson J. *New Critical Approaches to the Short Stories of Ernest Hemingway.* Durham, N.C.: Duke University Press, 1991.

Brenner, Gerry. *Concealments in Hemingway's Works.* Columbus: Ohio State University Press, 1983.

Brian, Denis. *The True Gen: An Intimate Portrait of Hemingway by Those Who Knew Him.* New York: Grove, 1988.

Burwell, Rose Marie. *Hemingway: The Postwar Years and the Posthumous Novels.* New York: Cambridge University Press, 1996. Important study of *The Garden of Eden* and *A Moveable Feast,* with particular emphasis on the symbolic importance of Eden to the author.

Carpenter, Humphrey. *Geniuses Together: American Writers in Paris in the 1920s.* London: Unwin Hyman, 1987.

Civello, Paul. "Hemingway's 'Primitivism': Archetypal Patterns in 'Big Two-Hearted River.'" *Hemingway Review,* 13 (Fall 1993): 1–16.

Comley, Nancy R., and Robert Scholes. *Hemingway's Genders: Rereading the Hemingway Text.* New Haven, Conn.: Yale University Press, 1994. Provocative analysis of Hemingway's representation of masculinity and femininity.

Cook, Dana. "Meeting Ernest Hemingway: A Miscellany of Fifty First Encounters and Initial Impressions." *Hemingway Review: Centennial Issue,* 18 (Spring 1999): 5–28.

Donaldson, Scott. *By Force of Will: The Life and Art of Ernest Hemingway.* New York: Viking, 1977. A thematic biography that examines how Hemingway transformed his life into his fiction.

Djos, Matts. "Alcoholism in Ernest Hemingway's *The Sun Also Rises*: A Wine and Roses Perspective on the Lost Generation." *Hemingway Review,* 14 (Spring 1995): 64–78.

Fabre, Michel. *From Harlem to Paris: Black American Writers in Paris, 1840–1980.* Urbana: University of Illinois Press, 1991.

Ferrero, David J. "Nikki Adams and the Limits of Gender Criticism." *Hemingway Review,* 17 (Spring 1998): 18–30.

Flanner, Janet. *An American in Paris: Profile of an Interlude Between Two Wars.* New York: Simon & Schuster, 1940. Reflections on expatriate Paris by a leading *New Yorker* contributor.

Fleming, Robert E. *The Face in the Mirror: Hemingway's Writers.* Tuscaloosa: University of Alabama Press, 1994.

Flora, Josepha. *Hemingway: A Study of the Short Fiction.* New York: Twayne, 1989.

Ford, Hugh. *Four Lives in Paris.* San Francisco: North Point Press, 1987. Excellent introduction to lesser-known expatriates, especially George Antheil and Kay Boyle.

Gaillard, Theodore L., Jr. "Hemingway's Debt to Cézanne: New Perspectives." *Twentieth Century Literature,* 45 (Spring 1999): 65–79.

Hanneman, Audre. *Ernest Hemingway: A Comprehensive Bibliography.* Princeton: Princeton University Press, 1967.

Hanneman. *Supplement to Ernest Hemingway: A Comprehensive Bibliography.* Princeton: Princeton University Press, 1975. Essential bibliographies; particularly important for researching essays and articles on Hemingway during his life.

Hart, Jeffrey. "Fitzgerald and Hemingway in 1925–1926." *Sewanee Review,* 105 (Summer 1997): 369–381.

Hemingway, Mary Welsh. *How It Was.* New York: Knopf, 1976. Hemingway's last wife recounts their life together in the 1940s and 1950s.

Johnston, Kenneth G. *The Tip of the Iceberg: Hemingway and the Short Story.* Greenwood, Fla.: Penkevill, 1987.

Joost, Nicholas. *Ernest Hemingway: The Little Magazines and the Paris Years.* Barre, Mass.: Barre, 1968.

Justice, Hilary K. "'Well, Well, Well': Cross-Gendered Autobiography and the Manuscript of 'Hills Like White Elephants.'" *Hemingway Review,* 18 (Fall 1998): 17–32.

Kennedy, J. Gerald. "Figuring the Damage: Fitzgerald's 'Babylon Revisited' and Hemingway's 'The Snows of Kilimanjaro,'" in *French Connections: Hemingway and Fitzgerald Abroad,* edited by Kennedy and Jackson R. Bryer. New York: St. Martin's Press, 1998, pp. 317–344.

Kennedy and Kirk Curnutt. "Out of the Picture: Mrs. Krebs, Gertrude Stein, and 'Soldier's Home.'" *Hemingway Review,* 12 (Fall 1992): 1–11.

Kert, Berniece. *The Hemingway Women: Those Who Loved Him—the Wives and Others.* New York: Norton, 1983. Essential background of the women who inspired Hemingway's female characters.

Larson, Kelli A. *Ernest Hemingway: A Reference Guide, 1974–1989.* Boston: G. K. Hall, 1990.

Leland, John. *A Guide to Hemingway's Paris.* Chapel Hill, N.C.: Algonquin, 1989.

Lewis, Robert W. *A Farewell to Arms: The War of the Words.* Boston: Twayne, 1991.

Lynn, Kenneth. *Hemingway.* New York: Simon & Schuster, 1987. Controversial biography that examines Hemingway's attitudes toward androgyny.

Mandel, Miriam B. *Reading Hemingway: The Facts in the Fictions.* Metuchen, N. J.: Scarecrow Press, 1995.

Mason, Alane Salierno. "To Love and Love Not." *Vanity Fair* (July 1999): 108–118, 146–152. Recently discovered letters cast new light on Hemingway's relationship with Jane Mason, the woman who inspired Margaret Macomber.

Meyers, Jeffrey. *Hemingway: A Life*. New York: Harper & Row, 1985. Solid biography; particularly insightful for its account of Hemingway's final years.

Miller, Linda Patterson. *Letters from the Lost Generation: Gerald and Sara Murphy and Friends*. Rutgers, N.J.: Rutgers University Press, 1991.

Morrison, Toni. *Playing in the Dark: Whiteness and the Literary Imagination*. New York: Vintage, 1992. The Nobel laureate explores the "Africanist presence" in American literature, including Hemingway's *To Have and Have Not* and *The Garden of Eden*.

Oliver, Charles M. *Ernest Hemingway A to Z: The Essential Reference to the Life and Work*. New York: Checkmark, 1999.

Raeburn, John. *Fame Became of Him: Hemingway as Public Writer*. Bloomington: Indiana University Press, 1977.

Reynolds, Michael S. *Hemingway's First War: The Making of A Farewell to Arms*. Princeton: Princeton University Press, 1976. Explores the background of Hemingway's third novel.

Reynolds. *The Sun Also Rises: A Novel of the Twenties*. Boston: Twayne, 1988.

Rovit, Earl, and Gerry Brenner. *Ernest Hemingway*. Boston: Twayne, 1986.

Sarason, Bertram D. *Hemingway and the Sun Set*. Washington, D. C.: NCR Microcard, 1972. Interviews and background on the Hemingway friends who inspired *The Sun Also Rises*.

Smith, Paul. *A Reader's Guide to the Short Stories of Ernest Hemingway*. Boston: G. K. Hall, 1989.

Spilka, Mark. *Hemingway's Quarrel with Androgyny*. Lincoln: University of Nebraska Press, 1990.

Stendahl, Renate. *Gertrude Stein in Words and Pictures*. Chapel Hill, N.C: Algonquin, 1994.

Stoneback, H. R. "From the rue Saint-Jacques to the Pass of Roland to the 'Unfinished Church of the Edge of the Cliff.'" *Hemingway Review*, 6 (Fall 1986): 2–29.

Svodoba, Frederic. *Hemingway's The Sun Also Rises: The Crafting of a Style*. Lawrence: University Press of Kansas, 1983.

Szalay, Michael. "Inviolate Modernism: Hemingway, Stein, Tzara." *Modern Language Quarterly*, 56 (December 1995): 457–486.

Tavernier-Courbin, Jacqueline. *Ernest Hemingway's A Moveable Feast: The Making of a Myth*. Boston: Northeastern University Press, 1991. Study of Hemingway's memoir, with particular emphasis on the posthumous editorial tinkering done by the author's wife and his editor.

Wagner-Martin, Linda. *"Favored Strangers": Gertrude Stein and Her Family*. Rutgers, N.J.: Rutgers University Press, 1995.

Wagner-Martin, ed. *Hemingway: Seven Decades of Criticism*. East Lansing: Michigan State University Press, 1999.

Watson, William Braasch. "The Other Paris Years of Ernest Hemingway: 1937 and 1938," in *French Connections: Hemingway and Fitzgerald Abroad*, edited by J. Gerald Kennedy and Jackson R. Bryer. New York: St. Martin's Press, 1998, pp. 141–160.

Watts, Emily. *Ernest Hemingway and the Arts*. Urbana: University of Illinois Press, 1971.

Wiser, William. *The Crazy Years: Paris in the Twenties*. New York: Atheneum, 1983.

Wiser. *The Great Good Place: American Expatriate Women in Paris*. New York: Norton, 1991. Informative minibiographies of such people as Caresse Crosby, Zelda Fitzgerald, and Josephine Baker.

Zwerdling, Alex. "The European Capitals of American Literature." *Wilson Quarterly,* 17 (Winter 1993): 126–137.

JOURNALS

The Fitzgerald/Hemingway Annual, edited by Matthew J. Bruccoli and C. E. Frazer Clark Jr. Englewood, Colo.: Information Handling Services, 1969–1979.

Hemingway Notes. Youngstown, Ohio: Youngstown State University Press, 1971–1981.

The Hemingway Review. Ada, Ohio: Ohio Northern University, 1981–1992; Pensacola, Fla.: University of West Florida Press, 1992–1993; Moscow, Idaho: University of Idaho Press, 1994– .

The Lost Generation Journal. Tulsa, Okla.: Literary Enterprises, 1973–1983.

MASTER INDEX

Emerson, Ralph Waldo 147, 154

"The End of an Avocation" (Hemingway) 160

The Enormous Room (Cummings) 18, 55, 140, 189–190

Esquire 104

"The European Capitals of American Literature" (Zwerdling) 68

Exile's Return (Cowley) 7, 19, 73, 138–139, 143

Exiles 8

F

Farah, Nuruddin 64

A Farewell to Arms (Hemingway) 18, 24, 45–46, 79, 81, 83–85, 101, 103, 109, 114–116, 141, 148–150

The Farm (Miró) 168

Faulkner, William 12, 112, 155

Fauset, Jessie 15

La Femme au chapeau (Matisse) 165

Fenton, Charles A. 149

"Fifty Grand" (Hemingway) 44

Finnegans Wake (Joyce) 65

Fire Dance (Fuller) 179

Fitzgerald, F. Scott 7, 12–13, 31, 42–49, 53–54, 80, 99–101, 106, 143–145, 147, 160, 185, 201

Fitzgerald, Zelda 31, 46, 48–49, 68, 100–101

Flappers and Philosophers (Fitzgerald) 42

Flaubert, Gustave 147

Flora, Joseph 103

For Whom the Bell Tolls (Hemingway) 45, 81, 88, 101, 103, 109, 111, 116–117, 148

Ford, Ford Madox 32, 66, 128–129, 133, 158, 169, 191, 199

Ford, Henry 50

Ford, Hugh 125

The 42nd Parallel (Dos Passos) 50

Fossalta, Italy 81–83, 114

Fountain (Duchamp) 169

Four Saints in Three Acts (Stein & Thompson) 72, 174, 176

France and Sherwood Anderson (Anderson) 25

France, Anatole 41

The French They Are A Funny Race (Mearson) 12

Freud, Sigmund 8–9

"From a Litterateur's Notebook" (Paul) 126

Frost, Robert 12, 36

Fuller, Henry Blake 147

Fuller, Loie 178

Fussell, Paul 18

G

García Lorca, Federico 9

The Garden of Eden (Hemingway) 49, 64, 87, 92–93, 107, 154–155, 159, 168, 198

Gellhorn, Martha. *See* Hemingway, Martha Gelhorn

Geography and Plays (Stein) 30, 33

"Get a Seeing-Eyed Dog" (Hemingway) 100

Gide, André 41

Goldman, Emma 140

Good Morning, Midnight (Rhys) 198

The Good Soldier (Ford) 129

Gordon, George, Lord Byron 9

The Great American Novel (Williams) 66

Great Companions: Critical Memoirs of Some Famous Friends (Eastman) 190

The Great Gatsby (Fitzgerald) 42–44, 46–49, 100–101, 143

"The Great War" *See* World War I

Green Hills of Africa (Hemingway) 39, 45, 52, 104–105, 108, 111, 139, 143, 145, 154

Gris, Juan 29, 168

Guardian Obelisk 67

H

H.D. *See* Doolittle, Hilda

Harding, Warren G. 13

Harper's Magazine 133

Havana, Cuba 52, 145

Hawthorne, Nathaniel 20, 69–70, 147

"He Do the Police in Different Voices" (Eliot) 40

The Heart to Artemis: A Writer's Memoirs (Bryher) 13, 190–191

"The Art of the Short Story" 44

Hemingway (Young) 149

"Hemingway and Europe" (Aldridge) 146

"Hemingway and the Decline of International Fiction" (Wegelin) 151

Hemingway Hoax (Haldeman) 192

Hemingway, Clarence 191

Hemingway, Ernest 12, 18, 59, 63, 73–74, 76, 164, 166–170, 174, 177–178, 180

   and Sherwood Anderson 24–28

   and John Dos Passos 49, 51, 53–54

   and T. S. Eliot 40–42

   and Expatriate Modernism 5, 7, 17–18, 20

   and F. Scott Fitzgerald 42–49

   and James Joyce 39–40

   modernist approach to writing 12

   and Paris 7

   and Ezra Pound 35–38

   and Gertrude Stein 28–35

   works on the expatriate experience 79–123

      characters 96–106

      plots 79–96

      symbols 112–121

      themes 106–112

Hemingway, Grace 28, 30

Hemingway, Hadley Richardson 25, 27, 30, 51, 54, 87–88, 90, 92, 100–101, 106, 155, 157, 159, 161–162

"Hemingway, Hadley, and Paris: The Persistence of Desire" (Kennedy) 155

Hemingway, Hemingway 65

Hemingway, Martha Gellhorn 87–88

Hemingway, Mary Welsh 87–88, 154, 158

Hemingway, Pauline Pfeiffer 27, 87–88, 108, 157, 159, 162, 168

"Hemingway: A Portrait" (Stein) 33

Hemingway: The Writer as Artist (Baker) 149

Hemingway's Chair (Palin) 192

Hemingway's Suitcase (Harris) 192

Henry and June: The Unexpurgated Diary of Anaïs Nin (Nin). See The Diary of Anaïs Nin, 1931–34 189

"Hills Like White Elephants" (Hemingway) 87, 90–91, 97, 109, 114, 116, 119, 125

Hitler, Adolf 17

Holder, Alan 70

"Homage to Switzerland" (Hemingway) 100

Hours Press 66

The House of the Seven Gables (Hawthorne) 69

Howells, William Dean 147

Hudson, Thomas 168

Hudson, W. H. 110

"Hugh Selwyn Mauberley (Life and Contacts)" (Pound) 36, 40

Hughes, Langston 15, 177

I

I Killed Hemingway (McCranor) 192

"I Want to Know Why" (Anderson) 25–26, 28

Idaho 124

"In Another Country" (Hemingway) 85, 117

In Our Time (Hemingway) 23, 27, 30, 40, 43, 50–51, 59, 76, 81, 84–88, 100, 106, 148, 160, 167

in our time (Hemingway) 23, 26, 40, 43, 51, 59, 65–66, 124

Incest: From a Journal of Love—The Unexpurgated Diary of Anaïs Nin, 1932–1934 (Nin). See The Diary of Anaïs Nin, 1931–34 189

"Indian Camp" (Hemingway) 65, 79

"An International Episode" (James) 153

Irving, Washington 20, 69, 147

Islands in the Stream (Hemingway) 154–155, 158, 168

It Was the Nightingale (Ford) 191

J

James I 129

James, Henry 20, 68–69, 79, 111, 124, 143, 146–148, 150–153

James, William 146

Jeune Fille aux Fleurs (Picasso) 166

Jolas, Eugene 124–125

Jones, Florence 177

Jones, James 20

Joyce, James 12, 39–40, 112, 128, 147, 155, 158

K

Kahane, Jack 67

Kansas City Star 149

Kennedy, J. Gerald 16, 107, 113, 155

Key West, Florida 52, 124, 148

Kiki. See Prin, Alice 170, 191

Kiki's Memoirs (Kiki) 191